D0198351

LIBRARY 09884
Argosy University
San Francisco Bay Area
1005 Atlantic Ave.
Alameda, CA 94501

Mentoring Dilemmas

Developmental Relationships Within Multicultural Organizations

Edited by

Audrey J. Murrell
University of Pittsburgh

Faye J. Crosby
University of California, Santa Cruz

Robin J. Ely
Columbia University

 LAWRENCE ERLBAUM ASSOCIATES, PUBLISHERS
1999   Mahwah, New Jersey   London

Copyright © 1999 by Lawrence Erlbaum Associates, Inc.
All rights reserved. No part of this book may be reproduced in any form, by photostat, microfilm, retrieval system, or any other means, without the prior written permission of the publisher.

Lawrence Erlbaum Associates, Inc., Publishers
10 Industrial Avenue
Mahwah, New Jersey 07430-2262

Cover design by Kathryn Houghtaling Lacey

Library of Congress Cataloging-in-Publication Data

Murrell, Audrey J.
Mentoring dilemmas : developmental relationships within multicultural organizations / Audrey J. Murrell, Faye J. Crosby, Robin J. Ely.
    p. cm.
Includes bibliographical references and index.
ISBN 0-8058-2632-7. — ISBN 0-8058-2633-5 (pbk.).
1. Mentoring in business. 2. Diversity in the workplace. 3. Mentoring. I. Crosby, Faye J., 1947- . II. Ely, Robin J. III. Title.
HF5385.M87   1998
658.3'124–dc21   98-24654
                                                           CIP

Books published by Lawrence Erlbaum Associates are printed on acid-free paper, and their bindings are chosen for strength and durability.

Printed in the United States of America
10 9 8 7 6 5 4 3 2 1

In memory of my most beloved and powerful mentors and role models, my father, Irvin M. Murrell, Esq., and my mother, Castella B. Murrell, MS

Audrey J. Murrell

~

To the memory of Mary Litchfield and to the memory of Jane Ruby

Faye J. Crosby

Contents

Foreword   xi
Sheila Wellington

Preface   xv

Part I   Theoretical Perspectives

1   The Developing Literature on Developmental   3
Relationships
Faye J. Crosby

2   Developmental Relationships of Black Americans   21
in the Academy
*Sharon R. Bowman, Mary E. Kite, Nyla R. Branscombe,
and Stacey Williams*

3   Asian Americans and Developmental Relationships   47
Sharon Goto

4   Gender Issues in Developmental Relationships   63
Regina M. O'Neill, Sylvia Horton, and Faye J. Crosby

Part II   Empirical Perspectives

5   At the Crossroads of Race and Gender: Lessons From   83
    the Mentoring Experiences of Professional Black Women
    Stacy Blake

6   Do Race and Sex Affect Employees' Access to and Help   105
    From Mentors? Insights From the Study of a Large
    Corporation
    Gail M. McGuire

7   Women's and Men's Role Models: The Importance   121
    of Exemplars
    Donald E. Gibson and Diana I. Cordova

8   Mitigating Perceptions of Racism: The Importance   143
    of Work Group Composition and Supervisor's Race
    Daria Kirby and James S. Jackson

9   Beyond the Simple Demography–Power Hypothesis: How   157
    Blacks in Power Influence White-Mentor–Black-Protégé
    Developmental Relationships
    David A. Thomas

Part III   Experiential Perspectives

10   Testing Theory by Practice   173
     Ellen McCambley

11   Mentoring With Class: Connections Between Social   189
     Class and Developmental Relationships in the Academy
     Sandra K. Hoyt

12   Mentoring at the Margin   211
     Audrey J. Murrell and Sandra Schwartz Tangri

Part IV   Conclusions

13 Where Do We Go From Here, and How Do We Get   227
    There? Methodological Issues in Conducting Research
    on Diversity and Mentoring Relationships
    Belle Rose Ragins

    Author Index   249

    Subject Index   259

Foreword

Sheila Wellington
Catalyst, New York

Organizations require renewal. Businesses, schools, governments, and churches that exist longer than a single lifetime need regeneration. Every social group must have ways to replace its departing members with new members, and each viable group must have ways to educate the new members.

We can look at the process of organizational renewal from two vantage points: that of the organization, which must devise ways to both train and socialize its new participants, and that of the newcomer, who must assimilate enough of the organization's norms in order to survive and flourish. From either vantage point, the process by which current group members guide new ones is of both practical and theoretical importance.

When new members closely resemble old ones, guidance can be a relatively simple task. When the protégé looks just like the senior person—only younger and more innocent—mentoring can proceed with minimal self-reflection. If the "new boy" has a life history and life circumstances that are just like those of the "old boy," then all the "old boy" has to do is to remember what private or secret information was useful and important for him to know and then pass that information on to the "new boy."

It is when members of the new generation differ from the old in important ways that organizational renewal ceases to be semi-automatic. Guiding the "new boy" who does not look just like oneself (who, indeed, may even be a girl) and whose background may be different from one's own is a task that requires not only the age-old knowledge and kindness but also new feats of empathy and imagination.

To recognize the special challenges of regeneration in a diverse workplace or educational setting is—to say the least—not to plead for a return to homogeneity. On the contrary, we know beyond a shadow of doubt that diversity can enhance organizational effectiveness. As any number of studies here at Catalyst have shown, the most vibrant organizations are those in which women as well as men assume positions of leadership and in which many cultures are represented and respected.

The demographics of America today and in the next century leave little hope or desire for continued organizational cloning. Change is not a matter of political correctness. Change is an imperative.

Good solid research provides us with the tools for making the most of change. That is why *Mentoring Dilemmas: Developmental Relationships Within Multicultural Organizations* is such an important book. Presenting the latest concepts and empirical work on questions of developmental relationships in organizations, *Mentoring Dilemmas* represents a splendid marriage between the ivory tower and the real world.

In *Mentoring Dilemmas: Developmental Relationships Within Multicultural Organizations*, a number of noted researchers discuss what scholars have found and are now finding to be true about mentors within their various roles in today's colleges and businesses. The findings are presented in ways that are useful not only to students but to educators, businesswomen, and businessmen as well. A look at a few representative chapters shows the union of theory and practice. Take, for example, Gibson and Cordova's (chap. 7) finding that visible women role models increased the number of women role models that men identified but not the number that women identified. Consider Blake's (chap. 5) conclusion that African American women in business trust White men to help them advance more than they trust White women. Imagine the implications of Crosby's (chap. 1) suggestion that to emphasize the emotional connection between the senior person and the more junior protégé—that is, to stress what most people mean by mentoring—is potentially to disadvantage women and minority men.

For much of my career, I worked in academic environments, largely in the Public Health and Psychiatry Departments at Yale. More recently, I moved from Yale to Catalyst to become its second President. At Catalyst, we work with corporations to effect positive changes on gender issues. I certainly know from both sets of experiences the importance of diversified mentoring relationships to organizations and individuals. It delights me to celebrate the significant contribution to our thinking about such issues that comes with the publication of *Mentoring Dilemmas: Developmental Relationships Within Multicultural Organizations*.

Preface

In 1995, a group of 15 women gathered in a house in Amherst, Massachusetts, to discuss the dilemmas facing them in diverse types of mentoring relationships. The product of these conversations shapes the content of this book, the title of which echoes the purpose of our discussions several years ago. As we met, it was clear to all of us that the world is changing. While organizations and the academy become more diverse, the need to recognize and develop talent within others becomes more critical and more complex. Herein lies the fundamental dilemma that parties to these important developmental relationships face. Our hope during that meeting was to help each other better understand the issues we were facing in our own diversified mentoring relationships as mentors, protégés, or both. We have the same goal for this book.

Our book is organized into three main parts, each with a different focus on mentoring perspectives: theoretical, empirical, and experiential. In Part I, the authors explore different theoretical perspectives on the issue of mentoring. Faye Crosby (chap. 1) discusses the literature on developmental relationships and explores some of the emerging themes within this area of work. In chapter 2, Sharon Bowman, Mary Kite, Nyla Branscombe, and Stacey Williams develop various theoretical models that help to explain the unique experience of Black Americans involved in developmental relationships within academic environments. Similarly, Sharon Goto (chap. 3) discusses the paucity of research that examines the challenges and obstacles facing Asian American students who seek mentoring relationships in order to survive on a traditional college campus. The final chapter in this section, written by Regina O'Neill, Sylvia Horton, and Faye Crosby, is a summary, exploration, and critique of the literature on gender and mentoring.

The next four chapters comprise Part II of this book and present empirical evidence, both qualitative and quantitative, relating to the impact of diverse mentoring relationships. In chapter 5, Stacey Blake describes the results of in-depth interviews with Black professional women about their struggles to advance within a traditional corporate environment. Addressing the issue of access and inclusion, Gail McGuire (chap. 6) presents results from a large survey of employees who discussed experiences with mentoring as a function of race and gender. Donald Gibson and Diana Cordova (chap. 7) further address the role of gender in developmental relationships, examining the impact of women's proportional representation in the upper echelons of organizations, or the role modeling and mentoring experiences of both men and women. Clearly, the notion of diversity and developmental relationships extends beyond the unique culture and environment of the United States. Daria Kirby and James Jackson (chap. 8) explore the impact of same- and cross-race supervisory relationships for Black British employees of large multinational organizations. The empirical section of the book concludes with a chapter in which David Thomas (chap. 9) explicates the functions that Black senior managers and executives serve in motivating White managers to form developmental relationships with Black protégés.

Part III of this book represents a unique contribution to the field by providing first-hand accounts of experiences in diverse mentoring relationships and key lessons learned from these experiences. In chapter 10, Ellen McCambley describes the two formal mentoring programs in which she was involved in a large corporation. These programs were designed to provide both career and psychosocial support to women and people of color attempting to break the glass ceiling within this organization. Sandra Hoyt (chap. 11) discusses the impact of mentoring on those who experience a different and often neglected glass ceiling that is erected as a result of people's poor and working class backgrounds. Audrey Murrell and Sandra Schwartz Tangri (chap. 12) provide additional reflections, each exploring the unique circumstances that surround their attempts to mentor from marginalized positions within their respective academic institutions.

Belle Rose Ragins, a prominent contributor to work in the area of diversified mentoring relationships, provides a commentary and conclusions in the final chapter of this book. Based on her highly productive career as a scholar investigating this topic, she provides clear insight into the issues that should be addressed in future research on diversity and mentoring. In addition, she offers some concrete suggestions for an approach that will provide valuable knowledge and understanding of developmental relationships in organizations.

The writing contained within the chapters of this book summarizes our attempt to understand the complex nature of diverse mentoring relationships. What this writing cannot adequately capture, however, is that our book is not just about diversified mentoring relationships. Our book was conceived as a result of diversified mentoring relationships. The planning of our conference, collaborations in the writing of chapters, and the overall joint editorship of this book each reflect important dimensions of the diverse relationships that we, as a collective, represent. Thus, we offer this book not simply as an academic discussion of diversified mentoring relationships but as a demonstration of what can be produced by meaningful collaborations among a diverse group of people who are themselves mentors and protégés of the highest quality.

ACKNOWLEDGMENTS

We acknowledge the generous financial support of the Schultz Foundation and of Smith College, which sustained the initial work on this project.

Many individuals helped with this book. We owe a special debt to Margie Jonnet, SunWok Eoh, Kimberly van Cleve, and Beth Patterson for their extraordinary efforts. Also earning our gratitude are Marilyn V. Patton, Casey Clark, Suzanne Klonis, and Lisa S. Markley, who made indirect but important contributions to the book. Lastly, Christie Smith has been a source of enlightenment and joy.

—*Audrey J. Murrell*
—*Faye J. Crosby*
—*Robin J. Ely*

I

Theoretical Perspectives

1

The Developing Literature on Developmental Relationships

Faye J. Crosby
University of California, Santa Cruz

In the late 1970s the well-known psychologist, Daniel Levinson of Yale University, was lead author on a book that represented the culmination of his career: *Seasons of a Man's Life* (Levinson, Darrow, Klein, Levinson, & McKee, 1978) Levinson's book rapidly became an international success. Translated into numerous languages, it sold record numbers of copies abroad and at home.

One arresting insight in *Seasons of a Man's Life* concerns the importance of mentors in the development of White middle-class men. Among the 40 men they interviewed, Levinson and his colleagues found that the presence of a mentor was essential in the smooth transition from young adulthood to authoritative maturity. The mentor, according to Levinson,

> may act as a teacher ... [and] ... as sponsor.... He [the mentor] may be a host and guide, welcoming the initiate into a new occupational and social world and acquainting him with its values, customs, resources, and cast of characters. Through his own virtues, achievements, and way of living, the mentor may be an exemplar that the protégé can admire and seek to emulate. He may provide counsel and moral support.... (p. 98)

To some, Levinson's insight has a timeless quality. The very word *mentor* calls to mind classical Greece. As perhaps everyone knows, Mentor was the

3

wise and caring servant to whom Odysseus entrusted oversight of the developing Telemachus, while he, the leader, was away from home on his famous adventures.

If timeless in some ways, in others Levinson's work seems very rooted in a specific historical context. The men whom Levinson studied grew to maturity at a period when the armed services, the professions and corporate management were all virtually homogeneous. Like Telemachus, the men in Levinson's study could expect all the public dramas of adulthood to play themselves out on a stage populated by others of the same gender and ethnicity. The context seems in some ways more antique than modern.

Today's world differs from that of the 1970s. The sons and daughters of Levinson's respondents face a very different public arena than that of their fathers. Contemporary schools and businesses are populated by White women and by people of color as well as by White men. How is Mentor to relate to Telemachus' sister and cousins and distant relatives with different skin tones and different cultures? How are they to respond to Mentor and to each other?

Ours is a book that looks at questions of developmental relations in the multicultural 1990s. Students of organizational behavior constitute our primary audience. Yet because abstractions without concrete referents are of more interest to the theologian than to the social scientist, we also include in our scope practitioners in the field of human resources. The chapters that follow include conceptual or theoretical pieces, reviews of the literature, discussions of specific studies, and firsthand accounts.

The fundamental challenge for any volume like ours is to differentiate between the enduring aspects of developmental relationships in organizations on the one hand and on the other, the more transient expressions of underlying processes. Accurate descriptions of local conditions are essential elements by which models of human interactions are built. In order to be useful, descriptions of specifics must not be confused with projections of what appears to be generally true.

The question of sexual attractions in the workplace offers a clear illustration of what is at issue. In 1983 Nancy Collins published the first quantitative study of mentoring issues at work. Collins reported that 99 of the 381 female respondents to answer the question about romance admitted that they had had sexual relations with their mentor (p. 121).

Would Collins' findings hold today? Men and women are often still attracted to each other—of this there is no doubt—yet given changing sexual mores of American business, it seems unlikely that 26 percent of contemporary cross-gender developmental relationships result in sexual intimacies. Such, at least, was the consensus of human resource professionals from the New York area attending a meeting in June 1997 (Blake & Crosby, 1997). The publicity around Monica Lewinsky, does not challenge their view that times have changed.

In this chapter appears the groundwork for the rest of the book. I start with a historical overview of how scholars and practitioners have approached the issues of developmental relations over the last quarter century. I then outline some questions that arise for those who would understand and promote mentoring across the boundaries of gender, ethnicity, and social class. As a means of facilitating the search for useful answers, I propose some terminology that, in my view, advances the work of theoretical and empirical researchers by enhancing the links between theory and practice.

HISTORY OF RESEARCH ON DEVELOPMENTAL RELATIONS

The decade of the 1970s promised expanded opportunities to many Americans. An unpopular and unfortunate war had ended. The victories of the Civil Rights Movement still felt fresh. The Women's Movement was gaining momentum, and educated liberal White men could still imagine that they would be allies to White women and to all people of color at no cost and with no change of self. Everybody was watching Sesame Street.

Given that scholarship reflects as well as shapes the times, it comes as no surprise that the 1970s was the decade when studies of healthy adult development gained special prominence. In 1976 Gail Sheehy published the best-selling book *Passages*, and in the same year an article entitled "The Mentor Connection: The Secret Link in the Successful Woman's Life" appeared in *New York Magazine.* In 1977 appeared George Vaillant's *Adaptation to Life*, in which a longitudinal study of a cohort of Harvard graduates reminded everyone that the "self-made man" is fiction. Anyone who couldn't understand Vaillant's insights (and many who could) would find in Rosabeth Kanter's brilliant tome *Men and Women of the Corporation*, also published in 1977, a searing analysis of the ways in which gendered conventions, including conventions about networking, facilitate or inhibit success. 1977 also brought with it Henning and Jardim's *Managerial Woman.* The next year the *Harvard Business Review* carried an article with the unambiguous title, "Everyone Who Makes It Has a Mentor" (Collins & Scott, 1978).

Meanwhile, *Seasons of a Man's Life* (Levinson et al., 1978), carrying its message that young men need mentors in their developmental journeys, was greeted with instant enthusiasm.

Over the course of the next few years there appeared a number of conceptual pieces (Cook, 1979; Fitt & Newton, 1981; Halcomb, 1980; Roche, 1979; Shapiro, Haseltine, & Rowe, 1978) in which vivid anecdotes or miniature studies were used to illustrate the authors' theoretical points. These articles enjoyed frequent citations throughout the 1980s. So did the one quantitative study of the era that showed that when the PhD candidate and dissertation advisor were of the same gender, the candidate was more productive than when the pair crossed genders (Goldstein, 1979).

By 1981 the initial burst of interest in mentoring and related topics was ending. One unresolved issue that continued to elicit attention was how to make sure that women received the same amount and same kind of mentoring as men. Underlying the gender question was, of course, the assumption that mentoring and sponsorship represented good practices, practices that benefited everyone, especially the protégé.

It was to the question of how women might find mentors and might manage their mentoring relationships that Linda Phillips-Jones and Nancy Collins turned their attention. In 1982 Phillips-Jones published her doctoral dissertation as a book entitled *Mentors and Protégés*. The next year came Collins' *Professional Women and Their Mentors*. Collins had contacted 600 impressive executive and managerial women from organizations in California and had received over 400 questionnaires. Collins supplemented her quantitative data with several dozen in-depth interviews.

Considering the richness of Collins' data, one might wonder why her book never received much attention in academic circles. Three explanations come to mind. First, as indicated in the subtitle of her book, Collins positioned her work as "a practical guide to mentoring for the woman who wants to get ahead" and thus fooled many scholars into thinking that she had fewer data than the more erudite-sounding works. Second, despite having quantitative data, Collins conducted no sophisticated analyses. All her statistics were descriptive, not inferential. Third, and probably most important, Collins' definitions lacked crispness. She outlined the components of mentoring but did not clearly differentiate the emotional or psychosocial functions of senior–junior alliances from the more instrumental functions.

A similar lack of conceptual crispness also characterized Michael Zey's study of 100 MBAs working in corporate America. Zey's book, *The Mentor Connection* (1984), proposed a hierarchy of developmental functions, rank ordered according to their importance. Believing that behaviors are more important than feelings, Zey assumed a four-tiered model with "protégé is recommended by mentor for promotion" two ranks above "mentor enhances protégé's sense of self" (p. 8). Because he did not support his controversial nosology with empirical data, Zey, like Collins, failed to capture a sustained scholarly audience.

Only with the publication of Kathy Kram's articles (Clawson & Kram, 1984; Kram, 1983; Kram & Isabella, 1985) and book (Kram, 1985) did the field begin to show the orderliness for which some well-known social scientists had loudly called (Hunt & Michael, 1983; Merriam, 1983). Through her famous in-depth qualitative study of 18 pairs of junior and senior managers in a New England utility company, supplemented by a qualitative study of peer pairs, Kram seemed to legitimate an entire field of study. *Mentoring at Work* (Kram, 1985) soon became and has since remained the classic publication in the area of developmental relationships.

With *Mentoring at Work*, contemporary scholarship on developmental relations begins. Kram's book has made its contribution by consolidating "available theories and empirical studies" (p. 2) and especially by systematizing concepts. Defining a developmental relationship as one that "contributes to individual growth and career advancement" (p. 4), Kram initially distinguishes between the classic mentor relationship and "other less involving, exclusive, and intricate forms like the sponsor relationship" and the peer support relationship (p. 4). Kram then draws on the work of Phillips-Jones (1982) and posits that there are two basic types of mentoring functions. The first type, career functions, involves sponsorship, exposure and visibility, coaching, protection, and challenging assignments. The second type of function, called psychosocial, includes, according to Kram, role modeling, acceptance and confirmation, counseling, and friendship. Whereas "career functions are those aspects of a relationship that enhance advancement in an organization" (p. 24), "psychosocial functions are those aspects of a relationship that enhance an individual's sense of competence, identity, and effectiveness in a professional role" (p. 32).

Expanding on Halcomb's (1980) ideas, Kram proposes in her book that developmental relationships can serve different functions at different stages in the life of a person's career. Kram also outlines the phases of the idealized mentoring relationship. Without ignoring the limitations of and problems with mentoring, especially within the context of what she calls "the complexities of cross-gender relationships" (p. 105), Kram clearly articulates the reasons that both mentoring and the mentoring alternatives (namely peer relationships) should bring benefit to organizations, to mentors, and especially to protégés.

Toward the end of her book, Kram describes conditions that facilitate the establishment of mentoring. Kram encourages organizations to remove the obstacles to effective mentoring and to educate their workforces about the benefits of mentoring. She also discusses "structural change strategies" (p. 173) such as modifying the reward system so as to link pay or promotions to how well managers develop subordinates but warns against the establishment of formal mentoring programs.

> Even if the match is not a poor one—that is, mentor and protégé like each other and want to build a relationship—both individuals can become anxious and confused about their new responsibilities as mentor or protégé. Seniors, when asked to mentor or coach, frequently have an idealized image of what this may entail. This image may cause considerable self-doubt and concern about their abilities to be successful. (p. 184)

"The risks," concludes Kram, "of a formal mentoring system are high, and the potential benefits have not been clearly demonstrated" (p. 185).

In the decade or so following the publication of *Mentoring at Work* has come a raft of substantial empirical studies of the antecedents, correlates, and consequences of being in a developmental relationship for women and men in a variety of settings. Some of the quantitative studies of developmental relationships use rigorous sampling procedures to obtain samples of respondents from lists of educated or professional people (Atkinson, Casas, & Neville, 1994; Bahniuk, Dobos, & Hill, 1990; Burke & McKeen, 1995; Chao, Walz, & Gardner, 1992; Corzine, Buntzman, & Busch, 1994; Dreher & Cox, 1996; Gaskill, 1991; Goh, 1991; Mobley, Jaret, March, & Lim, 1994; Ragins & Scandura, 1994; Struthers, 1995; Swerdlik & Bardon, 1988; Tepper, Shaffer, & Tepper, 1996; Whitely, Dougherty, & Dreher, 1991); other studies use equally appropriate and rigorous techniques to select respondents from one or more participating locations (Basow & Howe, 1980; Burke, McKeen, & McKenna, 1993; Erkut & Mokros, 1984; Fagenson, 1988, 1989; Hill, Bahniuk, & Dobos, 1989; Javidan, Bemmels, Devine, & Dastmalchian, 1995; Klaw & Rhodes, 1995; Ragins & Cotton, 1991, 1993; Ragins & McFarlin, 1990; Scandura, 1992). Most of the data in the quantitative studies come from people working in corporate settings (Burke et al., 1993; Burke & McKeen, 1995; Caruso, 1992; Dreher & Cox, 1996; Fagenson, 1988, 1989; Gaskill & Sibley, 1990; Goh, 1991; Ragins & Cotton, 1991, 1993; Ragins & McFarlin, 1990; Ragins & Scandura, 1994;

Scandura, 1992), but quantitative data also come from government workers (Javidan et al., 1995), lawyers (Mobley et al., 1994; Riley & Wrench, 1985), psychologists (Atkinson et al., 1994), university faculty (Hill et al., 1989; Struthers, 1995), students (Basow & Howe, 1980; Erkut & Mokros, 1984; Gilbert, 1985), and teenagers at risk (Klaw & Rhodes, 1995). Rates of responding vary from percentages as high as the mid-60s (Atkinson et al., 1994; Gilbert, 1985; Javidan et al., 1995; Struthers, 1995) and even 70% (Scandura, 1992) to less than 30% (Bahniuk et al., 1990; Dreher & Cox, 1996). Generally the response rates fall between 40% and 60% and are thus quite acceptable.

Although the majority of the academic articles published since the appearance of Kram's book present large scale quantitative studies, some articles contain small numerical studies (Bettencourt, Bol, & Fraser, 1994; Bowen, 1985; Ford & Wells, 1985; Kalbfleisch & Davies, 1991); some present qualitative studies (Ainslie & Pena, 1996; Maack & Passet, 1993; Stanulis, 1995; Thomas, 1989, 1990, 1993); some offer integrative reviews (Hale, 1995; Noe, 1988; Ragins, 1989, 1995, 1997) or conceptual pieces (Brinson & Kottler, 1993; Gilbert & Rossman, 1992; Olson & Ashton-Jones, 1992; Sandler, 1995); and some simply advocate for the concept of developmental relationships (Blackwell, 1989; Caudill & Carrington, 1995; Mathews, 1994–1995; Monaghan & Lunt, 1992; Redmond, 1990; Wilson & Elman, 1990). Of the qualitative studies, the insightful work conducted by David Thomas (1989, 1990, 1993) deserves special attention for its exquisite care in dealing with sensitive issues of race. Of the reviews, those of Belle Rose Ragins (1989, 1996, 1997) merit especially close reading for their thoroughness and intelligence on gender issues.

Only a very few academic studies have approached the topic of developmental relationships from the point of view of the senior person (Atkinson et al., 1994; Burke et al., 1993; Ragins & Cotton, 1993; Ragins & Scandura, 1994). Since the beginning, the bulk of studies on developmental relationships has looked at the topic from the angle of the protégé, and since the early 1980s, the academic studies have emphasized gender. Studies have documented which junior people seek and which have access to senior people. These studies show, by and large, that although junior women enter many more cross-gender developmental relationships than do men, there are few differences between the abilities of women and men to find mentors, sponsors, and role models (see O'Neill, Horton, & Crosby, chap. 4, this volume; Ragins, 1996). About the consequences of developmental relationships, the news for the junior person appears to be consistently positive. On the whole, despite early worries to the contrary (Noe, 1988; Olson & Ashton-Jones, 1992; Ragins, 1989), women derive as much measurable benefit as men from being sponsored or mentored.

Much less is known from the academic studies about ethnicity or race than about gender (see Blake, chap. 5, this volume; Bowman, Kite, Branscombe, & Williams, chap. 2, this volume; Goto, chap. 3, this volume; Kirby & Jackson, chap. 8, this volume). The vast majority of studies that specify the race or ethnicity of the participants contain a preponderance of Whites among the protégés. If most of junior people in the studies are White, so are virtually all the senior people. Indeed, it is really only now that mainstream scholars, so long focused on gender, have begun to acknowledge the role of race and ethnicity in developmental relationships (Blake, 1996; see also Nkomo, 1992).

MULTICULTURAL MENTORING

As issues of race and ethnicity have become increasingly important in business, so too have they appeared with increasing frequency on the research agendas of academics (Caruso, 1992; Catalyst, 1993). The change has illuminated holes in our understandings and has pointed out new directions to pursue through both basic and applied research. At the most fundamental level, the work of David Thomas (1989, 1990, 1993) amplifies questions that also arise from the work of others (e.g., Collins, 1983; Noe, 1988) about how the various aspects of a developmental relationship operate within different contexts to produce various kinds of benefits for the protégé.

At the heart of the matter are issues of trust, comfort, and rapport (Bowman et al, chap. 2, this volume; McCambley, chap. 10, this volume). Senior people might more readily act as instrumental sponsors than as psychosocial confidants for someone who differs from them on important dimensions of identity. Similarly, junior people may feel more suspicious of and behave more awkwardly around senior people who differ from them than around senior people who resemble them. Because most senior people in organizations today are still White men, insisting on the close emotional bond between a mentor and a protégé as the only vehicle for career advancement may unwittingly serve to reinforce the old (White) boys' network.

Scholars like Belle Rose Ragins (1989) and Herminia Ibarra (1995) have noted that under some conditions career advantages for a protégé can derive simply from having a senior person undertake instrumental functions on his or her behalf, whereas in other circumstances warm feelings may also be important. When a new recruit to an organization is part of a visible minority, might she or he seek instrumental connection with mainstream senior people and psychosocial support from other minority individuals who may be somewhat marginalized? Are some combinations more sustainable and more sustaining than others?

Noticing a Problem

Unfortunately, answers to questions such as these are hard to glean from the existing literature because, as Table 1.1 shows, most operational definitions used in the studies roll together the instrumental and emotional aspects of developmental relationships. The term *mentor* means different things to different scholars. It is hard to know to which aspects of mentoring the respondents are attending when they participate in the quantitative studies.

That psychosocial support and instrumental support are as distinct as Kram (1985) proposed as been shown empirically by at least three studies. First, Ragins and McFarlin (1990) developed the mentor role instrument (MRI), containing 33 different questions that assess 11 different functions of a developmental relationship. Five functions were instrumental in nature, and four were psychosocial. For example, to measure exposure, an instrumental function, Ragins and McFarlin had three items, including "helps me be more visible in the organization"; "creates opportunities for me to impress important people in the organization"; and "brings my accomplishments to the attention of important people in the organization." To measure acceptance, a psychosocial function, they had three other items including "accepts me as a competent professional"; "thinks highly of me"; and "guides my professional development." Developed with a small pilot sample, the different subscales of the inventory all showed good reliability with the approximately 181 protégés who were the respondents in the final study.

After Ragins and McFarlin (1990) showed that one could empirically distinguish the functions outlined by Kram (1985), Scandura (1992) demonstrated that the two main functions—instrumental and emotional—were distinct. Scandura administered an 18-item mentoring scale to 244 managers, 97% of whom were male (and most of whom were no doubt White). When Scandura factor analyzed the data, she found three discrete factors, which she labeled Social Support, Vocational, and Role Modeling. Each item loaded on one of the factors, and none loaded on more

TABLE 1.1

Sample Definitions of Mentoring Offered
by Researchers to Respondents

Date	Authors	Definition of Mentor Provided
1988, 1989	Fagenson	"Someone in a position power who looks out for you or gives you advice, brings your accomplishments to the attention of other people who have power in the company."
1989	Hill et al.	Administered a 10-page questionnaire asking about behaviors.
1989	Swerdlik & Bardon	"Mentoring exists when professional persons act as resources, sponsors, and transitional figures for another person entering the professional world. Mentors provide less experienced persons (mentees) with knowledge, advice, challenge, and support in their pursuit of becoming full members of a particular segment of life.... Mentors welcome less experienced persons into the professional world and represent skill, knowledge, and success that the new professionals hope someday to acquire...."
1990	Ragins & McFarlin	"A high-ranking, influential member of your organization who has advanced experience and knowledge and who is committed to providing upward mobility and support to your career."Also administered scale about 11 types of support.
1990	Thomas	"Someone who 'took an active interest in and concerted action to advance' your career." Also administered scale about 11 types of support.
1991	Gaskill	"A more experienced, higher ranking individual who aided with your professional development and career advancement beyond normal supervisory guidance."
1991	Goh	Administered an 11-item scale with items such as "My boss makes an effort to groom me for promotions."
1991	Kalbfleisch & Davies	"Member of the profession or organization who shares values, provides emotional support, career counseling, information and advice, professional and organizational sponsorship, and facilitates access to key organizational and professional networks."
1991	Ragins & Cotton	"A high-ranking, influential member of your organization who has advanced experience and knowledge and who is committed to providing upward mobility and support to your career."

1991	Whitely et al.	Administered 10-item scale of psychosocial or instrumental functions.
1992	Chao et al.	"Mentorship is defined as an intense work relationship between senior (mentor) and junior (protégé) organizational members. The mentor has experience and power in the organization and personally advises, counsels, coaches, and promotes the career development of the protégé. Promotion of protégé's career may occur through mentor's influence and power over other organizational members." Also administered scale with 14 psychosocial items and 7 career function items.
1993	Burke et al.	"Consider all the people younger than yourself whose careers you have influenced in a positive way over the last few years.... Choose one individual with whom you have shared an especially close relationship and whose career you have influenced the most ... " Administered a scale with six psychosocial and six career function questions.
1993	Maack & Passet	"Someone senior to you in the field who actively works for your advancement. A mentor can also be a role model."
1994	Atkinson et al.	"A mentor can be defined as a trusted and experienced supervisor or advisor who by mutual consent takes an active interest in the development and education of a younger and less experienced individual. A mentor differs from a traditional supervisor or advisor in that a mentor proactively seeks to enhance the development and education of a protégé while a traditional supervisor or advisor only promotes the development and education of a supervisee to the extent demanded by their position."
1994	Corzine et al.	"A higher level manager who has encouraged you and guided your career."
1995	Klaw & Rhodes	"Other than your parents or whoever raised you, do you have a role model or mentor who you go to for support and guidance? A mentor is not someone around your age or a boyfriend. He or she is an adult who is older than you, who has more experience than you, and who has taken a special interest in you."
1996	Dreher & Cox	"An individual who holds a position senior to yours who takes an active interest in developing your career.... The standard subordinate/supervisor relationship is not a mentoring relationship."
1996	Tepper et al.	Administered 16-item questionnaire.

than one factor, giving very firm empirical support to the distinction that Kram (1985) had drawn between the psychosocial and the career (instrumental) functions of the mentoring relationship. In a series of multiple regression analyses, Scandura (1992) found that scores on the social support scale statistically predicted salaries, whereas scores on the vocational scale statistically predicted promotions.

More recently, Tepper et al. (1996), included five different samples with a total of 569 full-time employed people as respondents to conduct a thorough psychometric study of a 16-item inventory. They confirmed the two distinct functions, instrumental and psychosocial, and found the two functions to be invariant across gender and stable across all samples.

For newcomers to organizations who might have better luck at establishing instrumental links than at establishing strong emotional ties, the forecast from studies like Scandura's is for variable weather. Some other recent academic studies have also rained on the parade. Whitely et al. (1991) examined the effects of sponsorship on earnings and promotions and initially found a huge effect among the 404 women and men in their random sample. Upon closer inspection, however, they discovered that all the effects occurred among respondents who had grown up in the middle and upper classes; for respondents who had grown up in working and lower classes, having had a sponsor brought no measurable benefit. Equally sobering are the results of a recent inquiry by Dreher and Cox (1996). MBAs in their study who had had a mentor earned significantly more money than those who had not had one— but only if the mentor was a White male. Respondents who had been mentored by a female or by a minority male did not earn more than those who had never been mentored. In contrast, protégés of White male mentors earned $22,454 more per annum on average than everyone else. Dreher and Cox also found that White male respondents earned on average $17,717 more than similar respondents who were female or were minority male. The low response rate means that Dreher and Cox's findings should be accepted only as tentative, but if they are replicated, the conclusion will be that there are rough seas for White women and ethnic minorities who seek to foster the careers of their more junior colleagues and for their junior colleagues who are invested in their being able to do so.

Reaching for Solutions: Clarifying Terms

How can the sailing be made smoother? Clearly, more research needs to be done. In line with feminist thinkers (e.g., Stewart, 1994), we believe that the quality of the research is enhanced by contextualizing it. One way to contextualize work is to look for the factors, such as one's social class of origin, that constrain observed connections between variables. Another way is to analyze situations in which behaviors do and do not occur. By examining, for example, the situations in which senior White men are or are not willing to sponsor women or minority men in their organizations, one can begin to chart more accurately the dynamics of cross-gender and cross-race developmental relationships.

A final means for achieving good contextually grounded research is to speak in terms that make sense to those whom we study. As mentioned previously, the bulk of the data on developmental relations come from corporate America. It makes sense, therefore, to describe the developmental processes in words that can readily be understood in corporate settings. Taking as our base the distinctions articulated by Phillips-Jones (1982) and Kram (1985) and following the more recent work of Thomas (1989, 1990, 1993), we see three functions that can be fulfilled by a senior person in a developmental relationship:

1. A role model is a senior person with whom a more junior person identifies emotionally and whom the more junior person wishes to emulate in some way. The role model, however, need feel no emotional attachment to the junior person. Indeed, the role model may not be aware that he or she is a role model for the junior person and may not even know of the existence of the junior person.

2. A sponsor is a senior person who gives instrumental help to a more junior person. Emotional attachment is not a necessary part of the sponsor–protégé relationship. The protégé must be able to trust that the sponsor will fulfill his or her duties vis-à-vis the protégé, but the protégé may have no other affective tie to the sponsor. Sponsors perform the career functions outlined by Kram (1985).

3. A mentor is a senior person who has an emotional investment in the development of a junior person. Interpersonal trust and emotional attachment exist on both sides. The mentor may or may not be able to effect much instrumental help for the protégé in the organization, but the mentor holds the protégé's interests at heart and provides socioemotional support to the protégé. Mentors perform the psychosocial functions outlined by Kram (1985).

A senior person may play more than one role in a developmental relationship. She or he may start out, for example, as a sponsor and by dint of working hard on behalf of a junior person, especially if the junior person shows gratitude and ability, may come to care about the welfare and well-being of the junior person. Indeed, at any one time a senior individual may be role model, sponsor, and mentor.

Given that an individual can fulfill more than one of the developmental roles at any given time, one may wonder what is served by our modification of Kram's concepts. Our answer is that our modifications simply refine the work of Kram and other pioneers in the field in order to capture as closely as possible the experiences people have in today's increasingly multicultural organizations.

Kram (1985) hinted that senior White men in most American organizations might feel more comfortable giving instrumental rather than emotional support (p. 184). Subsequent research (e.g., Struthers, 1995) has shown the wisdom of Kram's insight. Senior White men may feel worried when asked to mentor someone because the word *mentor* connotes a role that is laden with emotion (McCambley, chap. 10, this volume). If the task is to encourage beneficial developmental relationships, of which there are many kinds, why not define constructs in a way to fit the task?

The distinctions among role models, sponsors, and mentors look as valuable from the bottom–up perspective as from the top–down. Consider the African American woman who establishes deep rapport with her African American supervisor (Frierson, Hargrove, & Lewis, 1994). Like the fictional characters in Campbell's (1995) novel, *Brothers and Sisters*, she may wish to rely on her supervisor as an emotional and spiritual guide and may simultaneously need to acknowledge that her supervisor is relatively powerless to provide the kind of instrumental support that a sponsor could provide. Why not encourage a conceptual language to describe her realities (Nkomo, 1992)?

Not only do our terminological distinctions promise benefits for practice and research down the road, they also have the immediate benefit of allowing us to examine the validity of some assumptions. Zey (1984), for example, assumed that actions were more worthwhile than feelings. Is the assumption valid in all circumstances? Are there conditions under which emotional support or mutual caring matters more than sponsorship?

ENDNOTE

Ultimately, multicultural sponsorship and mentoring bring benefits not just to individuals but also to organizations. In addition to engendering contentment among both junior and senior employees, the uniting of people with diverse backgrounds into developmental relationships can encourage all parties to bring more of themselves to work, which in turn can facilitate productive questioning and problem solving (Thomas & Ely, 1996). When developmental relations only involve people who closely resemble each other, complacency and what Janis (1989) called *groupthink* too readily set in. Systems become ossified, and that is not a healthy state in today's athletic global economies. How much our existing organizations need to grow and change to accommodate the new talent coming into them and the new external conditions facing them remains to be seen. If the 1970s were obsessed with the issue of personal growth, perhaps the present era in which we usher in a new millennium will be smitten with the concept of growing communities.

REFERENCES

Ainslie, R. C., & Pena, E. (1996). Telemakhos' search: An illustration of therapeutic mentoring for multiply stressed youth. *Mind and Human Interaction, 7*, 202–212.

Atkinson, D. L., Casas, A., & Neville, H. (1994). Ethnic minority psychologists: Whom they mentor and benefits they derive from the process. *Journal of Multicultural Counseling and Development, 22*, 37–48.

Bahniuk, M. H., Dobos, J., & Hill, S. E. K. (1990). The impact of mentoring, collegial support, and information adequacy on career success: A replication. *Handbook of Replication Research, 5*, 431–451.

Basow, S., & Howe, K. G. (1980). Role model influence: Effects of sex and sex-role attitude in college students. *Psychology of Women Quarterly, 4*, 558–572.

Bettencourt, B. A., Bol, L., & Fraser, S. C. (1994). Psychology graduate students as research mentors of undergraduates: A national survey. *Psychological Reports, 75*, 963–970.

Blackwell, J. E. (1989, Sept.–Oct.). Mentoring: An action strategy for increasing minority faculty. *Academe, 8*, 14.

Blake, S. D. (1996). *The changing face of mentoring in diverse organizations.* Unpublished doctoral dissertation, University of Michigan, Ann Arbor.

Blake, S. D., & Crosby, F. J. (1997, June). *Multicultural mentoring.* Paper presented at fourth annual Smith Forum, New York, NY.

Bowen, D. D. (1985, February). Were men meant to mentor women? *Training and Development Journal*, 31–34.

Brinson, J., & Kottler, J. (1993). *Counselor Education and Supervision, 32*, 241–253.

Burke, R. J., McKeen, C. A., & McKenna, C. (1993). Correlates of mentoring in organizations: The mentors perspective. *Psychological Reports, 72*, 883–896.

Burke, R. J., & McKeen, C. (1995). Do managerial women prefer women mentors? *Psychological Reports, 76*, 688–690.

Campbell, B. M. (1995). *Brothers and sisters.* New York: Putnam.

Caruso, R. E. (1992). *Mentoring and the business environment: Asset or liability?* Brookfield: Dartmouth.

Catalyst. (1993). *Mentoring: A guide to corporate programs and practices.* New York: Catalyst.

Caudill, D. W., & Carrington, M. R. (1995, April). Marketing educators as mentors: Benefits for students. *Business Education Forum*, 34–36.

Chao, G. T., Walz, P. M., & Gardner, P. D. (1992). Formal and informal mentorships: A comparison on mentoring functions and contrast with nonmentored counterparts. *Personnel Psychology*, 45, 619–636.

Clawson, J. G., & Kram, K. E. (1984, May–June). Managing cross-gender mentoring. *Business Horizons*, 22–32.

Collins, E. G. C., & Scott, P. (1978, July–Aug). Everyone who makes it has a mentor. *Harvard Business Review*, 89100.

Collins, N. W. (1983). *Professional women and their mentors: A practical guide to mentoring for the woman who wants to get ahead.* Englewood Cliffs, NJ: Prentice-Hall.

Cook, M. F. (1979). Is a mentor relationship primarily a male experience? *The Personnel Administrator*, 24, 82–86.

Corzine, J. B., Buntzman, G. F., & Busch, E. T. (1994). Mentoring, downsizing, gender, and career outcomes. *Journal of Social Behavior and Personality*, 9, 517–528.

Dreher, G. F., & Cox, T. H., Jr. (1996). Race, gender, and opportunity: A study of compensation attainment and the establishment of mentoring relationships. *Journal of Applied Psychology*, 81, 297–308.

Erkut, S., & Mokros, J. R. (1984). Professors as models and mentors for college students. *American Educational Research Journal*, 21, 399–417.

Fagenson, E. A. (1988). The power of a mentor: Protégés and nonprotégés' perceptions of their own power in organizations. *Group and Organization Studies*, 13, 182–194.

Fagenson, E. A. (1989). The mentor advantage: Perceived career/job experiences of protégés versus nonprotégé's. *Journal of Organizational Behavior*, 10, 309–320.

Fitt, L. W., & Newton, D. (1981, MarchApril).When the mentor is a man and the protégée is a woman. *Harvard Business Review*, 56–60.

Ford, D. L., & Wells, L. (1985). Upward mobility factors among Black public administrators: The role of mentors. *Centerboard: Journal of the Center for Human Relations*, 3, 33–48.

Frierson, H. T., Hargrove, B. K., & Lewis, N. R. (1994). Black summer research students' perceptions related to research mentors' race and gender. *Journal of College Student Development*, 35, 475–480.

Gaskill, L. R. (1991). Same-sex and cross-sex mentoring of female protégés: A comparative analysis. *The Career Development Quarterly*, 40, 48–63.

Gaskill, L. R., & Sibley, L. R. (1990). Mentoring relationships for women in retailing. *Clothing and Textile Research Journal*, 9, 1–10.

Gilbert, L. A. (1985). Dimensions of same-gender student-faculty role-model relationships. *Sex Roles*, 12, 111–122.

Gilbert, L. A., & Rossman, K. M. (1992). Gender and mentoring process for women: Implications for professional development. *Professional Psychology: Research and Practice*, 23, 233–238.

Goh, S. C. (1991). Sex differences in perceptions of interpersonal work style, career emphasis, supervisory mentoring behavior, and job satisfaction. *Sex Roles*, 24, 701–710.

Goldstein, E. (1979). Effect of same-sex and cross-sex role models on the subsequent academic productivity of scholars. *American Psychologist*, 34, 407–410.

Halcomb, R. (1980, February). Mentors and the successful woman. *Across the Board*, 13–18.

Hale, M. M. (1995). Mentoring women in organizations: Practice in search of theory. *American Review of Public Administration*, 25, 327–339.

Henning, M. M., & Jardim, A. (1977). *The managerial woman.* New York: Doubleday.

Hill, S. E., Bahniuk, M. H., & Dobos, J. (1989). The impact of mentoring and collegial support on faculty success: An analysis of support behavior, information adequacy, and communication apprehension. *Communication Education*, 15–33.

Hunt, D. M., & Michael, C. (1983). Mentorship: A career training and development tool. *Academy of Management Review, 8,* 475–485.

Ibarra, H. (1995) Personal networks of women and minorities in management: A conceptual framework. *Academy of Management Review, 18,* 56–87.

Janis, I. (1989). *Crucial decisions: Leadership in policymaking and crisis management.* New York: Free Press.

Javidan, M., Bemmels, B., Devine, K. S., & Dastmalchian, A. (1995). Superior and subordinate gender and the acceptance of superiors as role models. *Human Relations, 48,* 1271–1284.

Kalbfleisch, P. J., & Davies, A. B. (1991). Minorities and mentoring: Managing the multicultural institution. *Communication Education, 40,* 266–271.

Kanter, R. M. (1977). *Men and women of the corporation.* New York: Basic Books.

Klaw, E. L., & Rhodes, J. E. (1995). Mentor relationships and the career development of pregnant and parenting African-American teenagers. *Psychology of Women Quarterly, 19,* 551–562.

Kram, K. E. (1983). Phases of a mentor relationship. *Academy of Management Journal, 26,* 608–625.

Kram, K. E. (1985). *Mentoring at work: Developmental relationships in organizational life.* Glenview, IL: Scott, Foresman.

Kram, K., E., & Isabella, L. A. (1985). Mentoring alternatives: The role of peer relations in career development. *Academy of Management Journal, 28,* 110–132.

Levinson, D. J., Darrow, C. M., Klein, E. G., Levinson, M. H., & McKee, B. (1978). *Seasons of a man's life.* New York: Knopf.

Maack, M. N., & Passet, J. E. (1993). Unwritten rules: Mentoring women faculty. Library *Science Review, 15,* 117–141.

Mathews, A. L. (1994-95, Winter). The diversity connections: Mentoring and networking. *The Public Manager,* 23–26.

Merriam, S. (1983). Mentors and protégés: A critical review of the literature. *Adult Education Quarterly, 33,* 161–173.

Mobley, G. M., Jaret, C., Marsh, J., & Lim, Y. Y. (1994). Mentoring, job satisfaction, gender, and the legal profession. *Sex Roles, 31,* 79–98.

Monaghan, J., & Lunt, N. (1992). Mentoring: Person, process, practice and problems. *British Journal of Educational Studies, 40,* 248–263.

Nkomo, S. (1992). The emperor has no clothes: Rewriting "Race in Organizations." *Academy of Management Review, 17,* 487–513.

Noe, R. A. (1988). Women and mentoring: A review and research agenda. *Academy of Management Review, 13,* 65–78.

Olson, G. A., & Ashton-Jones, E. (1992). Doing gender: (En)gendering academic mentoring. *Journal of Education, 174,* 114–127.

Phillips-Jones, L. (1982). *Mentors and protégés.* New York: Arbor House.

Ragins, B. R. (1989). Barriers to mentoring: The female manager's dilemma. *Human Relations, 42,* 1–22.

Ragins, B. R.. (1995). Diversity, power, and mentorship in organizations: A cultural, structural and behavioral perspective. In M. Chemers, M. Costanzo, & S. Oskamp (Eds.), *Diversity in organizations* (pp. 91–132). Newbury Park, CA: Sage.

Ragins, B. R., (1997). Diversified mentoring relationships in organizations: A power perspective. *Academy of Management Review, 22,* 482–521.

Ragins, B. R., & Cotton, J. L. (1991). Easier said than done: Gender differences in perceived barriers to gaining a mentor. *Academy of Management Journal, 34,* 939–951.

Ragins, B. R., & Cotton, J. L. (1993). Gender and willingness to mentor in organizations. *Journal of Management, 19,* 97–111.

Ragins, B. R., & McFarlin, D. B. (1990). Perceptions of mentor roles in cross-gender mentoring relationships. *Journal of Vocational Behavior, 37,* 321–339.

Ragins, B. R., & Scandura, T. A. (1994). Gender differences in expected outcomes of mentoring relationships. *Academy of Management Journal, 37,* 957–971.

Redmond, S. P. (1990). Mentoring and cultural diversity in academic settings. *American Behavioral Scientist, 34,* 188–200.

Riley, S., & Wrench, D. (1985). Mentoring among female lawyers. *Journal of Applied Psychology, 15,* 374–386.

Roche, G. R. (1979, Jan.–Feb.). Much ado about mentors. *Harvard Business Review,* 17–28.

Sandler, B. R. (1995, Spring). Women as mentors: Myths and commandments. *Horizons,* 105–106.

Scandura, T. A. (1992). Mentorship and career mobility: An empirical investigation. *Journal of Organizational Behavior, 13,* 169–173.

Shapiro, E. C., Haseltine, F. P., & Rowe, M. P. (1978). Moving up: Role models, mentors, and the patron system. *Sloan Management Review, 19*(3), 51–58.

Sheehy, G. (1976). *Passages: Predictable crises of adult life.* New York: Dutton.

Stanulis, R. N. (1995). Classroom teachers as mentors: Possibilities for participation in a professional development school context. *Teaching and Teacher Education, 11,* 331–344.

Stewart, A. J. (1994). Toward a feminist strategy for studying women's lives. In C. E. Franz and A. J. Stewart (Eds.), *Women creating lives: Identities, resilience, & resistance* (pp. 11–35). Boulder, CO: Westview Press.

Struthers, N. J. (1995). Differences in mentoring: A function of gender or organizational rank? *Journal of Social Behavior and Personality, 10,* 265–272.

Swerdlik, M. E., & Bardon, J. I. (1988). A survey of mentoring experiences in school psychology. *Journal of School Psychology, 26,* 213–224.

Tepper, K., Shaffer, B. C., & Tepper, B. J. (1996). Latent structure of mentoring function scales. *Educational and Psychological Measurement, 56,* 848–857.

Thomas, D. A. (1989). Mentoring and irrationality: The role of racial taboos. *Human Resource Management, 28,* 279–290.

Thomas, D. A. (1990). The impact of race on managers' experiences of developmental relationships (mentoring and sponsorship): An intra-organizational study. *Journal of Organizational Behavior, 11,* 479–491.

Thomas, D. A. (1993). Racial dynamics in cross-race developmental relationships. *Administrative Science Quarterly, 38,* 169–194.

Thomas, D. A., & Ely, R. J. (1996, Sept.–Oct). Making differences matter: A new paradigm for managing diversity. *Harvard Business Review,* 79–90.

Vaillant, G. (1977). *Adaptation to life.* Boston: Little.

Whitely, W., Dougherty, T. W., & Dreher, G. F. (1991). Relationship of career mentoring and socioeconomic origin to managers' and professionals' early career progress. *Academy of Management Journal, 34,* 331–351.

Wilson, J. A., & Elman, N. S. (1990). Organizational benefits of mentoring. *Academy of Management Executive, 4,* 88–94.

Zey, M. G. (1984). *The mentor connection.* Homewood, IL: Dow Jones-Irwin.

2

Developmental Relationships of Black Americans in the Academy

Sharon R. Bowman
Ball State University

Mary E. Kite
Ball State University

Nyla R. Branscombe
University of Kansas

Stacey Williams
University of Massachusetts

Most people in the United States have an active work life. That may consist of a variety of occupations over the lifespan or, more commonly, one occupation that is the focus of one's working life. For many, a career is more than just a job—it is an integral part of the self-concept and an important source of meaning in life (Baumeister, 1991). Many have internalized the American ideals of hard work, acquisition of job skills, and career advancement (Astin, 1984; Brown, Minor, & Jespen, 1991). For most of us to succeed in our careers, however, we need someone to help us navigate various obstacles, show us the ropes, and teach us the subtle aspects of the work environment. Given the complexity involved, the need for guidance in career development should not be surprising.

Increasingly, the best paid and most desirable jobs in the workforce require college educations. In fact, researchers have identified education as a more important predictor of economic success than ever before (see Bronfenbrenner, McClelland, Wethington, Moen, & Ceci, 1996; Major & Schmader, 1998). Given the importance of education, it is natural to ask: What factors influence the experience of Black Americans in college settings? How can ebony women and men flourish in the ivory tower? More specifically, what roles do developmental relationships involving mentoring and sponsorship play in the lives of Black American students and faculty? Finally, how might the academy be made more accessible and comfortable for Black Americans?

We begin our chapter with a review of the sobering statistics concerning the plight of Black Americans in educational settings. One could argue that one of the most serious problems plaguing the Black community is the failure of its students to be successful in the educational system. After examining why Black Americans do not fare well in the American educational system, we consider the impediments faced by Black American college students. We conclude by looking at the fate of Black American faculty members. In particular, we examine their problems and consider ways of nurturing budding Black American scholars.

As Henry (1994) noted, universities were originally conceived as unbiased institutions, where objective knowledge was dispensed to a select few, with the purpose of shaping the world for the better. Those ivory towers, however, were designed for and maintained by privileged White American males; there was a perception that the lack of ethnic, gender, and class diversity was due to the individual's inability to meet competitive standards, not as a problem with the selection process itself. Today's ivory towers continue to pose difficulties for ebony women (Allen, 1996; Henry, 1994; Taylor & Smitherman-Donaldson, 1989), whether they are students or faculty. This chapter describes the assistance that a sponsor or mentor can provide to someone navigating these ivory walls.

BACKGROUND

Black American students begin primary school with standardized test scores that are similar to their White American counterparts, but by the sixth grade they are two full grades apart in academic performance (Steele,

1997). Although the dropout rate of Black American students has fallen over the past 20 years, with more now completing high school (70%), they still score markedly below their White American counterparts on the verbal and mathematical portions of the Scholastic Assessment Test (see Russel, 1995). When we consider those who attend college, the proportion of White Americans who graduate is almost twice that of Black Americans (see Lang, 1988; Sigelman & Welch, 1991). As Garibaldi (1991) noted, lower graduation rates for Black Americans occur mainly at predominantly White American campuses. In contrast, Black colleges produce 40 percent of all Black American bachelor's degrees, even though Black colleges account for only 20% of the total Black American enrollment in higher education. Moreover, at predominately White American colleges, Black students are particularly underrepresented in mathematics and natural sciences (Cullotta & Gibbons, 1992; White & Parham, 1990). A similar pattern occurs in graduate education: Black colleges award one third of all masters' degrees Black Americans receive. In addition, Black American women have made gains in the PhDs received, but the number awarded to Black American men has declined (Steele, 1997). It seems that Black American colleges provide an environment that is more conducive to Black American achievement than do other college campuses.

Even when Black Americans successfully complete graduate study, problems emerge for them in obtaining academic positions. According to Wilson (1989), fewer Black American faculty were hired in 1979 than in 1975, even though the number of available faculty positions and the number of Black American PhDs increased over the same time period. Furthermore, once hired, Black Americans find it difficult to succeed in the academy. Black American women comprise less than 1%, and Black American men 1.6% of full professorships, compared to 9.9% for White American women and 83.2% for White American men (Carter, Pearson, & Shavlik, 1988, as cited in Wilson, 1989). Black Americans are approximately 12% of the U.S. population but less than 5% of full-time college and university faculty. Furthermore, of those minority faculty who are hired in a faculty position, only 60% earn tenure compared to 72% of nonminority faculty (Brinson & Kottler, 1993).

Black Americans, along with members of other underrepresented groups, are more likely to be found in administrative or student affairs positions than in the faculty ranks. Such positions, however, are not those that typically lead to promotion (e.g., affirmative action officers, heads of ethnic studies programs, or directors of remedial programs). Nor do they hold the status or recognition necessary for promotion, perhaps because they are seen as important but on the sidelines (Wilson, 1989). The ultimate of career opportunities in higher education, the college presidency, as well as other high ranks in academic administration, consist of very low proportions of Black Americans.

A number of studies have clearly demonstrated that Black Americans and their parents value education as much or more than White Americans (Cook & Curtin, 1987; Sigelman & Welch, 1991; Steinberg, Dornbusch, & Brown, 1992). Why, then, do Black Americans have such a relatively low success rate? Although some have advanced biologically based differences in intelligence as a potential explanation (e.g., Herrnstein & Murray, 1994; Jensen, 1969), this argument has received wide criticism (see Gould, 1996, for an excellent critique). Moreover, such reasoning flies in the face of evidence, discussed in this chapter, documenting that achievement can be significantly increased by relatively minor changes to current educational practices. Finally, this perspective typically ignores the fact that, even for studies finding ethnic and racial group differences, there are greater within-race differences than between-race differences (Suzuki & Valencia, 1997). More compelling are arguments that emphasize the clash between Afrocentric values of verve and movement, on the one hand, and mainstream values of immobility, order, and hierarchy in the classroom, on the other (Allen & Boykin, 1992; Fordham & Ogbu, 1986; Ogbu, 1990). From this perspective, it is the mismatch between the academic environment and the individual's cultural background that primarily contributes to the reduced success of Black Americans in the classroom.

Teachers' expectations also influence students' successes and their likelihood of staying in school (Allen, 1996). This literature suggests that students can improve their performance if they are given the chance to do so, but negative group-based expectancies can reduce those chances (Rosenthal & Jacobson, 1968). Teachers certainly hold expectations about student performance and ability, which in turn influence how teachers interact with those students (Jussim & Fleming, 1996). Teachers, for example, give more time and attention to students for whom they have high expectations (Jussim, 1989). Students respond to these different expectancies with behaviors that confirm them; students for whom the teachers have high expectations tend to perform better than students for whom the teachers have lowered expectations.

Evidence for the role that ethnic stereotypes play in this educational process is surprisingly scant (see Jussim & Fleming, 1996). Available data suggest, however, that expectancies for Black American university students are not equal to those held for their White American counterparts. Trujillo (1986) concluded from her research that professors act differently toward minority students and hold lower academic expectations for them, compared with White American students. She found that professors asked White American students significantly more complex questions, pushed them more to improve their responses, and gave longer responses to them compared to minority students. The literature on expectancy confirmation supports the proposition that this differential treatment can dramatically affect students' academic achievement.

Black American achievement is also affected by structural aspects of the academy. The ways in which material is presented and the assumptions professors make about the ways students learn can have a dramatic impact on student performance independent of ability or potential (e.g., Nelson, 1994). In his doctoral dissertation, Treisman (1985, cited in Fullilove & Treisman, 1990) began to explore factors associated with Black Americans who experienced low achievement in calculus despite high math entry scores. Rather than blame the students, Treisman set out to learn what experiences low achievers shared. In contrast with Chinese students, who were also a minority on campus but were highly successful in the course, Treisman found that Black Americans devoted less time to their mathematics studies, focused on computational errors rather than concepts, and did not seek assistance from each other or the teaching assistant. In response, Treisman invited these students to participate in an honors discussion class modeled after the success he saw in the Chinese students' study strategies. He described the program as highly selective, not remedial. He assigned homework that covered a variety of problem types. Although students could spend some time working alone, their primary responsibility during the classroom session was to help each other in collaborative groups. Although this aspect of the program took only 2 hours per week, its effects were impressive. Failure rates for non-program participants in this and follow-up programs (see Fullilove & Treisman, 1990) ranged from 33 to 41%, but for program participants only 4–7% failed. Moreover, participants were 2 to 3 times more likely to earn a B– or better. This success has been replicated in a variety of other science courses (see Nelson, 1994).

Recent work in psychology tells a similar story. Claude Steele and his colleagues have examined the extent to which Black American college students internalize negative stereotypes about their group and the degree to which such negative self-assessment interferes with scholastic performance. More specifically, Steele and Aronson (1995) argued that one of the reasons Black American students do poorly on standardized tests is because of stereotype threat. According to Steele (1997), this threat occurs "when one is in a situation or doing something for which a negative stereotype about one's group applies" (p. 614). Because negative stereotypes about Black Americans' academic abilities exist, when these individuals face achievement orientation situations, such as test taking, they are confronted with the possibility of confirming the group's negative stereotype. This extra burden may impede Black American's performance in certain situations (Steele & Aronson, 1995).

To test this notion, Steele and Aronson (1995) gave two groups of Black and White undergraduates a test composed of the most difficult verbal questions from the Graduate Record Exam. Before the test, one group was told that the purpose of the test was to examine the psychological factors involved in problem solving, whereas the other group was told that the exam was a test of verbal ability. Students also completed a reading task that measured, through response latency, the stereotypes that were activated in the students. Results showed that Black Americans who thought they were simply solving problems demonstrated less stereotype activation on the reading test than the other students. Furthermore, the Black American students who were in the nonthreatening situation performed as well as White Americans (who performed equally well in both situations), whereas the group of Black American students who labored under the belief that the test would measure their verbal ability performed significantly worse than all others. Thus, the threat that a negative stereotype might be applicable in that situation harmed performance.

Many Black American students attend predominantly White American institutions; for most of them the total immersion in a solidly White American environment is a new experience. Not only must they adjust to being away from home for the first time, they also must deal with their continued existence as minority group members in a White world. Many Black American students find themselves lost, unsure of where to turn and how to navigate the academic system. Often they do not have a Black American as either a roommate or a resident on their dormitory floor; they also may not have Black American students in their classes and will likely not be taught by Black American faculty. Is it any wonder, then, that Black American students are prone to problems with personal identity (Edmunds, 1984), may experience low self-esteem in such environments (Wesley & Boyd, 1994), and are at risk of quitting school?

DEVELOPMENTAL RELATIONSHIPS
FOR BLACK AMERICAN STUDENTS

Undergraduates and Developmental Relationships

Because most students are unclear about what their options are with schooling and what they need to do to achieve their goals, they need exposure to a variety of experiences during their college years. Many minorities and White Americans start their first year without considering carefully where their academic tracks might lead. By the end of the year, students have either settled in for the duration or they are leaving school for some period of time. Those who stay often recognize the importance of connecting with faculty members or others who can guide them through academic hurdles (LaFromboise, Coleman, & Gerton, 1993). These students turn to upperclassmen and women, graduate teaching assistants (TAs), or professors for guidance and advice.

On small campuses, finding guidance is relatively easy; professors are somewhat more available, and they have fewer students among whom to divide their energies. On a larger campus, however, students may have more difficulty locating a faculty member to serve as a mentor or sponsor. Particularly in large research universities, where demands on faculty time differ from those at teaching colleges and universities (Boyer, 1990), faculty may have little time for undergraduate mentoring. Students, especially in lower level classes, may be taught by graduate TAs more often than by professors. This is not to say that graduate students cannot create and sustain developmental relationships; in fact, they may be quite effective in this regard, providing a sense of direction to undergraduates and serving as role models for the next step in the process. Even so, graduate students simply do not have the resources or the power of a faculty member. Undergraduates so sponsored may not be receiving some forms of help that they need.

We propose that the college retention rate of Black American students could be improved with the assistance of sponsors and mentors for these students. Following the definitions set out in chapter 1 of this volume, we use the term *sponsor* to describe an organizationally senior person (e.g., a professor) who helps a junior person (e.g., a student) by providing instrumental help such as offering practical advice and information. A *mentor* may fulfill the sponsor's role but in addition exhibits an emotional attachment that is reciprocated by the junior person. Typically, mentors socialize the junior person into the profession; hence the mentor relationship is of longer term than that of a sponsor and involves greater commitment. In many instances, however, these terms have been used interchangeably in our chapter because the issues we discuss apply to both mentors and sponsors.

Most predominately White American college campuses have very few Black American faculty, and the majority of those faculty are in the lower echelons, working toward tenure and promotion. Both mentors and sponsors are scarce, and this poses a problem: The ability to identify with others in the educational context who share one's "stigmatizing condition" can be an important source of emotional well-being, alleviating feelings of aloneness and isolation (Branscombe & Ellemers, 1998; Jones, 1997). For students seeking a sponsor or mentor of the same sex, these problems are compounded because the available pool of potential sponsors is necessarily more limited (Gilbert, Gallessich, & Evans, 1983; Paludi et al., 1991).

Many minority faculty, concentrated in the lower ranks of the academic hierarchy, have difficulty getting through their daily workloads, teaching assignments, committees, and other requirements. Yet minority faculty have other duties laid at their feet because they are minority group members. For example, they may be expected to represent their minority group at various functions or to serve on several committees seeking a balance of dominant and minority group membership (Blakemore, Switzer, DiLorio, & Fairchild, 1997; Taylor & Martin, 1987). Many of these faculty do not have enough time left to help all the Black American students who come to them for support and guidance, and they may not all be willing to take on such a responsibility. Faculty can be quite selective about their protégés and about the amount of work they are willing to do to guide students through the system. Students whom faculty do not choose as protégés, for whatever reason, may feel left out and may be more likely to drop out of school altogether.

Given the realities of the present academic environment, Black American students face a difficult choice: They can seek out the rare professor of the same ethnicity, they can work with a professor of a different ethnicity, or they can try to cope without special connections to any faculty. Although ethnicity alone does not determine one's qualifications as an excellent mentor or sponsor, a body of literature suggests that cross-race mentor/sponsor–protégé relationships are less beneficial than same-race relationships (e.g., Moses, 1989; Sanders, 1991). One difficulty is that nonminority faculty may be somewhat uncomfortable with minority protégés (DeFour, 1991). White American faculty, as with everyone else, may prefer to work with people who are like them in significant ways (Byrne, 1971). This process, which Haslett and Lipman (1997) termed the principle of homogeneity, has an impact on the flow of information and opportunity. Senior-level faculty are more likely to share information with those who are like them. At the faculty level, for example, women and men agree that informal discussions of issues such as research and promotion and tenure are common, but women report that they are much less likely to be included in these discussions (Blakemore et al., 1997). This problem replicates itself in relationships between faculty and students, with faculty sharing more information about the inner workings of the academy with those with whom they feel most comfortable. Because of the informality of such discussions, their impact often goes unnoticed, but the outcome remains: Students who are different from those in power are left out of the loop and therefore have less information and less capacity to make the system work for them.

Minority students also fall through the cracks when it comes to mentoring because faculty assume that students will reach out if they want something. What faculty sometimes fail to realize is that assertive students of any race will certainly reach out, and that White American students, especially males, will be more likely to receive some tacit (or explicit) encouragement from the mentor or sponsor to do so. The rest of the students remain in limbo, however, struggling along in relative silence or dropping out. It is troublesome that this latter group is likely to include a disproportionate number of minority students.

Given the lack of available role models and sponsors, it is not surprising that those vying for these resources often rely on people outside the academy. Jackson, Kite, and Branscombe (1996) surveyed 125 Black American women undergraduates attending large predominately White American Midwestern universities regarding their developmental relationships. Participants came from primarily Black American neighborhoods (61%) and reported that the majority of their current friends were Black American (74%). The majority of the role models they selected were Black American women (72%), followed by Black American men (16%), White American men (7%), and White American women (5%). However, few of the role models of these college students were faculty members; instead, the vast majority of these role models (98%) were from outside the university setting altogether.

Jackson et al. (1996) also found that Black women who placed a high level of importance on their racial or gender identities were likely to report having Black American role models, particularly female role models. Hence, White American educational institutions are an especially barren source of mentors and sponsors for those who strongly identify with their devalued group memberships. Overall, the Black women in that study reported generally high levels of satisfaction with their role models. This satisfaction was significantly correlated with overall life satisfaction ($r = .31$). However, these findings may well have been influenced by the fact that most women identified a Black American woman as a role model. That is, whether levels of satisfaction would be lower in cross-race mentorships could not be assessed because so few respondents identified cross-race role models.

Obviously, ethnicity and gender by themselves do not determine the effectiveness of a mentor, and many individuals who are not Black American have served as effective mentors to Black American students. For those seeking to fulfill this role, Steele (1997) offered some wise counsel. If one sees emotional issues as too burdensome, for example, it may be most useful to emphasize instrumental help with tangible results, coupled with simple trust and optimism. Because the prevailing stereotypes make it plausible for minorities to worry that people in power will doubt their abilities, one way to counter this assumption is through the authority of "affirming adult relationships" (Steele, 1997, p. 624). This strategy was used in a mentoring program for incoming minority and other students at the University of Michigan; evaluation of this program showed that critical feedback to Black American students was very effective when it was paired with optimism about their potential. An especially useful strategy in helping minority students is to challenge them. Steele (1997) advised educators to select challenge over remediation. Giving challenging work conveys respect for one's potential. Remedial work only reinforces that minority students are being viewed stereotypically, which can potentially and subtly harm their performance.

Graduate Students and Developmental Relationships

Developmental relationships for graduate students require a different level of understanding and guidance than that needed for undergraduates. Graduate students interact with their professors and other senior people on a variety of levels, and the richness of the interpersonal relationship may be as much a factor in their education as any coursework (Kohatsu, 1991). Any attempts to complete graduate school without a sponsor, a mentor, or some type of support system may doom the student to a difficult process, if not failure.

On predominately White American college campuses, many Black American students lack adequate support. In Smith and Davidson's (1992) survey, one third of their sample of Black American graduate students reported receiving no help with their development from faculty, professional staff, or nonuniversity professionals. Another third of the students reported receiving support; a significant number of their supporters were White Americans. Nevertheless, even though only 4% of the faculty were Black American, fully 40% of the faculty and staff who worked with these students were Black American. This finding supports our earlier contention that Black American faculty have quite a heavy load if they choose to make themselves available to minority students for mentoring and sponsoring.

Although Black American graduate students may prefer Black American faculty as mentors, many academic departments have no Black American faculty members at all. Moreover, graduate students may be just as reluctant as undergraduates to step forward and request assistance. Underrepresented groups are often aware of inequities in their relationships with the powerful but are typically uncertain how to handle those inequities (e.g., Haslett & Lipman, 1997). Attempts to address the problem directly can result in negative labeling of the messenger or discounting of the message, particularly if those inequities are subtle and difficult to quantify.

What can be done to improve the mentoring of minority students? One important step is for White American faculty to put forth the effort to do so, precisely because there are insufficient minority faculty available (DeFour, 1991). Because a student plans to conduct research on minority issues that are not of direct interest to a White American faculty member does not mean the faculty member cannot contribute to the project. Nor does research on minority issues exist in a vacuum. A student studying Black American female adolescents' career development, for example, can certainly benefit by working with a White American faculty member interested in Whites' career development or adolescence. White American faculty can also direct their Black American graduate students to associations and conferences that may present a more multicultural framework than that exhibited in the department (e.g., the local or national Association of Black Psychologists; the Teachers College Cross Cultural

Roundtable on Education; Division 45 of the American Psychological Association). Some White American faculty have Black American colleagues on other campuses who can serve as distant resources (e.g., introducing the graduate student to a minority colleague at a conference or through a phone call). At a recent meeting of the American Psychological Association, Jessica Henderson Daniel spoke of the positive impact of meeting a prominent Latina on her career development. She further noted how important it was that her White American mentor initiated contact on her behalf with other Latina psychologists. Identification with others does not require geographic proximity; the lack of Black American role models on a student's home campus can be overcome by reaching out to those at a distance. We have often urged Black American graduate students in our own programs to make contact with Black American faculty around the country. One part of being a good mentor is simply knowing where to direct students so that they may acquire the needed information.

One approach to mentoring or sponsoring Black American students, especially for those who work with several students, is to create a hierarchy. Typically, students at different levels of development (e.g., some advanced doctoral students, some masters' students, perhaps some undergraduates) all request advice and guidance from the same person. Overworked faculty members can save time (and their sanity) by directing students to sponsor each other. They may closely mentor the advanced graduate students, who will probably spend the most time with them and have the most complicated needs as they plan their careers. These students, in turn, can sponsor the masters' students. More senior students likely know what their junior counterparts need and are perhaps better able to provide certain kinds of guidance and support than the faculty member. Finally, masters' students (and doctoral students) may advise and sponsor undergraduate women and men. With such a strategy, faculty mentors may touch many more lives indirectly than they ever could in a direct fashion (Bettencourt, Bol, & Fraser, 1994).

DEVELOPMENTAL RELATIONSHIPS
FOR BLACK AMERICAN FACULTY

Although all faculty members are senior to the students and can thus be role models, sponsors, or mentors to people more junior than themselves, some faculty are also relatively new professionals themselves. These younger faculty are sometimes adopted as protégés by other more experienced faculty and administrators.

All junior faculty can benefit from being part of a developmental relationship (Gilbert et al., 1983; Riley & Wrench, 1985), but ethnic minority faculty may benefit even more than others. According to Epps (1989), "African American faculty encounter a culture that rejects them as legitimate participants in the life of the academy" (p. 25). A comparably large proportion of minority faculty experience difficulties finding a support network among the faculty and administrators at many universities. The Black American faculty member is often found on the periphery rather than in mainstream teaching and research. Because Black American women, as members of two traditionally oppressed groups, experience the double jeopardy of the "high visibility of a woman of color and the societal invisibility of a woman" (Eckardt, 1989, p. 52), they may be the ones most in need of a good mentor or sponsor (Allen, 1996).

Mentors and sponsors in academic settings provide the protégé with more than a safe place to vent his or her woes; they also model how to succeed in academic life. A good mentor provides emotional support, encouragement, and a trusting environment during the early developmental process. It is therefore important that the mentor be in a position to support the protégé (Jacobi, 1991), recognizing in particular that such relationships vary considerably both in duration and level of intimacy. The good sponsor serves as the protégé's advocate in public forums, and helps her or him navigate the department and university's political environment. The sponsor also provides knowledge about research and teaching methods and may even collaborate with the protégé on research, helping the protégé get her own research program off the ground (Unger & Crawford, 1996).

Having a senior person who is also a minority group member may prove especially helpful to junior minority people. The more experienced and wiser colleague can help the inexperienced one avoid some of the pitfalls of the academy, especially as the senior person may have experienced and overcome problems that the junior person now faces. A minority mentor or sponsor who has been questioned on his or her interpersonal style in the past, for example, can help the protégé weigh the pros and cons of using a similar approach to interacting with colleagues.

Minority faculty are typically ready and willing to fill the role of senior person to a junior faculty member. Atkinson, Casas, and Neville (1994) surveyed ethnic minority psychologists and found that almost half had mentored at least one novice professional and that the overwhelming majority of those protégés were ethnic minorities. That ethnic minority psychologists are mentoring others is an excellent sign, as it may result in even more minorities entering and remaining in the field. Ethnic minority psychologists who mentor may perceive themselves as giving back to the community while gaining a sense of personal satisfaction from helping the protégé. However, the drawback is that these psychologists are sacrificing some of the energy that they could be directing toward their own development, perhaps making them less effective than they otherwise would be and leading to a higher burnout rate than their White American colleagues experience (e.g., Caplan, 1993; Davies, Lubelska, & Quinn, 1994).

Problems Crossing the Ethnic Line

The ironic outcome is that developmental relationships may be most difficult to arrange for those who need them most. Minority faculty who are advanced enough to serve as mentors are a scarce resource. Although working with a cross-race sponsor or mentor is an option, it can create other issues for junior faculty who are Black American. Such issues may be especially problematic when the cross-race sponsor is of the other sex and hence is doubly different from the protégé.

Cross-race developmental relationships pose several noticeable difficulties. The difficulties may be diminished if the senior person is sensitive, but given the racist nature of the wider society, they cannot be completely eradicated. First, developmental relationships, by their very nature, are hierarchical. The fact that the mentor or sponsor has more power and status, by virtue of tenure in the academic system, can create its own tension. Members of minority groups often are relegated to a low status and treated as subordinates in society. Once they enter the academy, they may not be willing to accede to secondary status when they have worked equally hard for the same educational credentials as their White American (male) colleagues. Senior professors tend to express opinions about what is best for all junior faculty, from what courses to teach to whether they possess promotional merit. Junior faculty may not find this behavior comforting; in fact, they may interpret it as paternalistic. Minority faculty may feel patronized even more keenly than White American faculty. As Brinson and Kottler (1993) pointed out, many members of minority groups have a distrust of White Americans, especially White American males, based on years of oppression and cultural misunderstandings.

Gender Issues

The importance of gender in mentor–protégé relationships is not certain. A survey of minority psychologists who have served as mentors for students, interns, and novice professionals found that they perceived same-sex relationships just as positively as other-sex relationships (Atkinson et al., 1994). Even so, the actual mentoring process may differ for men and women mentors (Gilbert et al, 1983; Paludi et al., 1991). Women graduate students and faculty members emphasize the psychosocial functions of mentoring (e.g., role modeling, encouraging, counseling, collegial behaviors), whereas men prefer the instrumental functions of mentoring (e.g., educating, job coaching, protecting the protégé). Women believe they are not encouraged in their fields of study and not introduced to the professional network (see also Blakemore et al., 1997); women also sometimes believe their male mentors avoid them—a problem male protégés do not report. Paludi et al. (1991) found that male mentors perceived themselves as helping to shape the careers of their male protégés but that they viewed their female protégés as needing remedial assistance.

These findings suggest that people do better with a same-sex mentor or sponsor and that when given a choice, people select same-sex role models (e.g., Jackson et al., 1996). Women with research interests outside the mainstream (i.e., topic areas in which White men are typically not interested) may particularly benefit from female guidance. Scott (1992) noted that same-sex sponsorships allow female protégés to identify more closely with the sponsor. For women faculty, however, such relationships can be one more project to take on while they themselves are circumventing the barriers. If female sponsors are overwhelmed by the demands of their role, they may have difficulty giving their protégés the attention they need. Finally, women entering a male-dominated field may survive better if they have a male mentor who can teach them how to enter and survive the inner circle. Hence, factors other than gender may be equally, if not more, important in selecting an appropriate sponsor.

Professional Development of Black American Faculty

Professionals must choose carefully where and how to spend their time. Brinson and Kottler (1993) reported that Black American professors are often encouraged to get involved with ethnic service activities (e.g., departmental or campus-wide minority awareness committees). The problematic nature of this situation is exacerbated if they are not equally exposed to nonminority-related professional endeavors, such as grant writing or other professional development opportunities. Black American faculty may perceive these omissions as suggesting that "... there are certain jobs that are designed for members of their race" (Brinson & Kottler, 1993, p. 245). In contrast, White American faculty may believe it is helpful to encourage minority faculty to get involved in ethnic committees, but they erroneously assume that all minority faculty are interested in focusing on minority issues. Being a member of a particular group does not automatically determine one's research and applied interests. In fact, many minority group members may wish to work in research and service areas not explicitly involving their group membership so that they can avoid the charge of bias or the claim that their work is not sufficiently rigorous or theoretical.

When senior faculty do not introduce their minority colleagues to vital areas of professional development, they may inadvertently leave them unable to meet the exacting standards necessary to achieve tenure. Service on minority-related committees is often pushed on minority faculty, yet these activities are often not as valued as other activities in tenure decisions. Untenured faculty may well receive a mixed message if senior faculty encourage them to fulfill certain roles but later do not reward them for those efforts. If senior faculty do not explain these facts of life to Black American faculty members, they may not be around in seven years to sponsor someone else.

As Black American junior faculty navigate the academic environment, there is little doubt that they will be and feel noticed. Individuals who differ from the majority stand out and capture others' attention (McArthur, 1981; Taylor & Fiske, 1978). Being a token influences both how those individuals behave and how others perceive them. Such effects also appear to be nearly inevitable; there are salience effects both when the perceiver is focusing on the target and when the perceiver is distracted (Taylor, Fiske, Etcoff, & Ruderman, 1978). More often than not, then, the salient individual is placed in a no-win situation—seemingly no behavior escapes scrutiny.

Although the consequences of this perceptual salience are not always negative (e.g., Yoder & Sinnett, 1985), many times the individual who is different feels isolated and discounted (Yoder, 1985; Yoder, Adams, Grove, & Priest, 1985). Tokens, compared to members of the majority group, report feeling more anxious and concerned about their social interactions (Ickes, 1984), and they are less able to remember the opinions expressed by other group members (Lord & Saenz, 1985). In response to such situations, many Black American faculty tend to step back, be reserved, and observe the environment before deciding how to interact within it. As Brinson and Kottler (1993) noted, other colleagues may interpret this behavior as showing a lack of interest in departmental issues, aloofness, or a lack of competence. Yet those who choose a more assertive interpersonal style may find that others perceive them as aggressive or pushy. Unfortunately, either strategy can preclude comfortable interactions with colleagues (Yoder, 1985). As a consequence, Black American faculty may find that they are not considered for more prestigious departmental or university committees or are not invited to informal gatherings that encourage discussions of promotion, tenure, and salary increases. These problems can be compounded in departments where junior faculty are a numerical minority anyway. For minority faculty, "these feelings ... are often exacerbated when they believe they must surrender parts of their cultural identity in an effort to fit into the prevailing environment" (Brinson & Kottler, 1993, p. 246).

Black American faculties' expectations of White American mentors and sponsors vary. Thomas (1993) showed that cross-race developmental relationships are more likely to develop into true mentoring relationships when there is symmetry in the two parties' views on the role race plays in the organization and are more likely to remain purely instrumental, sponsoring relationships when there is asymmetry. His findings suggest that if race is a salient issue for protégés, it is all the more important that they believe that the mentor or sponsor has concern for their welfare and is considering their individual needs and talents. These protégés will also expect the mentor or sponsor to be culturally sensitive, which includes having some knowledge and appreciation of their culture's values. The White American mentor or sponsor willing to work with a minority protégé will need to understand and accept the protégé's worldview and recognize that his or her own perspective may influence how others will interpret the protégé's behaviors. For example, the protégé's tendency to spend social time with other Black American women on campus may be interpreted as isolationist, although the protégé views it as a means of self-protection or a reality check. The same mentor or sponsor may see nothing wrong with a White American male protégé spending time with other White American males, even though that behavior may occur for similar reasons.

Complicating all developmental relationships is the protégés' struggle to ensure that their mentors or sponsors see them as individuals, not simply as representatives of their category. Prejudice is more likely to occur when people are considered members of a group rather than individuals (e.g., Fiske & Neuberg, 1990). Yet mentors need to be sensitive to cultural and ethnic issues as well. In other words, protégés need for mentors and sponsors to remember that they are Black American but also to forget that they are Black American. Some mentors may have limited experiences, with only media-based knowledge or stereotypes on which to rely. Some of this knowledge may be accurate, but other information may not be (Jussim, McCauley, & Lee, 1995; Ryan, 1995). In either case, assuming that everything one knows about Black American culture is true of the individual can create an uncomfortable distance between the mentor or sponsor and the protégé and may damage both the relationship and the mentor's credibility. Yet assuming that Black Americans are "just like White Americans" can be equally problematic.

These points are most salient if and when the protégé feels comfortable enough to discuss possibly discriminatory experiences with the mentor or sponsor. For example, the protégé may feel uncomfortable with apparently racist statements made by another faculty member but be unsure how to handle it. If the protégé is comfortable with the mentor, she or he may raise the issue with that person. If the mentor or sponsor's initial response conveys the message that minorities are too sensitive to such issues, all further communication is likely to be affected. It will become clear that certain parts of the protégé's life experiences will not be honored by the mentor or sponsor and are therefore taboo subjects. In this case, both members of the dyad lose. Instead, the mentor or sponsor will need to recognize that such incidents indeed occur in the daily experience of minorities. Just because it does not happen to or is not interpreted as necessarily discriminatory or racist by the White American mentor does not make it less probable, less real, or less painful to the Black American person who sees it that way.

One of the most difficult reactions that White American mentors may have to combat when interacting with their Black American protégés is that of White guilt (see Helms, 1993; Steele, 1990, for a detailed discussions of this construct). Before any honest discussion of race and racism can begin, White American mentors and sponsors must consider the possibility that their behavior is affected by their own feelings of collective guilt. White Americans who are low in identification with their racial group (i.e., do not think of themselves as being White American) may feel particularly guilty when the unfairness of their privileged position is made salient. However, feelings of guilt concerning what one's own group has historically done to members of the minority group are probably not relevant to the specific interaction between the mentor and the protégé. Rather than being productive, such negative emotional responses could even provoke White Americans who do not have a strong sense of their racial identity to attempt to escape such an uncomfortable situation. However, in highly identified White Americans (i.e., those who categorize themselves in racial terms, value their White American racial group membership, and embrace their racial status as legitimate), the likely response to collective feelings of White guilt is rather different. When these individuals have experiences that make group-based inequality salient—particularly ones in which their own group is favored—they may attempt to justify the situation. As mentors, their justification may be to blame the protégé who is a victim of discrimination in order to deal with their own emotional predicament. It would be too difficult for highly identified White Americans to accept negative views of their own group (i.e., that their group has obtained its position by oppressing minority groups through discriminatory treatment). In support of this reasoning, recent studies (Branscombe, 1998; Branscombe, Schiffhauer, & Valencia, 1997) have revealed that highly identified White Americans who are asked to examine the privileges that they receive as a result of their racial group membership show increases in modern racism scores. In contrast, those low in White racial identification experience self-esteem losses and attempt to distance themselves from their group membership under the same conditions. As a result, such low-identified White American mentors may attempt to atone and apologize for the discriminatory behavior of other members of their group (Doosje, Branscombe, Spears, & Manstead, 1998) or simply avoid the situation entirely.

One final problem is an unwillingness on the part of some ethnic minority faculty to meet the senior dominant group member halfway. Given the level of cultural mistrust on the part of some Black Americans, it is very easy, perhaps almost second nature, to question anything said by a White American (Jones, 1997). If the protégé does not give the mentor a chance, the relationship will be stalled. It is important for the protégé to recognize that the mentor may not have much knowledge about Black American culture but is interested in helping him or her make progress in the academy. Without such trust in the White American mentor, protégés may unwittingly undermine the mentor's ability and willingness to help (Watkins, Terrell, Miller, & Terrell, 1989). In such cases, being patient and learning about White American academic culture while learning to achieve within it will be important. The protégé who assumes that all White Americans are alike will be just as much a part of the problem as the mentor who assumes that all Black Americans are alike. Both members of the dyad can learn from each other. Neither member carries the whole burden for the relationship; they must work together to make it successful.

Overcoming Problems

Brinson and Kottler (1993) provided several other recommendations for Black American junior faculty seeking a faculty member for a developmental relationship. First and foremost, the protégé should take responsibility for finding a sponsor, recognizing that there may be some reluctance on a White American colleague's part to approach the new faculty member. The potential protégés should identify some preferred sponsors, begin to approach them, and express interest. If rebuffed initially, protégés should try to determine whether the rebuff is cultural or possibly a personal issue for that individual (after all, not everyone wants to or feels able to be a sponsor). Administrative-level programs that encourage or provide mentors may alleviate some of these difficulties, but such programs must consider what makes a good match between mentors and protégés.

In identifying a mentor, protégés should be selective, deciding what their most important needs are and seeking them out in a potential mentor. They should choose someone who has a positive reputation, who garners the respect of others, and who seems to model behaviors that they would like to develop. Protégés should be aware that they may need to select several mentors for different purposes and develop varying levels of intimacy with them. Some mentors may be perfect for discussing the politics of the system and learning how to navigate it. Other mentors may be more comfortable and more available for issues related to race and gender. Mentors may have varying levels of status and influence in the university, or they may be members of different departments or on different campuses. Often it helps to have a variety of trusted professionals to use as sounding boards. Protégés will also need to detail their needs to the mentor. If seeking certain information from the mentor, they should tell him or her; mentors are not mind-readers! They might seek supportive or helpful feedback on initial drafts of manuscripts in progress or suggestions after reviewing initial teacher evaluations. Expressing one's professional needs will make the relationship more profitable for both the mentor and the protégé and may help the mentor feel more comfortable with the relationship.

Regardless of the resources available in one's own department, faculty also need to cultivate a support group. This may include other Black Americans on campus (e.g., recent hires in other academic or student affairs departments), friends from other universities in similar positions, or colleagues through professional organizations. Having other Black American colleagues (male or female) available, even if only through periodic e-mail contacts, can be quite affirming. When trying to deal with racism and sexism, for example, Black American women have been shown to benefit from the feedback and opinions of other Black American women, who are most likely to have also had similar experiences (Lykes, 1983). These other resources can provide considerable support and validation to Black American faculty members (Ibarra, 1995).

Brinson and Kottler (1993) also make some important suggestions for White American mentors and sponsors. First and foremost, the mentor must develop a genuine interest in minority issues on campus and in the community. Mentors should understand that the adjustment issues of the typical new faculty member will probably be exacerbated for new Black American faculty members. Black Americans may have difficulties locating appropriate housing, for example. White American colleagues, when asked for advice, may recommend "good" (White American) communities and steer the new faculty member away from "bad" (Black American) communities, without consciously realizing the message they're sending. As a result, the Black American faculty member can be left without an accurate sense of the new community. As another example, the new Black American faculty member may have more difficulty than a White American colleague getting assistance on campus, especially if he or she appears in person at various offices. She or he may be consistently mistaken for a student, misdirected to the wrong place, or ignored altogether. The resulting frustration from such treatment is bad enough without having White American colleagues respond to the situation with jokes or dismissals.

It is not enough to have some vague knowledge that there are some minority faculty on campus. White American mentors and sponsors who are truly interested in working with minority colleagues should begin to develop their own levels of cultural sensitivity. They should get involved with minority organizations and activities on campus and in the community. They should begin to develop a level of sensitivity to cultural differences. When minority students on campus raise complaints in the school paper, they should pay heed and try to understand their issues, not dismiss them out of hand. The same is true for events in the community. Asking a minority woman to enter one's White community without having some sense of what she is walking into is at least naive if not hostile.

The White American mentor or sponsor should also discuss minority issues and mentoring with minority colleagues already on campus. These individuals can reflect on their own experiences on campus and in the community and suggest ways to improve things for new minority colleagues. The mentor should be prepared to listen to protégés' experiences, without reframing their statements and telling them how wonderful things really are. The point of such discussions is to learn how minority staff perceive their world, not to make them see it the "right" way. Mentors and sponsors who can step out of their own experiences and enter someone else's will be much better able to mentor a colleague struggling with racial, or any other, issues.

If the White American mentor or sponsor has worked through some of the earlier suggestions for developing sensitivity, he or she is ready to reach out to a minority colleague. As Brinson and Kottler (1993) commented, anyone who has escaped the experience of not belonging, of feeling different from everyone else, is fortunate. Many of us who have had such experiences probably wished that someone would have reached out to us, sensed our discomfort, and tried to bridge the gap. White American mentors and sponsors who candidly acknowledge that they have not had the same experiences as Black American protégés can still recount personal feelings about similar, relevant situations. The ability to make the connection could bridge the gap between the mentor and protégé quickly and do wonders for the new colleague's morale and confidence.

PARTING THOUGHTS

Wilson and Justiz (1988) contended that the declining participation of minorities in higher education will have severe repercussions for future generations of Americans. Without effort, we will lose the promise of those Black Americans who are now being overlooked in the American educational system. How are Black Americans to be retained and promoted in the system? A helping hand and guidance are surely part of the answer. The importance of sponsorships and mentoring can not be overstated (O'Connell & Russo, 1980; Riley & Wrench, 1985).

As one of Henry's (1994) Black American women colleagues said, "I do not consider myself to be more intelligent than other Black American women for getting or staying in University, I just happened to be lucky enough to be in the right place at the right time" (p. 54). It is planning, not luck, however, that will ultimately increase the number of ebony women and men in the ivory tower. The implementation—by individuals, departments, and campuses—of suggestions such as the ones we have outlined will aid in increasing the numbers of Black American students and faculty who successfully navigate the American system of higher education.

REFERENCES

Allen, B. A., & Boykin, A. W. (1992). African-American children and the educational process: Alleviating cultural discontinuity through prescriptive pedagogy. *School Psychology Review, 21*, 586–596.

Allen, B. (1996). Staying within the academy. In K. F. Wyche & F. J. Crosby (Eds.), *Women's ethnicities* (pp. 9–26). Boulder, CO: Westview.

Astin, H. S. (1984). The meaning of work in women's lives: A sociopsychological model of career choice and work behavior. *The Counseling Psychologist, 12*, 117–126.

Atkinson, D. R., Casas, A., & Neville, H. (1994). Ethnic minority psychologists: Whom they mentor and benefits they derive from the process. *Journal of Multicultural Counseling and Development, 22*, 37–48.

Baumeister, R. F. (1991). *Meanings of life.* New York: Guilford.

Bettencourt, B. A., Bol, L., & Fraser S. C. (1994). Psychology graduate students as research mentors of undergraduates: A national survey. *Psychological Reports, 75*, 963–970.

Blakemore, J. E., Switzer, J. Y., DiLorio, J. A., & Fairchild, D. L. (1997). Exploring the campus climate for women faculty. In N. Benokraitis (Ed.), *Subtle sexism: Current practices and prospects for change* (pp. 54–71). Thousand Oaks, CA: Sage.

Boyer, E. L. (1990). *Scholarship reconsidered: Priorities of the professoriate.* Princeton, NJ: The Carnegie Foundation for the Advancement of Teaching.

Branscombe, N. R. (1998). Thinking about one's gender group's privileges or disadvantages: Consequences for well-being in women and men. *British Journal of Social Psychology, 37*, 167–184.

Branscombe, N. R., & Ellemers, N. (1998). Coping with group-based discrimination: Individualistic versus group-level strategies. In J. L. Swim & C. Stangor (Eds.), *Prejudice: The target's perspective* (pp. 243–266). New York: Academic Press.

Branscombe, N. R., Schiffhauer, K., & Valencia, L. (1997). *Consequences of thinking about White privilege or disadvantage and degree of White identification for self-esteem and racism.* Manuscript submitted for publication.

Brinson, J., & Kottler, J. (1993). Cross-cultural mentoring in counselor education: A strategy for retaining minority faculty. *Counselor Education and Supervision, 32*, 241–253.

Bronfenbrenner, U., McClelland, P., Wethington, E., Moen, P., & Ceci, S. J. (1996). *The state of Americans: This generation and the next.* New York: Free Press.

Brown, D., Minor, C. W., & Jespen, D. A. (1991). The opinions of minorities about preparing for work: Report of the second NCDA national survey. *The Career Development Quarterly, 40*, 5–19.

Byrne, D. E. (1971). *The attraction paradigm.* New York: Academic Press.

Caplan, P. J. (1993). *Lifting a ton of feathers: A woman's guide for surviving the academic world.* Toronto, Canada: University of Toronto Press.

Cook, T. D., & Curtin, T. R. (1987). The mainstream and the underclass: Why are the differences so salient and the similarities so unobtrusive? In J. C. Masters & W. P. Smith (Eds.), *Social comparison, social justice, and relative deprivation: Theoretical, empirical, and policy perspectives* (pp. 217–264). Hillsdale, NJ: Lawrence Erlbaum.

Cullota, E., & Gibbons, A. (Eds.). (1992, November 13). Minorities in science [Special section]. *Science, 258*, 1176–1232.

Davies, S., Lubelska, C., & Quinn, J. (1994). *Changing the subject: Women in higher education.* Bristol, PA: Taylor and Francis.

DeFour, D. C. (1991). Issues in mentoring ethnic minority students. *Focus, 5,* 1–2.

Doosje, B., Branscombe, N. R., Spears, R., & Manstead, A. S. R. (1998). Guilty by association: When one's group has a negative history. *Journal of Personality and Social Psychology, 75.*

Eckardt, A. (1989). Double jeopardy: racism and sexism. In *Black-Women-Jew: Three wars for human liberation* (pp. 51–59). Bloomington: Indiana University Press.

Edmunds, G. J. (1984). Needs assessment strategy for Black students: An examination of stressors and program implications. *Journal of Non-White Concerns in Personnel and Guidance, 12,* 48–56.

Epps, E. G. (1989). Academic culture and the minority professor. *Academe, 75,* 23–26.

Fiske, S. T., & Neuberg, S. L. (1990). A continuum of impression formation, from category-based to individuating processes: Influences of information and motivation on attention and interpretation. In M. P. Zanna (Ed.), *Advances in experimental social psychology,* (Vol. 23, pp. 1–74). New York: Academic Press.

Fordham, S., & Ogbu, J. U. (1986). Black students' school success: Coping with the "burden of acting White." *The Urban Review, 18,* 176–206.

Fullilove, R. E., & Treisman, P. U. (1990). Mathematics achievement among African American undergraduates at the University of California, Berkeley: An evaluation of the Mathematics Workshop Program. *Journal of Negro Education, 59,* 463–478.

Garibaldi, A. M. (1991). The role of historically Blacks colleges in facilitating resilience among African-American students. *Education and Urban Society, 21,* 103–112.

Gould, S. J. (1994). The mismeasure of man (2nd ed.). New York: Norton.

Gilbert, L. A., Gallessich, J. M., & Evans, S. L. (1983). Sex of faculty role model and students' self-perceptions of competency. *Sex Roles, 9,* 597–607.

Haslett, B. B., & Lipman, S. (1997). Micro inequities: Up close and personal. In N. Benokraitis (Ed.), *Subtle sexism: Current practice and prospects for change,* (pp. 34–53). Thousand Oaks, CA: Sage.

Helms, J. (1993). Toward a model of White racial identity development. In J. E. Helms (Ed), *Black and White racial identity: Theory, research and practice* (pp. 49–66). Westport, CT: Praeger.

Henry, M. (1994). Ivory towers and ebony women: The experiences of Black women in higher education. In S. Davies, C. Lubelska, & J. Quinn (Eds.), *Changing the subject: Women in higher education* (pp. 42–57). Bristol, PA: Taylor and Francis.

Herrnstein, R. J., & Murray, C. (1994). *The bell curve: Intelligence and class structure in American life.* New York: Free Press.

Ibarra, H. (1995). Race, opportunity, and diversity of social circles in managerial networks. *Academy of Management Journal, 38,* 673–703.

Ickes, W. (1984). Compositions in black and white: Determinants of interaction in interracial dyads. *Journal of Personality and Social Psychology, 47,* 330–341.

Jackson, C. H., Kite, M. E., & Branscombe, N. R. (1996, August). *African-Americans' mentoring experiences.* Paper presented at the meeting of the American Psychological Association, Toronto, Canada.

Jacobi, M. (1991). Mentoring and undergraduate academic success: A literature review. *Review of Educational Research, 61,* 501–532.

Jensen, A. R. (1969). How much can we boost IQ and scholastics achievement? *Harvard Educational Review, 39,* 1–123.

Jones, J. M. (1997). *Prejudice and racism* (2nd ed.) New York: McGraw-Hill.

Jussim, L. (1989). Teacher expectation: self-fulfilling prophecies, perceptual biases, and accuracy. *Journal of Personality and Social Psychology, 57,* 469–480.

Jussim, L. J., & Fleming, C. (1996). Self-fulfilling prophecies and the maintenance of social stereotypes: The role of dyadic interactions and social forces. In C. N. Macrae, C. Stangor, & M. Hewstone (Eds.), *Stereotypes and stereotyping* (pp. 161–192). New York: Guilford.

Jussim, L. J., McCauley, C. R., & Lee, Y. (1995). Why study stereotype accuracy and inaccuracy? In Y. Lee, L. J. Jussim, & C. R. McCauley (Eds.), *Stereotype accuracy: Toward appreciating group differences* (pp. 189–214). Washington, DC: American Psychological Association.

Kohatsu, E. L. (1991). Mentoring graduate students in psychology: What has happened to it or is there such a thing? *Focus, 5,* 12–13.

LaFromboise, T., Coleman, H., & Gerton, J. (1993). Psychological impact of biculturalism: Evidence and theory. *Psychological Bulletin, 114,* 395–412.

Lang, M. (1988). The Black student retention problem in higher education: Some introductory perspectives. In M. Lang & C. A. Ford (Eds.), *Black student retention in higher education* (pp. 3–11). Springfield, IL: Charles Thomas Publishers.

Lord, C. G., & Saenz, D. S. (1985). Memory deficits and memory surfeits: Differential cognitive consequences of tokenism for tokens and observers. *Journal of Personality and Social Psychology, 49,* 918–926.

Lykes, M. B. (1983). Discrimination and coping in the lives of Black women: Analyses of oral history data. *Journal of Social Issues, 39,* 79–100.

McArthur, L. Z. (1981). What grabs you? The role of attention in impression formation and causal attribution. In E. T. Higgens, C. P. Herman, & M. P. Zanna (Eds.), *Social cognition: The Ontario Symposium,* (Vol. 1, pp. 201–246). Hillsdale, NJ: Lawrence Erlbaum.

Major, B., & Schmader, T. (1998). Coping with stigma through psychological disengagement. In J. K. Swim & C. Stangor (Eds.), *Prejudice: The target's perspective* (pp. 219–241). New York: Academic Press.

Moses, Y. T. (1989). *Black women in academia: issues and strategies,* Washington, DC: Association of American Colleges Project on the Status of and Education of Women.

Nelson, C. E. (1994). Critical thinking and collaborative learning. *New Directions for Teaching and Learning, 59,* 45–58.

O'Connell, A. N., & Russo, N. F. (Eds.). (1980). Models for achievement: Eminent women in psychology. *Psychology of Women Quarterly, 5,* 6–10.

Ogbu, J. U. (1990). Minority education in comparative perspective. *Journal of Negro Education, 59,* 45–57.

Paludi, M. A., DeFour, D. C., Craithwaite, J., Chan, B., Garvey, C., Kramer, N., Lawrence, D., & Haring-Hidore, M. (1991). Academic mentoring for women: Issues of sex, power, and politics. *Focus, 5,* 7–8.

Riley, S., & Wrench, D. (1985). Mentoring among women lawyers. *Journal of Applied Social Psychology, 15,* 374–386.

Rosenthal, R., & Jacobson, L. (1968). *Pygmalion in the classroom: Teacher expectation and pupils' intellectual development.* New York: Holt, Rinehart, and Winston.

Russel, C. (1995). *The official guide to the American marketplace* (2nd ed.). Ithaca, NY: New Strategist Publications.

Ryan, C. S. (1995). Motivations and the perceivers' group membership: Consequences for stereotype accuracy. In Y. Lee, L. J. Jussim, & C. R. McCauley (Eds.), *Stereotype accuracy: Toward appreciating group differences* (pp. 3–27). Washington, DC: American Psychological Association.

Sanders, D. W. (1991). Minority issues in mentor-protégé relationships. *Focus, 5,* 13.

Scott, M. E. (1992). Designing effective mentoring program: Historical perspectives and current issues. *Journal of Humanistic Education and Development, 30,* 167–175.

Sigelman, L., & Welch, S. (1991). *Black Americans' views of racial inequality: The dream deferred.* Cambridge, MA: Cambridge University Press.

Smith, E. P., & Davidson, W. S. (1992). Mentoring and the development of African American graduate students. *Journal of College Student Development, 33,* 531–539.

Steele, C. M. (1997). A threat in the air: How stereotypes shape intellectual identity and performance. *American Psychologist, 52,* 613–629.

Steele, C. M., & Aronson, J. (1995). Stereotype threat and the intellectual test performance of African-Americans. *Journal of Personality and Social Psychology, 69,* 797–811.

Steele, S. (1990). *The content of our character: A new vision of race in America.* New York: St. Martin's Press.

Steinberg, L., Dornbusch, S. M., & Brown, B. B. (1992). Ethnic differences in adolescent achievement: An ecological perspective. *American Psychologist, 47,* 723–729.

Suzuki, L. A., & Valencia, R. R. (1997). Race-ethnicity and measured intelligence: Educational implications. *American Psychologist, 52,* 1103–1114.

Taylor, D. A., & Smitherman-Donaldson, G. (1989). "And ain't I a woman?" African-American women and affirmative action. *Sex Roles, 21,* 1–12.

Taylor, S. E., & Fiske, S. T. (1978). Salience, attention, and attribution: Top of the head phenomena. In L. Berkowitz (Ed.), *Advances in experimental social psychology* (Vol. 11, pp.249–288). New York: Academic Press.

Taylor, S. E., Fiske, S. T., Etcoff, N. L., & Ruderman, A. J. (1978). Categorical and contextual bases of person memory and stereotyping. *Journal of Personality and Social Psychology, 36,* 778–793.

Taylor, S. E., & Martin, J. (1987). The present-minded professor: Controlling one's career. In M. P. Zanna & J. M. Darley (Eds.), *The compleat academic: A practical guide for the beginning social scientist* (pp. 23–60). New York: Random House.

Thomas, D. A. (1993). Racial dynamics in cross-race developmental relationships. *Administrative Science Quarterly, 38,* 169–194.

Trujillo, C. M. (1986). A comparative examination of classroom interactions between professors and minority and non-minority college students. *American Educational Research Journal, 23,* 629–642.

Unger, R. K., & Crawford, M. E. (1996). *Women and gender: A feminist psychology* (2nd ed.). New York: McGraw-Hill.

Watkins, C. E., Terrell, F., Miller, F. S., & Terrell, S. L. (1989). Cultural mistrust and its effects on expectational variables in Black client-White counselor relationships. *Journal of Counseling Psychology, 36,* 447–450.

Wesley, A. L., & Boyd, P. (1994). *Translating research into practice: The impact of mentoring for African-American college students.* Proceedings of the 1994 Minority Student Today Conference, San Antonio, TX.

White, J. L., & Parham, T. A. (1990). *The psychology of Blacks: An African-American perspective* (2nd ed.). Upper Saddle River, NJ: Prentice-Hall.

Wilson, R. (1989). Women of color in academic administration: Trends, progress, and barriers. *Sex Roles, 21,* 85–97.

Wilson, R., & Justiz, M. (1988). Minorities in higher education: Confronting a time bomb. *Educational Record, 68,* 8–14.

Yoder, J. D. (1985). An academic woman as a token: A case study. *Journal of Social Issues, 41,* 61–72.

Yoder, J. D., Adams, J., Grove, S., & Priest, R. F. (1985). To teach is to learn: Overcoming tokenism with mentors. *Psychology of Women Quarterly, 9,* 119–131.

Yoder, J. D., & Sinnett, L. M. (1985). Is it all in the numbers? A case study of tokenism. *Psychology of Women Quarterly, 9,* 413–418.

3

Asian Americans and Developmental Relationships

Sharon Goto
Pomona College

Asian American and mentoring are not words that are frequently paired. A computerized search of articles published between 1974 and 1995 revealed no articles on the mentorship of Asian Americans in business or educational settings. Buried within one volume (Thomas, 1991) was a clue as to what might account for the lack of attention: Asian Americans tend not to have mentors, nor do they participate in mentoring programs. At Culbertson Industries Defense Application Laboratory, R. R. Thomas (1991) interviewed successful managers in five categories: White men, White women, African Americans, Hispanic Americans, and Asian Americans. Asian Americans were least likely to say they had had a mentor. Overall, 62% of the respondents had a mentor, but only 43% of the Asian Americans were mentored. Meanwhile, 54% of the African Americans and 53% of the Hispanic Americans had mentors. In addition, Asian Americans were significantly less satisfied with their mentoring experiences than were other minorities.

If there has been little attention to the mentoring needs of Asian Americans, there has been even less attention to the contributions that Asian Americans might make as mentors or sponsors to others. White organizations have a culturally narrow definition of what constitutes leadership, which generally does not include skills often associated with Asian Americans, such as good listening abilities and a desire for harmony (Sue, Zane, & Sue, 1985). To the extent that people turn to those whom they perceive as leaders to serve in mentoring and sponsoring roles, Asian Americans are therefore unlikely candidates.

In this chapter I look at some reasons why Asian Americans might not have mentoring or sponsoring relationships at their schools and places of work. My narrative augments the literature on ethnicity with a few reflections from my own experiences as a fourth-generation Japanese American. I also present some preliminary data from an ongoing study of Asian American youth at an elite West Coast private college to illustrate the beliefs that serve both to facilitate and to hinder participation in a structured mentoring program. The chapter ends with suggestions for ways to improve the quality of the mentoring experience for Asian Americans.

WHY DON'T ASIAN AMERICANS HAVE MENTORS?

Perhaps We Have Perfect Success Already

One reason that Asian Americans do not have mentors may be that, as a group, they are so successful that they don't need them. Asian Americans have been called the successful minority or the model minority. If, for example, planned mentoring programs are designed to help people succeed in school and advance at work, then perhaps Asian Americans do not join or are not targeted because they have already succeeded and already have easy access to advancement.

The media often draws attention to the educational successes of Asian American children and youth. Asian Americans capture proportionately more top scores and national prizes in science and math than would be expected. We are disproportionately represented at the country's leading colleges and universities. In general, Asian Americans are thought to be very well prepared to enter and participate in the American work force (Woo, 1994).

In employment, the image is again one of success. Asian Americans experience less unemployment than other ethnic minority groups (Woo, 1994). Approximately two thirds of Asian Americans working full time are employed in white-collar occupations. The percentage of Asian Americans working as professionals, salespersons, technicians, managers, and in administrative support jobs is greater than the percentage of European Americans working in the same areas (Bennett, 1991, as cited in Der, 1993). Asian Americans in the paid labor force earn more money per capita than people from other ethnic minority groups and even more money than White people (Tomasson, Crosby, & Herzberger, 1996). At first blush, the picture is one of relative success.

Closer investigation of the status of Asian Americans yields a different story, however. The reason is that the Asian American population is extremely diverse. Based on similarity of physical appearance and cultural values, over 25 subgroups of Asian Americans and Asian/Pacific Islander Americans exist (Uba, 1994). Some of the most populous groups are Cambodian, Chinese, Filipino, Indonesian, Japanese, Korean, Samoan, Thai, and Vietnamese.

In addition to ethnic and national origin differences, there are differences among Asian Americans in acculturation. Some Asian Americans (e.g., Chinese Americans or Japanese Americans) are more likely to have been in the United States for four or more generations, whereas others are more likely to be recent immigrants. These generational differences are associated with differences in English language proficiency and acculturation.

Corresponding to the diversity of backgrounds are differences in social class and education. Although Asian Americans generally fare well with respect to education, about one third of Southeast Asians have had no schooling (Ong & Hee, 1993). Among those obtaining advanced degrees, a large proportion—about 25%—are foreign nationals (Ong & Hee, 1993). Many of these people do not identify with Asian Americans, as they intend to return immediately to their homeland after finishing their educations in the United States.

Economically, the actual diversity is far greater than the cover story leads one to expect. Whereas Asian Indians, Chinese, Japanese, Koreans, and Filipinos tend to occupy white-collar positions, Vietnamese, Laotians, Hmongs, Hawaiians, and other Pacific Islanders tend to be employed in blue-collar work (U.S. Bureau of the Census, as cited by Der, 1993). For every Asian American household earning over $75,000 per annum, another earns less than $10,000 (Ong & Hee, 1993). Furthermore, well-paid Asian Americans tend to cluster in parts of the country where the cost of living is high. By making adjustments in the income figures to take into account cost of living, the data show that Asian Americans earn fewer "real" dollars than White Americans.

Given the massive amount of stereotyping associated with the myth of the model minority, it is not surprising to find firm evidence of racial discrimination against Asian Americans. A thorough review shows that Asian Americans enjoy a smaller dollar return on their educations than do White Americans. The U.S. Commission on Civil Rights found in 1988 that being of "Asian descent" adversely affected one's chances of moving into a management position. This unfortunate finding held true even when it was controlled statistically for such factors as "education, work experience, English ability, urban residence, industry of employment, ... and marital and disability status" (Woo, 1994, p. 42).

Despite the diversity of Asian American experiences, Asian Americans are perceived within many organizations to fit narrow roles. Blank and Slipp (1994) interviewed numerous Asian Americans about their experiences in private companies, government agencies, and educational institutions. Asian American employees complained that others do not perceive them to be well suited for top-level management positions. Instead, they reported, others think of them as excelling only in science, math, and technical subjects.

In view of the diversity of experiences and the documented discrimination against Asian Americans, the model minority myth takes on an insidious tinge. The myth conceals the real problems Asian Americans face at schools and at work and prevents them from being addressed.

The myth is invidious also. It has been used in the past, both implicitly and explicitly, to pit Asian Americans against other minority groups. The underlying argument has been that opportunities, not barriers, exist for minorities. Because Asian Americans have succeeded by themselves, so can others, or so the argument goes. Hispanic Americans and African Americans need only capitalize on opportunities to succeed. Certainly, the myth compliments nobody.

In sum, the perception of great and uniform success is misguided. The evidence does not support the perception that Asian Americans are so successful that we do not need to be mentored (or to mentor!). If the issue is one of need, then the need is there!

The evidence does suggest, however, that Whites who might serve as sponsors and mentors seek out Asian American protégés only in rare circumstances. Whites, as we have seen, hold a number of stereotypes about Asian Americans and these stereotypes may lead Whites to overlook Asian Americans' need for contact. If Whites believe that Asian Americans do not make good leaders, then White businesspeople may be especially slow to dismantle any of the barriers that prevent Asian Americans and Whites from entering into developmental relationships with one another.

Perhaps Mentoring is a Culturally
Incongruent Path to Success for Asian Americans

Asian Americans need to find ways to be more successful at school and at work, but perhaps mentoring is a culturally incongruous route to success. That is, there may be cultural reasons that Asian Americans are reluctant to seek out or accept help from mentors and sponsors, especially from those who are White.

Collectivism as a Cultural Value.   The many diverse Asian cultures share at least one important attribute: We are all collectivist. Individualism is a strong Western characteristic but not an Asian one.

Collectivism is a cultural construct that scholars have traditionally conceptualized as the opposite of individualism (Hofstede, 1984). Both individualistic and collectivist cultures place significance on the individual person and on meaningful and stable in-groups such as the family or the work group. Individualistic cultures, however, value the needs and desires of the individual over the needs and desires of the group. In those situations where a conflict occurs between the individual and the group, in an individualistic society, the individual's needs and desires prevail. In a collectivist society, by contrast, if a conflict occurs, the group's desires take precedence (Triandis, Bontempo, Villareal, Asai, & Lucca, 1988).

Collectivist societies tend to differ from individualistic societies accordingly. Individuals in a collectivist culture worry about being a burden on others, particularly on those whom they perceive to be part of their group, whether this be a work or nonwork group. Those in an individualistic society are more likely to judge interactions on equity terms. Collectivists tend to draw a stronger distinction between in-group members and out-group members than do individualists (Leung, 1988). Collectivists may perceive in-group members as being extremely trustworthy and out-group members as being extremely untrustworthy. In contrast, individualists may perceive in-group members as only moderately trustworthy and out-group members as only moderately untrustworthy.

For Asian Americans, the primary group is the family. Because the family's needs and desires tend to influence the individual's needs and desires, the head of the family often wields considerable influence over the lives of the children. Often the family, especially the parents, make decisions regarding the careers of the children (Leong, 1991). This holds true particularly for males.

Finally, Asian cultures tend to be more hierarchical than individualistic ones. Power distance is a cultural construct that differentiates collectivist from individualistic societies (Hofstede, 1984). Power distance refers to the distinction of "status consistency versus equality" (p. 68). A high power-distant culture tends to maintain strict hierarchies. Here, status differentials must be supported by societal norms, superiors, and subordinates. By contrast, a low power-distant culture tends to maintain equality in relationships. Hofstede's (1980) data suggest that Asian cultures are marked by relatively high power distance whereas the dominant American culture is low in power distance.

Formality is a consequence of power distance. Uba (1994) pointed out that formality is an important aspect of Asian American culture. A research team was going to interview elder, first-generation Japanese Americans. The interviewers were instructed to avoid prolonged eye contact with the elders, to bring small gifts for them, and to refuse the first offer of refreshments. The effect of the formal behavior was to make the elders feel relaxed and confident!

Triandis et al. (1988) created the terms *idiocentrism* and *allocentrism* to apply to people who live in individualistic and collectivist cultures, respectively. One can have an idiocentric or an allocentric personality type. One could describe the typical Asian American from any of a number of different Asian groups as an allocentric person living in an individualistic culture.

Asian Americans must balance their traditional Asian heritage with American culture. They must constantly negotiate the cultural clash between individualism and collectivism. Certainly, recent immigrants face the issues in a different way from those whose families have lived here for generations, but unless one assumes total assimilation, one must acknowledge the struggle that even fifth-generation Asian Americans may feel. As a fourth-generation Japanese American, I, for example, have none of the language problems of recent immigrants, but I relate deeply to the struggle of retaining beloved Asian values, attitudes, and beliefs, despite the bombardment of American ideals. Balancing individualism and collectivism is a constant issue.

Developmental Relationships and the Allocentric Asian American.
Most schools and businesses in which Asian Americans learn and work have few Asian Americans in positions of authority. If Asian Americans view Whites as distrusted out-group members, they may be reluctant to enter into developmental relationships with them.

Overcoming distrust of out-group members is not the only problem, however. Asian American students and workers may shy away from developmental relationships because they may not wish to be a burden to others. Being considerate of the work that others do for them, Asian Americans may worry about how much time and effort a sponsor or mentor needs to devote to the developmental relationship. Asian Americans may feel uncomfortable with the notion of engaging in informal discussions with their elders. Thus, they may avoid situations in which a naturally occurring mentoring relationship is likely to develop, and may refuse to participate in formal mentoring programs altogether.

Culturally Asian Models of Mentoring. Asian culture may also be a hindrance to the development of mentoring relationships for Asian Americans because Asian culture contains models of mentoring that are different from Western models. As a result, Asian Americans may expect different outcomes from mentoring or may be accustomed to different types of mentor-like relationships, which may discourage them from seeking or recognizing opportunities for developing mentoring relationships built on the Western model. For example, in Japanese culture, there is a mentor-like relationship between a teacher (*sensei*) and the student, and between senior *sempai* and junior *kohai* peers. Chinese and Korean cultures have similar mentor-like roles: *Qian-bei* and *hou-bei* refer to senior and junior peers, respectively, in Chinese culture; *son-bei* and *hu-bei* refer to the same relationships in Korean culture. *Da-gei* is the title of a "big brother" in Chinese culture, and *hyung* is used by a younger male to refer to an elder male in Korean culture. These roles are intended to serve many of the functions of the Western mentor.

Culturally Asian mentor-like relationships differ from their Western counterparts in that they are much more formally hierarchical and they blur the distinction between family and social ties. For example, formal language, formal titles, deference, and other forms of reverence are expected between student and teacher and even between junior and senior peers. Through relationships within families and in other settings, Asian Americans learn the behaviors that are appropriate for nonfamilial relationships. Furthermore, they may come to rely on these Asian mentor-like relationships for career-related guidance and may not understand the need to pursue such relationships in work or school contexts.

Although Asian Americans may not explicitly use their culture's labels to describe a mentor in a work or school setting, they may hold a set of expectations that their culture has defined for appropriate behavior and outcomes from such relationships. For example, many Asian Americans may assume that those who are senior to them—who hold potentially mentor-like positions in relation to them—will automatically give them timely guidance and nurture the relationship. As protégés, they may not expect to have to seek such guidance and nurturance actively, holding instead the expectation that the person with the greater power will initiate this. In this way, Asian Americans' beliefs about mentoring may reflect non-Western models of relationships that they would rarely be able to achieve at school or work in this culture.

In conclusion, establishing developmental relationships—especially with Whites—may be a culturally incongruous path to success for Asian Americans. This difficulty may be because of their collectivist culture or because of the culturally based expectations they hold for such relationships.

PRELIMINARY DATA
FROM A MENTORING PROGRAM

Although by no means definitive, preliminary data from a study of Asian American undergraduate students help shed light on these issues. The foregoing review suggests at least two reasons for Asian Americans' relative lack of engagement with mentors and sponsors. First, Whites may not actively pursue Asian Americans as protégés, perhaps because they perceive Asian Americans as already successful and therefore without need for such relationships. Second, Asian Americans themselves may avoid both the mentor and protégé roles because they hold certain culturally specific beliefs about mentoring that inhibit their taking on such roles. In this study, several colleagues and I focused on the latter explanation by examining Asian Americans' beliefs about mentoring.

More specifically, we interviewed 25 Asian American students at an elite West Coast private college to assess their beliefs about a formal program the college had designed to facilitate developmental relationships between younger and older Asian American students. We eliminated from our investigation many of the cultural differences between protégés and mentors, as well as the issue of distrust of non-Asians. This enabled us to focus instead on how these students' cultural backgrounds might have influenced their perceptions of mentoring.

The Program

The mentoring program at the college was aimed at facilitating the transition of Asian American students into a liberal arts college. Students who perceived adjustment into a highly competitive, close-knit academic community to be a difficult process had initiated the program. When we conducted our study (C. Kim, Goto, Bai, T. Kim, & Wong, 1998), the program was in its fifth year. The design of the program was simple. It matched successful Asian American sophomores, juniors, and seniors (as mentors) with Asian American first-year students (as protégés). The idea was that official mentor program activities such as workshops would foster mentoring relationships.

All Asian American first-year students were eligible to participate in the program as protégés and were assigned mentors who actively encouraged them to do so. Ultimately, however, it was the protégés' decision about whether or not to take advantage of the mentoring opportunity and participate in the program. Levels of participation were generally high; each year, about two thirds of those eligible chose to participate. Participants' levels of investment in the program varied, however: Some dyads actively pursued their mentoring relationship whereas others showed disinterest. The purpose of our study was to understand better how the program looked from the vantage point of the potential protégé (for more details of the study, see Kim, Goto, Bai, Kim, & Wong, 1998).

Participants

We randomly selected 25 students (10 men and 15 women) to participate in the study from the pool of self-identified Asian American college freshmen. The mentoring program had not yet officially begun for this group of freshmen, and we were interested in learning more about the factors that would shape their decisions about whether or not to participate. Our sample was predominantly Chinese American (36%), Korean American (20%) and Japanese American (16%). The number of generations that their families had lived in America gave an indication of their acculturation and ranged from one to five, with a mode of two. In other words, most participants had been born in the United States, but their parents were immigrants. Fifty-two percent of the sample spoke English as their first language.

Data Collection and Results

Data collection involved interviewing our sample of eligible program participants about their beliefs and their reference groups. We developed the belief questions in accordance with the theory of reasoned action (Fishbein & Ajzen, 1975), which is a widely used framework for understanding and predicting people's intention to perform specific behaviors (in this case, participating in the mentoring program). Open-ended questions allowed us to hear about the respondents' perceptions without imposing our own expectations.

Beliefs. We asked three questions to elicit beliefs about participating in the mentoring program. First, we asked, "In your opinion, what are the advantages or benefits of participating in mentoring programs here on campus?" Second, we asked, "In your opinion, what are the disadvantages or drawbacks of participating in mentoring programs here on campus?" Finally, we asked, "Is there anything else that you associate with participating in mentoring programs on campus?"

Content analysis showed that in response to the set of questions about beliefs, students expressed predominantly positive opinions toward the mentoring program. Most of the Asian American students believed that the mentoring program would help them at school. Sixty percent thought that the mentoring program would help them to "meet new people," would "lead to a successful college career," or would "ease the transition to college." Nine respondents felt that the mentoring program would help them to find "people to guide me" or "help me to solve problems."

Over half the participants thought the program would affirm their culture. For example, 54% of the respondents thought the mentoring program would help foster cultural identity. Typical sentiments were that the program would "foster cultural learning," "strengthen ... ethnic identity," and "support Asian heritage."

When asked, 44% of the respondents could think of no disadvantages to the mentoring program. Others cited two disadvantages of the program: Eight worried that the program was ethnocentric, and eight believed the program served to exclude unfairly some other racioethnic groups.

After we interviewed the 25 original participants, we interviewed an additional six eligible program participants to explore further some emerging trends. By this time, the program was well underway. Three of the six we interviewed were fully involved in the mentoring program, and three had chosen not to participate. These follow-up interviews confirmed that some Asian American students were concerned about being singled out for mentoring. One eligible protégé said "to strengthen our identity is bad because it is a 'love yourself' view and teaches us not to love others. It increases the fractioning." Some first-year students whose primary goal was to fit in worried that the program brought unwanted attention to cultural differences.

Reference Groups. Three questions in the interview addressed whether any individuals or groups influenced respondents' consideration about whether or not to participate in the mentoring program. Participants had less to say in response to these questions than to the belief questions. Nevertheless, some interesting findings emerged.

Fifty-two percent of the respondents said that they thought their assigned mentors would like them to be active in the program. Twenty-eight percent admitted that they felt pressure from other Asian Americans to join the program. In contrast, three respondents thought that other Asian American students disliked the idea of them participating in the program, and two respondents believed that the White majority culture disapproved of their participation.

Summary and Conclusions

Analysis of the interviews with 25 first-year students showed stronger support than disapproval of the Asian American mentoring program. Most potential protégés saw the program as congruent with their needs as they made the transition to college. They perceived mentors as able, at least potentially, to help them make the adjustment into the new environment and to help pave the way to their success. The small literature on mentoring programs in college, which reports that ethnic minorities benefit from mentoring (Frierson, Hargrove, & Lewis, 1994; Locke & Zimmerman, 1987; Thile & Matt, 1995), suggests that these perceptions were probably accurate.

Interestingly, however, there was a thread of resistance to the culturally specific mentoring program among some respondents. Some of students viewed the fact that the program was targeted at Asian Americans as separatist. Perhaps because of their collectivist orientation it was important to them that they be included as part of, rather than identified as separate from, the larger community. This finding, together with the finding that others felt that the program was an important way to affirm their ethnic identity—suggests formal mentoring programs designed to match mentor–protégé pairs on the basis of shared ethnic minority group membership may be greeted, at least by Asian Americans, with mixed feelings. On the one hand, such programs may be especially attractive to Asian Americans who for a variety of reasons appear not to develop these relationships informally, especially with Whites; on the other hand, Asian Americans may also resist such programs, perhaps in efforts to sustain the myth of their model status or to downplay their differences from the dominant culture. Thus, it appears that formal mentoring programs that target Asian Americans should address these concerns explicitly.

LESSONS

When our pilot study is viewed in light of what is known about the situations of Asian Americans in colleges and businesses, at least two questions arise. First, how can work organizations achieve some of the same enthusiasm for developmental programs we found at the college level, while minimizing the resistance? Second, how can we maximize the success of all mentoring programs that involve Asian Americans?

One basic answer to both questions involves education. Education is one of the ways Kram (1985) suggested organizations can maximize both the popularity and the effectiveness of mentoring programs. Education certainly seems crucial in the multicultural setting. In particular, the first step is to educate both majority and minority members about the facts that dispel the model minority myth. Whites will benefit from confronting their stereotypes about Asian Americans and especially from learning about the diversity of traditions and situations that exist within the general category. Asian Americans will benefit from learning the truth: It is especially important that students not measure themselves against an unrealistically inflated image of intellectual prowess and deny themselves the benefits of mentoring.

The second step is to educate everyone about the meanings of different behaviors. Protégés need to know about the intentions of the senior person, especially when the senior person is ethnically unfamiliar to them. Meanwhile, White sponsors and especially White mentors need to know how to interpret the junior person's behaviors. As an example, when I was a student, I realized the value of an education and was extremely appreciative of my sponsors. I also found myself extremely conscious of not being a burden to them. My concern was manifested in my taking efforts to ensure that I spent the absolute minimum amount of time with them. I would find myself in meetings talking about business issues and then leaving as quickly as possible for fear of taking too much of their time.

As a faculty member, I now see that pattern of behavior from the mentor's perspective. Some Asian American students seem to be very concerned about not taking up too much of my time. They quickly usher themselves out of my office without an extra word being said. Clearly, their fear of being a burden is detrimental to my acting as an effective mentor or sponsor. It does not allow the time needed to develop as comfortable a working relationship as we might otherwise have. It would be a great benefit to an Asian American protégé to understand that important socialization into ways of thinking and acting are often more likely to occur through informal social interactions than through formal businesslike instruction.

Mentors and sponsors should also make efforts to ensure that their would-be Asian American protégés understand that the benefits of mentoring go both ways. I am careful to show that I value the new perspectives and expertise that my students bring—like knowledge about Asian models of mentoring! I explicitly communicate that I, too, am rewarded when they do well. It should be no wonder then that I look forward to long, enriching relationships with my students.

Another issue that is rife with misconceptions involves deference to authority. In one study, Asian American employees indicated that they found themselves unwilling to refuse any request, even if the request were undoable, because of their high respect for authority (Blank & Slipp, 1994). These employees felt that asking a question might be perceived as insubordinate behavior. The high regard for authority (i.e., high power distance) was accompanied by an expectation that the authority would act in the employee's best interest. Employees felt, for example, that their seniors would recommend them for promotion if they were qualified without their having to express an explicit interest in promotion.

Within any developmental relationship, Asian American students and employees should be encouraged to ask questions and to express opinions. Asian American students and workers need to learn that they are performing a service, not a disservice, to their sponsor or mentor if they offer their perspective. For their part, senior people should be educated about the meanings of silence. Mentors and sponsors should learn not to interpret the absence of questions and suggestions to mean that neither problems nor ambitions exist.

Similarly, everyone can be educated as to the functions and meanings of assertiveness. Asian Americans are often seen as wholly unassertive. One Filipino American budget analyst said

> Our reticence and discipline are held against us. People think that we can't communicate well and that we can't assert ourselves as managers because our styles may be different from mainstream Americans. We're seen only as achievers, accomplishing a given task, but not as initiators or go-getters. (Blank & Slipp, 1994, p. 38)

There is a good deal of research on assertiveness among Asian Americans because of its important implications. Self-report studies indicate that Asian Americans act less assertively than White Americans and that Asian Americans find assertiveness more stressful than do White Americans (Fukuyama & Greenfield, 1983). Studies involving role playing, however, suggest that Asian Americans behave no less assertively than their White American counterparts when the situation calls unambiguously for assertiveness (Sue, Ino, & Sue, 1983). Ayabe (1971) and Zane, Sue, Hua, and Kwon (1991) have found assertiveness to be more contextually dependent for Asian Americans than for White Americans. Both Asian American and White employees might, for example, be more assertive with a co-worker than with a supervisor, but for Asian Americans the differential might be greater.

Effective mentoring programs might encourage Asian American students and workers to develop a situation-specific strategy for behaving assertively. The strategy could be culturally congruent and effective. Asian cultures tend to demand more situationally specific behavior. For example, one's behavior varies dramatically depending on to whom one speaks. From a Western perspective, this change of behavior may be misunderstood as inconsistent or fraudulent. In my own experience, coming to understand the Asian-influenced, contextual nature of my own behavior as a cultural strength enabled me to use it actively as a strategy. I no longer perceive assertiveness as a purely rude, American behavior. Sometimes it is functional and appropriate. As an Asian American woman, I am now seldom hindered by a lack of assertiveness at work. However, when interacting with my grandmother I remain ever careful to be deferential!

PARTING THOUGHTS

More and more students in the United States are Asian American. Asian Americans also represent a growing percentage of the work force. Those of us who are in positions of authority should use our culturally based knowledge to help junior people learn to balance Western ways with Eastern traditions. We should also take the time to educate our White colleagues about how to interpret Asian American behavior so as to make the most of the growing talent pool.

Meanwhile, young Asian American students and workers may gain much from joining mentoring programs. When joining a new organization or starting at a new school, potential protégés may do well to seek out other Asian Americans. As time goes on, however, protégés may gain extra benefit from working with sponsors and mentors of all cultural backgrounds. What ambitious junior people gain through both formal and informal programs enables them to do more than simply advance their careers; it also increases their ability to make worthwhile contributions to a variety of organizations and cultural groups.

REFERENCES

Ayabe, H. (1971). Deference and ethnic difference in voice levels. *Journal of Social Psychology, 85,* 181–185.

Blank, R., & Slipp, S. (1994). Asian Americans. *Voices of diversity* (pp. 36–55). New York: American Management Association.

Der, H. (1993). Asian Pacific Islanders and the "glass ceiling"—New era of civil rights activism? In *The state of Asian Pacific America: Policy issues to the year 2020* (pp. 215–232). Los Angeles: LEAP Asian Pacific American Public Policy Institute and UCLA Asian American Studies Center.

Fishbein, M., & Ajzen, I. (1975). *Understanding attitudes and predicting social behavior.* Englewood Cliffs, New Jersey: Prentice-Hall.

Frierson, H. T., Jr., Hargrove, B. K., Lewis, N. R. (1994). Black summer research students' perceptions related to research mentors' race and gender. *Journal of College Student Development, 35,* 475–480.

Fukuyama, M. A., & Greenfield, T. K. (1983). Dimensions of assertiveness in an Asian American student population. *Journal of Counseling Psychology, 30*(3), 429–432.

Hofstede, G. (1984). *Culture's consequences, international differences in work-related values.* Beverly Hills, CA: Sage.

Kim, C., Goto, S. G., Bai, M., Kim, T., & Wong, E. (1998). *An application of the theory of reasoned action to a culture-specific Asian American mentoring program.* Manuscript submitted for publication.

Kram, K. (1985). *Mentoring at work: Developmental relationships in organizational life.* Glenview, IL: Scott Foresman & Co.

Leong, F. T. L. (1991). Career development attributes and occupational values of Asian American and White American college students. *The Career Development Quarterly, 39,* 221–230.

Leung, K. (1988). Some determinants of conflict avoidance. *Journal of Cross-cultural Psychology, 19,* 125–136.

Locke, D. C., & Zimmerman, N. A. (1987). Effects of peer-counseling training on psychological maturity of black students [Special issue: Blacks in U.S. higher education]. *Journal of College Student Personnel, 8*(2), 525–532.

Ong, P., & Hee, S. J. (1993). Work issues facing Asian Pacific Americans. *The state of Asian Pacific America: Policy issues to the year 2020* (pp. 141–152). Los Angeles: LEAP Asian Pacific American Public Policy Institute and UCLA Asian American Studies Center.

Sue, D., Ino, S., & Sue, D. (1983). Nonassertiveness of Asian Americans: An inaccurate assumption? *Journal of Counseling Psychology, 30,* 581–588.

Sue, S., Zane, N. W. S., & Sue, D. (1985). Where are the Asian American leaders and top executives? *P/AAMHRC Review, 4,* 13–15.

Thile, E. L., & Matt, G. E. (1995). The ethnic mentor undergraduate program: A brief description and preliminary findings, *Journal of Multicultural Counseling and Development, 23,* 116–126.

Thomas, R. R., Jr. (1991). *Beyond race and gender.* New York: American Management Association.

Tomasson, R. F., Crosby, F. J., & Herzberger, S. (1996). *Affirmative action: The pros and cons of policy and practice.* Washington, DC: American University Press.

Triandis, H. C., Bontempo, R., Villareal, M. J., Asai, M., & Lucca, N. (1988). Individualism and collectivism: Cross-cultural perspectives on self-ingroup relationships. *Journal of Personality and Social Psychology, 54,* 323–338

Uba, L. (1994). *Asian Americans: Personality patterns, identity, and mental health.* New York: Guilford.

Woo, D. (1994). *The glass ceiling and Asian Americans: A research monograph.* Washington, DC: U.S. Department of Labor, Glass Ceiling Commission.

Zane, N., Sue, S., Hu, L.-T., & Kwon, J.-H. (1991). Asian American assertion: A social learning analysis of cultural differences. *Journal of Counseling Psychology, 38,* 63–70.

4

Gender Issues
in Developmental
Relationships

Regina M. O'Neill
Suffolk University

Sylvia Horton
Smith College

Faye J. Crosby
University of California, Santa Cruz

Many discussions of developmental relationships make reference to the heroic myths of ancient Greece. What people seem to remember is that when Odysseus left to fight the Trojan War, he entrusted the education of his son Telemachus to his wise and trusted counselor and friend, Mentor. What they seem to forget is that Mentor, according to Homer, was sometimes really the goddess Athena in disguise. Right from the start gender has been a complicating factor in developmental relationships.

The purpose of our chapter is to review the literature on gender and developmental relationships. Inspired particularly by the work of Belle Rose Ragins (1989; Ragins & Cotton, 1991, 1993; Ragins & McFarlin, 1990; Ragins & Sundstrom, 1990; Scandura & Ragins, 1993), we take as a given that gender issues have less to do with the essential characteristics of women and men than with stereotypes and the distribution of power and status within organizations. Our chapter complements Ragins' (e.g., 1989,

1995) excellent reviews of gender and developmental relationships by taking a social psychological approach to the area.

At the heart of our chapter are three clusters of questions.

1. What effect does gender have on the amount of help people give and receive? In other words, are women and men equally likely to enter into developmental relationships, as either the senior person or the protégé?
2. How does gender affect the quality of the experience of being in a developmental relationship, either from the point of view of the senior person or
   from the point of view of the protégé?
3. How does gender influence the outcomes of developmental relationships?
   Do women and men reap the same benefits from being protégés? Do women
   and men confer the same benefits as each other when they sponsor or mentor
   junior people?

These questions are ever more pressing because of the accelerating participation of women in the labor force. Statistics from the Department of
Labor project an increase in the percentage of working-age women in the
paid labor force from 55% in 1986 to 61.4% in the year 2000. Until the new
millennium, women are expected to make up approximately 63% of the
new labor-force growth. The percentage of women in managerial positions
in the United States has risen from 32% in 1983 to 41% in 1991 and is expected to grow even higher in years to come (Catalyst, 1997). Fostering female talent is not just a politically correct move; it is a real economic
necessity.

GENDER AND THE FREQUENCY OF
DEVELOPMENTAL RELATIONSHIPS

Ours is a sexist society. Social psychological studies have shown that people
have stereotypes about men and women (Lott, 1997). The masculine stereotype depicts men as tough, aggressive, forceful, dominant, risk taking,
adventurous, and able to endure pressure. In general, masculinity has been
associated with an instrumental orientation that focuses on getting the job
done. The feminine stereotype, on the other hand, depicts women as emotionally supportive, kind, compassionate, gentle, helpful, and warm. In general, femininity has been associated with an expressive orientation and
concern for the welfare of others (Eagly & Crowley, 1986; Eagly & Steffen,
1984, 1986).

Sex-stereotypic thinking on the part of decision makers, coupled with the legacy of institutional sexism, results in sex discrimination at school and in the workplace (American Association of University Women, 1994; Ginsburg, 1997; Kahn & Crosby, 1985). Although we have made great strides toward gender equality since World War II (Clayton & Crosby, 1992; Tomasson, Crosby, & Herzberger, 1996), significant problems remain. A recent study conducted by Brett and Stroh (1997), for example, shows that women still lag behind comparable men in terms of employment opportunities and compensation. As they climb the corporate ladder, women and men are given less and less equal footing (Catalyst, 1993).

Are Women Less Likely Than Men to Be Protégés?

Given the extent of documented sex prejudice and discrimination in the workplace, it would be logical to expect women to have a harder time than men finding mentors and sponsors. The expectation of unequal access to mentors and sponsors was certainly one of the guiding principles of early work (Collins & Scott, 1978; Cook, 1979; Fitt & Newton, 1981), including the pioneering work of Kathy Kram (1985) and Nancy Collins (1983). Scholars with similar expectations have offered conceptualizations (e.g., Auster, 1984; Bowen, 1986; Farylo & Paludi, 1985; Gilbert & Rossman, 1992; Hetherington & Barcelo, 1985; Nichols, Carter, & Golden, 1985; Noe, 1988b), reviewed the existing literatures (e.g., Burke & McKeen, 1990; Paludi, Meyers, Kindermann, Speicher, & Haring-Hidore, 1990; Ragins, 1989), or conducted qualitative studies (e.g., Clawson & Kram, 1984; Maack & Passet, 1993).

How can one test the expectation? One way is to ask women and men whether they have had role models, sponsors, or mentors. By knowing the sample size and the number of people who have been protégés, it is a fairly simple matter to calculate the percentages of women and men who have had the help of more senior people in their organizations.

In the simplest terms, the gender of a junior person does not influence the person's probability of becoming a protégé. Across a number of studies using a variety of conceptual and operational definitions, no sex discriminatory pattern emerges regarding the sheer likelihood of having had a mentor, sponsor, or role model.

The first study to use quantitative data to compare the probability of women and men receiving developmental help was published by Ellen Fagenson (1988; see also Fagenson, 1989). Fagenson distributed a questionnaire to a stratified random sample of women and men in high and low level jobs in a large health care company. Respondents were asked to indicate whether or not they had a mentor, and a mentor was defined as "someone in a position of power who looks out for you, or gives you advice, or brings your accomplishments to the attention of other people who have power in the company" (Fagenson, 1988, p. 186). Thirty-seven percent of the respondents claimed to have a mentor. Although high-level workers were much more likely than low-level ones to have a mentor, there were no sex differences at either level.

Similarly, studying three research and development firms, Ragins and Cotton (1991) found no differences in the percentages of women and men who could be characterized as having been protégés in developmental relationships. Fifty-five percent of the men and 50% of the women had had at least one mentor or sponsor. Virtually identical percentages of women and men—slightly under 18% in both cases—had had extensive mentoring. These similarities in actual percentages were especially striking because more women than men in the survey said they needed to have a mentor and because women perceived more barriers to obtaining a mentor than did men.

The studies by Fagenson (1988, 1989) and Ragins and Cotton (1991) are not isolated examples. A number of other studies of developmental relationships in the workplace have substantiated these findings. Swerdlik and Bardon (1988), Dreher and Ash (1990), Cox and Nkomo (1991), Whitely, Dougherty, and Dreher (1992), Turban and Dougherty (1994), and Baugh, Lankau, and Scandura (1996) all report that men and women acknowledge in equal measure having been protégés. A number of other studies have included gender as a variable and found no gender effects, implying that women and men are equally likely to receive developmental help (Bahniuk, Dobos, & Hill, 1990; Chao, Walz, & Gardner, 1992; Corzine, Buntzman, & Busch, 1994; Dreher & Cox, 1996; Whitely, Dougherty, & Dreher, 1992). One study (Goh, 1991) found that men supervisors excluded women subordinates from work-related discussions more often than men subordinates, but overall men and women subordinates reported equal amounts of inclusion in work discussions at the office.

In fact, two recent studies—one of managers (Thomas, 1990) and the other of lawyers (Mobley, Jaret, Marsh, & Lim, 1994)—found that women were more likely than men to have been someone's protégé. In the study of lawyers, however, the apparent gender difference was due to the fact that women in the sample were more likely to be at the associate level whereas men were more likely to be partners.

What about gender differences in academic settings? A vast number of studies have been concerned with career development in corporate and professional settings. Yet students' experiences in school are also important in professional development.

A number of activists like M. Elizabeth Tidball (e.g., 1986) assume that women students have a more difficult time than men finding mentors and sponsors. Indeed, part of the rationale for the continued existence of women's colleges is that there women have greater access to mentors (Conway, 1989). By implication, coeducational environments are seen as difficult places for women to find mentors.

Although the empirical research is scant, it suggests little gender difference. Busch (1985) conducted a study of mentoring during graduate education among 432 education department faculty. She found that those who had been mentored were significantly more likely to mentor others and that the percentages of men and women who had been mentored were approximately equal. When Keith and Moore (1995) questioned over 300 doctoral students in 40 different departments of sociology, they found no differences in the degree to which women and men students acknowledged having had access to mentors.

Only one study in the last two decades has found that women claim to have been mentored less than men (Wilson & Reschly, 1995). In that study, however, the measure of mentoring was a single item in a long inventory of items, and the sample was relatively small (87 men and 89 women with doctorates in school psychology). There were no gender differences in responses to a similar question about role models. In short, the data show virtually no difference between women and men in access to mentors.

Are Women Less Likely Than Men to Have Mentors, Sponsors, and Role Models of the Same Gender?

Even though women and men appear equally likely to be the junior person in a developmental relationship, there is clear evidence that men are more likely than women to have a mentor or sponsor at work who is of their own gender. The men participants in Swerdlik and Bardon's (1988) study named 294 senior men as mentors and only 76 senior women. The women participants in the study named 187 senior women and 278 senior men. In the study by Hill, Bahniuk, Dobos, and Rouner (1989) of faculty at two universities, 96% of the men and 70% of the women claimed to have had male mentors. Ragins and McFarlin (1990) also found that a greater proportion of women protégés were in cross-gender developmental relationships (48 of 66) compared to men (11 of 115). Similarly, the survey conducted by Ragins and Cotton (1991) revealed 77 cross-gender developmental relationships for the women and 19 for the men, whereas same-gender relationships numbered 40 for the women and 114 for the men. More recently, Hale's (1995) review of research conducted in government organizations showed that women were divided equally as protégés of men and women, whereas men worked almost exclusively as the protégés of other men. Independently, Javidan, Bemmels, Devine, and Dastmalchian (1995) found the same result in their study of three governmental organizations.

The scarcity of men who are guided by senior women is apparent in educational settings as well as in work settings. Four separate studies (Basow & Howe, 1985; Erkut & Mokros, 1984; Farylo & Paludi, 1985; Gilbert, 1985) have shown that men students cite men teachers and family members as influential people or role models but do not cite women teachers or family members. Although hard numbers examined in the aggregate show that men students consistently look to same-gender mentors, the young men in the Farylo and Paludi (1985) study indicated that they did not think gender was an important factor in their choice of role models, suggesting a lack of self-awareness. Two studies (Basow & Howe, 1985; Gilbert, 1985) have shown that women students also seek role models of their own sex; one study (Erkut & Mokros, 1984) showed no particular preference among women in this respect.

Are Women Less Likely
Than Men to Have Protégés?

One reason that junior men are more likely to have same-gender developmental relationships than junior women may be that senior women are less willing or able to serve in mentor roles. It is conceivable that senior women may be reluctant to pair with junior men as protégés or that they are so overburdened in their workplaces that they seek to escape altogether from the role of being anyone's sponsor or mentor. After all, if senior women resist these roles, then junior women who seek mentors or sponsors would have no one to turn to except senior men.

Once again, the data are not copious, but they are clear. In Collins' (1983) classic study, 315 of 387 professional women considered mentoring important enough to go out of their way to do it. No woman in Collins' study declared herself unwilling to mentor.

Gender comparisons tell the same story. Although women anticipate more drawbacks to mentoring relationships than do men, senior women are as likely as senior men to want to be mentors (Ragins & Cotton, 1993). Senior women guide and promote junior members of their organizations as frequently as men do (Ragins & Scandura, 1994), and at least one study (Ragins & McFarlin, 1990) has shown that women mentor men and women equally whereas men mentor men more frequently than they mentor women.

The relative scarcity of developmental pairs including a senior woman and a junior man, therefore, seems more likely the result of small numbers of senior women rather than their attitudes or preferences. In academia, for example, faculties, especially at the senior levels, are still inhabited largely by White males (Clark & Corcoran, 1986). This is particularly true in the sciences. As recently as 1992, for example, most major academic chemistry departments had their first female faculty member on tenure track (Amato, 1992), and in 1990–1991, the top 10 math departments had 50 tenure-track men and only 3 tenure-track women. Even in psychology, where women were being awarded nearly half the doctorates by 1980, the proportion of women full professors in graduate departments of psychology for that year was 182 out of 2,073, or 8.8% (Russo, Olmedo, Stapp, & Fulcher, 1981). The greater number of men in senior faculty positions means that there are more men than women in positions to mentor both graduate students and junior faculty members.

In a study of 90 graduate students in psychology, Cronan-Hillix, Gensheimer, Cronan-Hillix, and Davidson (1986) found that, although about half (53%) reported having mentors, only 13 percent had women mentors. (Although the term *mentor* was not defined, it was clear to students that a mentor did not necessarily include their advisers because both mentored and nonmentored students had advisers.) This percentage appeared to be a function of the small number of women faculty: Of 61 full-time faculty in the psychology department, only 12 were women, 4 of whom were full professors, compared to 49 men faculty, 34 of whom were full professors. No men students had women mentors, whereas women students had women mentors in the proportion that women faculty were available for mentoring.

Of course, in business women are even more scarce at the upper reaches than in academia. Catalyst's (1996) census of women in corporate leadership positions makes for depressing reading. Only 3% of officers of Fortune 500 companies are women. In one in-depth analysis of developmental relationships in a corporate setting, McCambley (chap. 10, this volume) found that although women were ready to mentor, they held so few of the positions in senior management that men tended more often to serve in those roles instead.

THE NATURE OF THE MENTORING EXPERIENCE

Some have suggested that women and men look for different qualities in senior guides. In an early review, Ragins (1989) proposed that women may look for socioemotional support in a mentor, whereas men may look for instrumental help. In one study of graduate students seeking role models, Gilbert (1985) found that the female students cared more than men about the lifestyles and values of their role models. Although men students were as likely as women students to seek out role models, their criteria for selection may have been more instrumental.

If women and men respond to different aspects of developmental relationships, they may also respond differently to the same experiences. Although there are few gender differences in the quantity of developmental relationships, there may be many gender differences in the quality of the experience. Burke and his colleagues have suggested, for example, that mentors give psychosocial help to junior women and instrumental help to junior men (Burke, 1984; Burke & McKeen, 1990; Burke, McKeen, & McKenna, 1990, 1993).

Studies show, however, that women and men receive equal amounts of instrumental and psychosocial help. Ragins and McFarlin (1990) developed a 59-item inventory, which they called the Mentor Role Instrument (MRI), asking men and women employees in three research and development firms about the kinds of help they have received from their men and women mentors. On the instrument Ragins and McFarlin defined a mentor as "a high-ranking, influential member of your organization who has advanced experience and knowledge and who is committed to providing upward mobility and support to your career" (pp. 326–327). In a series of analyses looking at instrumental help, socioemotional help, friendship, and role modeling, Ragins and McFarlin obtained no effects for the gender of the protégé: The help women received was of the same nature as the help men received.

Thomas (1990) administered a Career Experience Questionnaire to White and Black men and women in a Northeast utility company. He measured 11 types of support junior managers received from a person who "took an active interest in and concerted action to advance" their careers (p. 483) and found that protégés received more psychosocial support in same-race than in cross-race developmental relationships. Gender, however, was unrelated to the amount of psychosocial or instrumental support protégés received.

Tepper, Shaffer, and Tepper (1996) provided further confirmation of these findings. With five different samples of people from diverse backgrounds and a 16-item scale developed from Noe's (1988a) work, they confirmed the empirical distinction between instrumental and socioemotional help and found no gender differences in the amount of either type of help protégés received.

What about approaching the question of gender differences from another angle? Do men and women differ in the kinds of help they give to others? The typical expectation is that senior men will give instrumental help whereas senior women will give psychosocial help. With only a few exceptions, however, most of the research has shown that women and men generally provide the same sort of mentoring. In Ragins and McFarlin's (1990) industry study, for example, there were no sex differences in senior people's reports of the kinds or amounts of help they give to their protégés. Similarly, in a mailed survey to women working in retail stores, Gaskill (1991) found that of the more than 200 women who responded, 135, or 65% acknowledged that they had been helped by at least one more senior retail executive. In response to items about socioemotional and instrumental help (which Gaskill developed from Kram's 1985 work), there was no difference between the kind of help men gave and the kind of help women gave. In a much smaller interview study of 28 African American summer research assistants, Frierson, Hargrove, and Lewis (1994) found that although White male teachers established somewhat less rapport with their protégés than did White female teachers or teachers of color, there were no main effects for mentor gender.

The same story emerged with a quite different sample. Looking at the experiences of 165 women professors who acknowledged that they had been mentored at some point in their careers, Struthers (1995) could uncover no differences in the types of help they had received from their male and female guides. Struthers did find that the higher the rank of the more senior person, the more likely the woman was to report having received instrumental help from that person and the less likely she was to report having received psychosocial help. This finding suggests that what appear to be stereotypical gender differences may be misleading when mentors' sex is confounded with other factors, such as rank. If men tend to occupy the more senior ranks and those in the more senior ranks are more likely to dispense instrumental help, it could appear that men mentors are more likely than women to provide instrumental help. The untrained observer might then erroneously conclude that gender differences are real and robust. Struthers' (1995) finding also sheds light on McGuire's (chap. 6, this volume) finding that the type of help a mentor gives depends on his or her gender and the gender of the protégé and supports her suspicion that the gender differences she found derive from differences in rank.

Despite the absence of gender differences in the studies reviewed, it seems plausible that the greater frequency of cross-sex developmental relationships for women may nevertheless provide women with a different set of mentoring experiences than men. Some have suggested, for example, that in a cross-sex mentoring relationship both parties may assume stereotypical behaviors (Clawson & Kram, 1984; Kram, 1985). Uncertain and ambiguous situations seem to call for familiar or traditional behavior (Kram, 1985). In the case of a male mentor and a female protégé, the mentor may act as a protector and helper, indicating that he is powerful and dominant (Kram, 1985), whereas the female protégé may come to rely excessively on him for guidance and advice, thus implying that she cannot act autonomously. In this way, this relationship may elicit stereotypical behaviors that imply a more powerful and knowing male and a more supplicant female, reinforcing the power dynamics that are inherent in the hierarchical relationship (Kram, 1985). At the same time, the woman mentor–woman protégé dyad may unconsciously remind the junior woman of her experiences with her mother, arousing infantile expectations and frustrations (Heinrich, 1995), which in turn may influence her mentor's reactions to her.

Although we found no quantitative research that addressed these speculations directly, some data suggest that the gender composition of the dyad affects the quality and nature of the developmental relationship. In the Ragins and McFarlin (1990) study, the gender composition of the mentor–protégé dyad influenced neither the type—instrumental versus psychosocial—nor amount of help the mentor gave; however, two important interaction effects suggest that the sex composition of the dyad mattered. First, the junior women were more likely to perceive role models among their female mentors than among their male mentors (e.g., "this person represents who I want to be"), whereas men in the sample appeared to identify slightly more with their male mentors than with their female mentors. Second, both the women and the men reported that they avoided socializing with their other-sex mentors after hours.

Ragins and McFarlin's (1990) finding about the avoidance of socializing is not surprising in view of the problem of sexuality in the workplace. Where cross-gender relationships might be especially detrimental is in their potential to lead to sexual involvement or the perception of others of sexual involvement (Clawson & Kram, 1984; Devine & Markiewicz, 1990; Fitt & Newton, 1981; Ragins, 1989; Ragins & Cotton, 1991). Since the beginning of scholarship on the topic, observers have worried about sexual involvement between mentor and protégé. Fitt and Newton (1981) noted that 10% of their cross-gender mentoring pairs had been romantically involved. Among the professional women in Collins' study, a quarter admitted to having had affairs with their male mentors. Approaching matters from the other side, Fitzgerald, Weitzman, Gold, and Ormerod (1988) found that 25% of male faculty in their study reported having had sexual relationships with students (interestingly, only one thought he might be guilty of sexual harassment).

Sexual involvement can produce anxiety and confusion for both members of the relationship. Special harm may await the junior woman in the romance. Looking back on their situations, many women in Collins' study felt that the sexual liaisons had been harmful to them, and none felt they had been helpful.

Sexual liaisons between mentors and protégés can also create problems for organizations. As Clawson and Kram (1984) noted, every mentoring relationship has two aspects: an internal one and an external one. The internal relationship is what transpires between the two individuals, and the external relationship is among the two individuals and the rest of the organization (Kram, 1985; Clawson & Kram, 1984). Even a false appearance of sexual intimacies can stir up unproductive feelings among those outside the relationship.

CONSEQUENCES
OF DEVELOPMENTAL RELATIONSHIPS
FOR MALE AND FEMALE PROTÉGÉS

Women and men are equally likely to acknowledge that they have been someone's protégé, but women are more likely than men to have been in a cross-gender developmental relationship. Research suggests that for most developmental relationships, gender matching or mismatching may not matter, but for some proportion, it does—especially because of sexual tensions. In other ways not yet measured by researchers, differences in the quality of the mentoring experience may exist. Perhaps women have access to senior guides who are older or younger, more or less experienced, or more or less powerful than the senior guides to whom men have access; women may feel more comfortable than men asking for and receiving help; or possibly women worry more than men about appearing anything less than perfectly competent and therefore avoid asking for help.

If the nature of the developmental relationship varies noticeably for women and men, the educational and employment consequences should also differ. It may well be that men benefit from having a role model, sponsor, or mentor more than women do. Certainly, if men are mentored by men and if senior men are more highly placed than senior women, then developmental relationships may serve to exaggerate rather than to eliminate gender asymmetries at school and at work (Nichols, Carter, & Golden, 1985). Such was the reasoning of an early and much cited study in which Goldstein (1979) looked at the number of publications from young men and women scholars who had had male and female dissertation advisers. Goldstein found that same-gender pairs led to greater productivity than cross-gender pairs.

Nevertheless, over the last two decades, the hypothesis that developmental relationships might differentially benefit women and men has not received empirical support. Fagenson's meticulous study of managers in a large firm showed developmental relationships to benefit protégés by providing access to important people and resources (Fagenson, 1988), greater career mobility, and greater opportunity (Fagenson, 1989). The benefits were obtained equally for women and for men.

Other studies show the same pattern as Fagenson's study. In 1985 Whitely, Dougherty, and Dreher (1991) mailed surveys to recent MBAs from three universities, about a quarter of whom were female. They measured a construct that they called secondary mentoring and that corresponds to Kram's (1985) variable of career functions and to Crosby's (chap. 1, this volume) variable of sponsorship. Respondents who had a sponsor had earned more promotions and higher salaries than others. The association remained statistically significant even after the researchers controlled for demographic and motivational variables. Although women earned less than comparable men, the positive impact of sponsorship was the same for both. The lack of gender differences is especially noteworthy because the detailed analysis was sensitive to other differences that could have seemed less important initially than gender. For example, they showed that mentoring aided only those people whose family of origin was middle class or upper-middle class.

A number of other studies provide further confirmation that sponsoring and mentoring benefits women as much as men. Chao et al. (1992) conducted an alumni survey and found that although informal (freely chosen) mentoring experiences are associated with higher job satisfaction and higher salaries than are formal mentoring programs, there were no gender effects. Among bankers, Corzine et al. (1994) found that women and men who have been protégés express greater job satisfaction and escape more from career plateauing than other women and men and that the effects are equally visible in the two sexes. Mobley et al. (1994) reported the same strong impact of mentoring on job satisfaction among women as among men.

Only one study showed clearly the mediating effects of gender on the relationship between protégé and nonprotégé status and career outcomes, but these were in the opposite direction than researchers have hypothesized. In a comparison of executive men and women who had or had not been mentored (Baugh et al., 1996), according to their self-reports, nonmentored men were distinctive from mentored men in many ways: Nonmentored men reported lower organizational commitment, lower job satisfaction, lower career expectations, and higher role ambiguity. In contrast, nonmentored women differed from mentored women only in that they reported lower career expectations. In other words, in this mailed-questionnaire study, failure to have a mentor proved more detrimental for the men than for the women.

Although the gender of the protégé does not seem to influence the effects of mentoring or sponsorship, the gender—and ethnicity—of the senior person may well exert a very powerful effect on outcomes. Dreher and Cox (1996) sent questionnaires to MBAs from nine schools in a consortium. Slightly over a quarter of the MBAs responded to the questionnaire, yielding a sample of 742 men and 276 women. The researchers asked all respondents if they had had a mentor in their careers and defined a mentor as "an individual who holds a position senior to yours, who takes an active interest in developing your career" and who typically is not the direct supervisor. Participants in the study provided information about their mentors and about themselves. Salary was one of the self-referential pieces of information. They found that MBAs who had had a mentor earned substantially higher salaries than other MBAs, but only if the mentor were a White male. Female mentors and male mentors of color brought no additions to income.

The income advantage of the protégés of White males, relative to all others in the sample, amounted to somewhere between $16,840 and $22,454 per annum, depending on the other factors considered in the calculations.

The dynamics behind the Dreher and Cox finding have some interesting implications. Senior white men in that study tended to give instrumental help of the type that Crosby (chap. 1, this volume) calls sponsorship. Of course, whether other studies will corroborate their findings remains to be seen. The research suggests that if senior White men in corporations were involved in formal sponsorship programs in which they were assigned some measurable tasks and provided providing instrumental help to women and people of color, but were not expected to develop instant friendships and close emotional ties, some progress toward gender equity might be made.

WHAT NOW?

Ragins (1989) suggested that organizations that want to become or remain competitive may wish to increase the pool of skilled managers. Such an increase will come if they remove barriers that keep women artificially excluded from power. Involving women in developmental relationships certainly seems to be a prime way to effect such change.

Before individuals and organizations rush to action, we must give some thought to the potential pitfalls. Olson and Ashton-Jones (1992) and Nichols et al. (1985) have warned us that the hierarchical nature of developmental relationships may simply reinforce the patriarchy of the larger society. More specifically, the prevalence of unhelpful sexual or romantic feelings in cross-gender relationships has prompted some scholars and activists to advocate for developmental relationships that differ from the old-fashioned mentoring ones that Kram (1985) and others (e.g., Zey, 1984) described. Some organizations are instituting mentoring circles or groups in which several senior people share responsibility for several junior people (Catalyst, 1993; McCambley, chap. 10, this volume). Other authorities propose that when organizations develop formal programs, they emphasize sponsorship, with its relative lack of emotional content, rather than mentorship (Crosby, chap. 1, this volume).

As diversity gains more of a foothold in various organizations, some interesting questions arise. Following Nkomo (1992), Ibarra (1993; Ibarra & Andrews, 1993), Ragins (1997), and others (e.g., Hoyt, chap. 11, this volume), we think it will be imperative to track the changing effects of gender, social class, and ethnicity on mentoring relationships and access to power. Dreher and Cox (1996) concluded that only White men mentors bring economic advantage to protégés; would their depressing conclusion remain true, for example, among a sample of women managers and executives in a female-friendly firm (Katz & Katz, 1996)? Would female-dominated or sex-balanced organizations look the same as the traditional, male-dominated ones in terms of gender, developmental relationships, and access to resources? Answers to these and a host of similar questions will deepen our knowledge of the basic social psychology of organizational life while making positive and practical change in the world.

REFERENCES

Amato, I. (1992). Profile of a field: Chemistry. Women have extra hoops to jump through. *Science, 255,* 1372–1378.

American Association of University Women. (1994). *Shortchanging girls, shortchanging America.* Washington, DC: American Association of University Women.

Auster, D. (1984). Mentors and protégés: Power-dependent dyads. *Sociological Inquiry, 54,* 142–153.

Bahniuk, M. H., Dobos, J., & Hill, S. E. K. (1990). The impact of mentoring, collegial support, and information adequacy on career success: A replication. *Journal of Social Behavior and Personality, 5,* 431–451.

Basow, S., & Howe, K. (1985). Role-model influence: Effects of sex and sex-role attitude in college students. *Psychology of Women Quarterly, 4,* 558–572.

Baugh, S. G., Lankau, M. J., & Scandura, T. A. (1996). An investigation of the effects of protégé gender on responses to mentoring. *Journal of Vocational Behavior, 49,* 309–323.

Bowen, D. D. (1986). The role of identification in mentoring female protégés. *Group and Organization Studies, 11,* 1–2, 61–74.

Brett, J., & Stroh, L. (1997). Jumping ship: Who benefits from an external labor market career strategy? *Journal of Applied Psychology, 82*(3), 331–341.

Burke, R. J. (1984). Mentors in organizations. *Group and Organization Studies, 9,* 353–372.

Burke, R. J., & McKeen, C. A. (1990). Mentoring in organizations: Implications for women. *Journal of Business Ethics, 9,* 317–332.

Burke, R. J., McKeen, C. A., & McKenna, C. S. (1990). Sex differences and cross-sex effects on mentoring: Some preliminary data. *Psychological Reports, 67,* 1011–1023.

Burke, R. J., McKeen, C. A., & McKenna, C. S. (1993). Correlates of mentoring in organizations: The mentor's perspective. *Psychological Reports, 72,* 883–896.

Busch, J. W. (1985). Mentoring in graduate schools of education: Mentors' perceptions. *American Educational Research Journal, 22*(2), 257–265.

Catalyst. (1993). *Mentoring: A guide to corporate programs and practices.* New York: Catalyst.

Catalyst. (1996). *The 1996 census of women corporate officers and top earners.* New York: Catalyst.

Catalyst. (1997, October). *Infobrief: Women in business. A Snapshot.* New York: Catalyst.

Chao, G. T., Walz, P. M., & Gardner, P. D. (1992). Formal and informal mentorships: A comparison of mentoring functions and contrast with nonmentored counterparts. *Personnel Psychology, 45,* 619–636.

Clark, S. M., & Corcoran, M. (1986). Perspectives in the professional socialization of women faculty: A case of accumulative disadvantage? *Journal of Higher Education, 57*(1), 20–43.

Clawson, J. G., & Kram, K. E. (1984). Managing cross-gender mentoring. *Business Horizons*, *27*(3), 22–31.

Clayton, S. D., & Crosby, F. J. (1992). *Justice, gender, and affirmative action*. Ann Arbor, MI: University of Michigan Press.

Collins, E. G. C., & Scott, P. (1978, Aug.–Sept.). Everyone who makes it has a mentor. *Harvard Business Review*, 89–100.

Collins, N. (1983). *Professional women and their mentors*. Englewood Cliffs, NJ: Prentice-Hall.

Conway, J. J. (1989). Higher education for women. *American Behavioral Scientist*, *32*, 633–639.

Cook, M. F. (1979). Is the mentor relationship primarily a male experience? *Personnel Administrator*, *24*(11), 82–86.

Corzine, J., Buntzman, G., & Busch, E. (1994). Mentoring, downsizing, gender and career outcomes. *Journal of Social Behavior and Personality*, *9*, 517–528.

Cox, T. H., & Nkomo, S. M. (1991). A race and gender group analysis of the early career experience of MBAs. *Work and Occupations*, *18*, 431–446.

Cronan-Hillix, T., Gensheimer, L. K., Cronan-Hillix, W. A., and Davidson, W. S. (1986). Students' views of mentors in psychology graduate training. *Teaching of Psychology*, *13*(3), 123–127.

Devine, I., & Markiewicz, D. (1990). Cross-sex relationships at work and the impact of gender stereotypes. *Journal of Business Ethics*, *9*, 333–338.

Dreher, G. F., & Ash, R. A. (1990). A comparative study among men and women in managerial, professional, and technical positions. *Journal of Applied Psychology*, *75*(5), 1–8.

Dreher, G. F., & Cox, T. H. (1996). Race, gender, and opportunity: A study of compensation attainment and the establishment of mentoring relationships. *Journal of Applied Psychology*, *81*(3), 297–308.

Eagly, A. H., & Crowley, M. (1986). Gender and helping behavior: A meta-analytic review of the social psychology literature. *Psychological Bulletin*, *100*, 283–308.

Eagly, A. H., & Steffen, V. J. (1984). Gender stereotypes stem from the distribution of women and men into social roles. *Journal of Personality and Social Psychology*, *46*, 735–754.

Eagly, A. H., & Steffen, V. J. (1986). Gender and aggressive behavior: A meta-analytic review of the social psychology literature. *Psychological Bulletin*, *100*, 309–330.

Erkut, S., & Mokros, J. R. (1984). Professors as models and mentors for college students. *American Educational Research Journal*, *21*, 399–417.

Fagenson, E. A. (1988). The power of a mentor: Protégés' and nonprotégés' perceptions of their own power in organizations. *Group and Organization Studies*, *13*(2), 182–194.

Fagenson, E. A. (1989). The mentor advantage: Perceived career/job experiences of protégés versus non-protégés. *Journal of Organizational Behavior*, *10*(4), 309–320.

Farylo, B., & Paludi, M. (1985). Developmental discontinuities in mentor choice by male students. *The Journal of Social Psychology*, *125*, 521–522.

Fitt, L. W., & Newton, D. A. (1981). When the mentor is a man and the protégé a woman. *Harvard Business Review*, *58*(2), 56–60.

Fitzgerald, L., Weitzman, L., Gold, Y., & Ormerod, M., (1988). Academic harassment: Sex and denial in scholarly garb. *Psychology of Women Quarterly*, *12*, 329–340.

Frierson, H. T., Jr., Hargrove, B., & Lewis, N. R. (1994). Black summer research students' perceptions related to research mentors' race and gender. *Journal of College Student Development*, *35*, 475–480.

Gaskill, L. R. (1991). Same-sex and cross-sex mentoring of female protégés: A comparative analysis. *Career Development Quarterly*, *40*, 48–63.

Gilbert, L. A. (1985). Dimensions of same-gender student-faculty role-model relationships. *Sex Roles, 12,* 111–123.

Gilbert, L., & Rossman, K. (1992). Gender and the mentoring process for women: Implications for professional development. *Professional Psychology: Research and Practice, 23,* 233–238.

Ginsburg, R. B. (1997, September 12). *In remembrance of Sophia Smith.* Speech delivered at Smith College.

Goh, S. (1991). Sex differences in perceptions of interpersonal work style, career emphasis, supervisory mentoring behavior, and job satisfaction. *Sex Roles, 24,* 701–710.

Goldstein, E. (1979). Effect of same-sex and cross-sex role models on the subsequent academic productivity of scholars. *American Psychologist, 34,* 407–410.

Hale, M. (1995). Mentoring women in organizations: Practice in search of theory. *American Review of Public Administration, 25,* 327–339.

Heinrich, K. T. (1995). Doctoral advisement relationships between women. *Journal of Higher Education, 66,* 447–469.

Hetherington, C., & Barcelo, R. (1985, Fall). Womentoring: A cross-cultural perspective. *Journal of NAWDAC,* 12–15.

Hill, S. K., Bahniuk, M. H., Dobos, J., & Rouner, D. (1989). Mentoring and other communication support in the academic setting. *Group and Organization Studies, 14*(3), 355–368.

Ibarra, H. (1993). Personal networks of women and minorities in management: A conceptual framework. *Academy of Management Review, 18,* 56–87.

Ibarra, H., & Andrews, S. (1993). Power, social influence, and sense making: Effects of network centrality and proximity on employee perceptions. *Administrative Science Quarterly, 38,* 277–303.

Javidan, M., Bemmels, B., Devine, K., & Dastmalchian, A. (1995). Superior and subordinate gender and the acceptance of superiors as role models. *Human Relations, 48,* 1271–1284.

Kahn, W., & Crosby, F. J. (1985). Discriminating between attitudes and discriminatory behavior: Change and stasis. In L. Larwood, B. A. Gutek, & A. H. Stromberg (Eds.), *Women and work, an annual review* (Vol. 1, pp. 215–238). Beverly Hills, CA: Sage.

Katz, P., and Katz, M. (1996). The feminist dollar: The wise woman's buying guide. New York: Plenum.

Keith, B., & Moore, H. A. (1995). Training sociologists: An assessment of professional socialization and the emergence of career aspirations. *Teaching Sociology, 23,* 199–214.

Kram, K. E. (1985). *Mentoring at work: Developmental relationships in organizational life.* Glenview, IL: Scott, Foresman.

Lott, B. (1997, August). *Carolyn Wood Sherif address: Learning gender roles.* Paper presented at the American Psychological Association Annual meeting.

Maack, M., & Passet, J. (1993). Unwritten rules: Mentoring women faculty. *Library and Information Science Research, 15,* 117–141.

Mobley, M., Jaret, C., Marsh, K., & Lim, Y. (1994). Mentoring, job satisfaction, gender and the legal profession. *Sex Roles, 31,* 79–98.

Nichols, I., Carter, H., & Golden, M. (1985). The patron system in academia: Alternative strategies for empowering academic women. *Women's Studies International Forum, 8,* 383–390.

Nkomo, S. (1992). The emperor has no clothes: Rewriting "race in organizations." *Academy of Management Review, 17,* 487–513.

Noe, R. (1988a). An investigation of the determinants of successful assigned mentoring relationships. *Personnel Psychology, 41,* 457–479.

Noe, R. (1988b). Women and mentoring: A review and research agenda. *Academy of Management Review, 13*(1), 65–78.

Olson, G., & Ashton-Jones, E. (1992). Doing gender: (En)gendering academic mentoring. *Journal of Education, 174*, 114–127.

Paludi, M. A., Meyers, D., Kindermann, J., Speicher, H., & Haring-Hidore, M. (1990). Mentoring and being mentored: Issues of sex, power, and politics for older women. *Journal of Women and Aging, 2*, 81–92.

Ragins, B. R. (1989). Barriers to mentoring: The female manager's dilemma. *Human Relations, 42*(1), 1–22.

Ragins, B. R. (1995). Diversity, power, and mentorship in organizations: A cultural, structural, and behavioral perspective. In M. Chemers, M. Costanzo, & S. Oskamp (Eds.), *Diversity in organizations* (pp. 91–132). Newbury Park, CA: Sage.

Ragins, B. R. (1997). Diversified mentoring relationships in organizations: A power perspective. *Academy of Management Review, 22*, 482–521.

Ragins, B. R., & Cotton, J. L. (1991). Easier said than done: Gender differences in perceived barriers to gaining a mentor. *Academy of Management Journal, 34*, 939–951.

Ragins, B. R., & Cotton, J. L. (1993). Gender and willingness to mentor in organizations. *Journal of Management, 19*(1), 97–111.

Ragins, B. R., & McFarlin, D. B. (1990). Perceptions of mentor roles in cross-gender mentoring relationships. *Journal of Vocational Behavior, 37*, 321–339.

Ragins, B. R., & Scandura, T. A. (1994). Gender differences in expected outcomes of mentoring relationships. *Academy of Management Journal, 37*, 957–971.

Ragins, B. R., & Sundstrom, E. (1990). Gender and perceived power in manager–subordinate relations. *Journal of Occupational Psychology, 63*, 273–287.

Russo, N. F., Olmedo, E. L., Stapp, J., & Fulcher, R. (1981). Women and minorities in psychology. *American Psychologist, 36*, 1315–1363.

Scandura, T. A., & Ragins, B. R. (1993). The effects of sex and gender role orientations on mentorship in male-dominated occupations. *Journal of Vocational Behavior, 43*(3), 251–265.

Struthers, N. J. (1995). Differences in mentoring: A function of gender or organizational rank? *Journal of Social Behavior and Personality, 10*, 265–272.

Swerdlik, M., & Bardon, J. (1988). A survey of mentoring experiences in school psychology. *Journal of School Psychology, 26*, 213–224.

Tepper, K., Shaffer, B. C., & Tepper, B. J. (1996). Latent structure of mentoring function scales. *Educational and Psychological Measurement, 56*, 848–857.

Thomas, D. A. (1990). The impact of race on managers' experiences of developmental relationships (mentoring and sponsorship): An intra-organizational study. *Journal of Organizational Behavior, 11*, 479–492.

Tidball, M. E. (1986). Baccalaureate origins of recent natural science doctorates. *Journal of Higher Education, 57*, 606–620.

Tomasson, R., Crosby, F. J., & Herzberger, S. (1996). *Affirmative action: The pros and cons of policy and practice*. Washington, DC: American University Press.

Turban, D. B., & Dougherty, T. W. (1994). Role of protégé personality in receipt of mentoring and career success. *Academy of Management Journal, 37*, 688–702.

Whitely, W., Dougherty, T. W., & Dreher, G. F. (1991). Relationship of career mentoring and socioeconomic origin to managers' and professionals' early career progress. *Academy of Management Journal, 34*, 331–351.

Whitely, W., Dougherty, T. W., & Dreher, G. F. (1992). Correlates of career-oriented mentoring for early career managers and professionals. *Journal of Organizational Behavior, 13*(2), 141–154.

Wilson, M. S., & Reschly, D. J. (1995). Gender and school psychology: Issues, questions, and answers. *School Psychology Review, 24*, 45–61.

Zey, M. G. (1984). *The mentor connection*. Homewood, IL: Irwin.

II

Empirical Perspectives

5

At the Crossroads of Race and Gender: Lessons From the Mentoring Experiences of Professional Black Women

Stacy Blake
Harvard University

The Negro is a sort of seventh son, born with a veil, and gifted with second sight in this American world, a world which yields him no true self-consciousness, but only lets him see himself through the revelation of the other world. It is a peculiar sensation, this double consciousness, this sense of always looking at one's self through the eyes of others, of measuring one's soul by the tape of a world that looks on in amused contempt and pity. One ever feels his twoness, an American, a Negro; two souls, two thoughts, two unreconciled strivings; two warring ideals in one dark body, whose dogged strength alone keeps it from being torn asunder.

—DuBois, 1903

DuBois published this statement in the early 19th century to describe Blacks' experiences of living in America, a society based largely on denial of respect and full rights to Blacks. Although this statement is dated in the early 19th century, it is aptly descriptive of the experiences that Blacks face in America today. What DuBois described as double consciousness is currently defined as biculturalism, or living in two worlds. DuBois' statement is particularly descriptive of the corporate experience of Blacks and other ethnic minorities. A second and third generation of Black college graduates have graduated from America's universities and run to corporate America to reap the benefits of their education: the cars and the houses in suburbia, the vacations and the clothes, jewelry and electronic gadgets. Yet the mantle of education, earned oftentimes at elite universities, is not enough to ward off the harsh effects of racism. Fernandez (1981) found in his study of 4,202 managers from 10 companies that of all the racial groups included in the study (Hispanics, Asians, Native Americans, Blacks, and Whites), the greatest burden of racism has fallen on Blacks. Differences between Blacks and Whites in terms of income, promotability, satisfaction, and other organizational outcomes are well documented (Braddock & McPartland, 1987; Cox & Nkomo, 1991; Davis & Watson, 1982; Fernandez, 1981). Even after a variety of factors such as education, socioeconomic status, age, and background are held constant, research shows that Blacks are still fighting to gain equality with Whites in the corporate sector. Blacks are pulled to succeed in the predominantly white corporate sector yet are also drawn to the Black community. By necessity, Blacks are often bicultural, moving back and forth between their professional spheres and the Black community (Bell, 1990).

Although both Black men and women face the effects of racism and the stresses of being bicultural, Black women are in an even more tenuous position within the labor market. Black women are at the intersection of two of the most pervasive prejudices in America, racism and sexism. There has been debate within the academy as to whether Black women are in a position of advantage or a position of disadvantage as a result of the intertwining of race and gender (Nkomo, 1988). Proponents of the former position assert that because of their membership in two disadvantaged groups protected by affirmative action (EEO), Black women are the beneficiaries of preferred status over Black men and White women. Advocates of the latter position argue that Black women are doubly disadvantaged. Beale (1979) coined the term *double jeopardy* to describe the dual discriminations of racism and sexism facing Black women. As Nkomo (1988, p. 137) stated, "They must constantly battle the assumption that they are both racially and sexually inferior."

Essed (1991) noted that the inability to separate the specific impact of either race or gender leads to a form of gendered racism that suffuses the experiences of Black women. For the most part Black women face the challenges of gendered racism in silence, as their experiences have been excluded from scholarly analysis. hooks (1989) found that when she "began the long search in history, sociology, and psychology texts for material, I was surprised that Black women were rarely a category in anyone's index, that when we were written about we rarely rated more than a few sentences or paragraphs" (p. 150). The management literature is no exception (Bell, 1990; Essed, 1991; Evans & Herr, 1991; Nkomo, 1988; Scott, 1989). Too often it is assumed that through a study of Black males, the Black woman is understood. Alternatively, studies of White women are assumed to encompass the experiences of their Black counterparts. Both assumptions are erroneous and detrimental; both render Black women invisible (King, 1988).

The purpose of this chapter is to combat that invisibility in the study of one domain of Black women's lives at work. In the organizational mentoring literature, there is a conspicuous absence of research on Black women. Mentoring was defined by Thomas (1990) as the relationship between juniors and seniors (in terms of age or experience) that exists primarily to support the personal (or psychosocial) and career development of the junior person. These relationships provide a wide range of developmental functions (including coaching and counseling) and require both individuals to invest considerable time and emotion in the relationship.

Mentoring in the organizational setting has recently gained attention in the management literature. The past 10 years have seen a proliferation of research investigating the effects of mentoring on a variety of organizational outcomes (Burke, 1984; Burke & McKeen, 1989; Dreher & Ash, 1990; Dunbar, 1990; Hill & Kamprath, 1991; Kram, 1985; Kram & Hall, 1989; Kram & Isabella, 1985; Missrian, 1982; Noe, 1988; Thomas, 1989; Zey, 1984). Much of the early work in mentoring research was done using white male samples (Collins & Scott, 1978; Dalton, Thompson, & Price, 1977; Gould, 1972; Levinson et al., 1978; Roche, 1979). A growing number of scholars has recognized that women seeking to enter mentoring relationships face myriad challenges and obstacles as a result of gender biases. Thus a body of literature has developed to address the concerns of women in the mentoring process (Clawson & Kram, 1984; Collins, 1983; Fitt & Newton, 1981; Halcomb, 1980; Nieva & Gutek, 1981; Noe, 1986; Ragins, 1989). Most of these studies have included White women as respondents to questionnaires and interviews. Scholars have looked at the impact of race on the mentoring experiences of Black managers in the corporate sector (Cox & Nkomo, 1991; Davis & Watson, 1982; Deinard & Friedman, 1991; Hill & Kamprath, 1991; Ibarra, 1993; Thomas, 1989, 1990). Yet the voices of Black women, which are different from those of Blacks who happen to be men and different from those of women who happen to be White, are still largely unheard. This silence compelled me to mount this research project.

This study is a qualitative analysis of the mentoring experiences of Black professional women in the corporate setting. I conducted the study with Kram's (1983) definition of mentoring in mind—a developmental relationship in which a senior person provides both psychosocial and instrumental support to a junior person. The participants in my study relied on this definition. This definition is significant because much of participants' experience in developmental relationships involved feelings of disappointment that their mentors failed to provide the psychosocial functions Kram described as essential to the mentoring relationship. In the spirit of holding onto this sense of disappointment, I do not use Crosby's (chap. 1, this volume) term, sponsorship, to describe those developmental relationships that fell short of my participants' expectations for psychosocial support. Sponsorship is a valuable kind of developmental relationship in its own right; it is not sponsorship that my participants experienced, I contend, but rather unfulfilled mentorship.

Through informal interviews, a number of themes emerged concerning Black women's experiences of mentoring. Two prominent themes were that there is a general lack of Black role models who might serve as mentors for the women involved in the study and that Black women's relationships with White women mentors are largely characterized by mistrust, which may be grounded in the historical interaction between women of these cultural groups. In this chapter, I discuss the implications of these findings for Black women's mentoring relationships, as well as practical and theoretical considerations for managers and researchers.

METHODS

I collected the data for this study between October and December of 1992. Once I received approval from the human subjects review committee, I conducted two semistructured, informal, recorded interviews at the homes of two Black women in the Detroit metropolitan area. To identify these women, I used a reference technique. Through referrals from colleagues and friends, I gathered names of professional Black women in the Detroit area who might consent to participate in the study. Of the three women I initially contacted, two agreed to participate in the study. In addition to the two individual interviews, I held a semistructured, recorded group interview with nine Black women in a hotel meeting room in the Philadelphia metropolitan area. Women who participated in the group interview were participants in an annual social gathering of Black professional women. I gained access to this group through my own membership of 7 years.

I presented each woman who participated in the study with a list of interview questions to serve primarily as a guide. I asked each woman if she objected to being audiotaped and assured her that I would maintain her confidentiality. I changed all names to protect their confidentiality as well as the confidentiality of the people about whom they talked. In addition to audiotaping, I took notes in both the individual and the group settings.

I collected demographic information from all 11 participants. The women in this sample ranged in age from 37 to 52 years. All participants had some college education; most had advanced professional degrees (MBA or JD). They were employed in a variety of occupations ranging from corporate management to governmental agencies. Their salaries ranged from $51,000 to over $100,000.

After the interviews, the tapes were transcribed, and I integrated my field notes, as well as any other personal observations, into the final transcription. I then coded part of the transcription of the first interview using in-vivo coding, a line-by-line restatement of the relevant information. I took care during this process to use the verbatim language of the participants. This transcription was particularly important because my extensive reading of the mentoring literature threatened to overpower the voices of the Black women whose very exclusion had prompted this study. Chesler's (1987) suggestion to avoid the theoretical literature until after the discovered framework is stabilized is a warning against this tendency to test only prior conceptualizations. From these restatements, a set of code categories emerged. I repeated this process with another segment of data from the second interview.

The next step was to take the code categories and apply them to the remaining data. Through this process, I was constantly comparing the raw data with the categories I had generated. I adjusted the categories to reflect new information and engaged in the comparison process again. Thus, through the use of Glaser and Strauss' (1967) method of constant comparison, I felt relatively secure that the code categories were truly reflective of the participants' experiences. By the third interview, I decided to switch lenses from a micro perspective to a more macro orientation. I analyzed this transcription and generated conceptual themes. I compared these themes to those I had created in the two earlier interviews through the in-vivo process. Throughout this process, I looked for common themes and indicators of mentoring among the participants.

Moving to the next step, memo writing, was a breath of fresh air after the tedium and intensity of generating themes and coding. Glaser (1987, p. 83) described the writing of theoretical memos as the "core stage in the process of generating theory, the bedrock of theory generation." I used this opportunity to let my mind run free and explore possible connections and emergent themes. This process was fruitful because through the memos I identified that most, if not all, women in my study were first-generation businesswomen and that this commonalty may have implications for their subsequent mentoring experiences.

I became particularly sensitized to Black women's mentoring relationships across race and gender. In the following sections, I explore what I learned from these women about the factors that characterized their relationships with Black men, White men, and White women. In particular, I focus here on their relationships with White women because they seemed to be the most emotionally laden for my participants and because there was a good deal of variability in the quality of those relationships within my sample.

BLACK WOMEN'S MENTORING RELATIONSHIPS

One respondent compared her experience of striking out and doing freelance work to "walking into a room with no lights on." The Black women in my sample were often pioneers, jumping into new territories, as they moved into middle and upper management without the guidance of Black women before them:

> I came at a time when there was, as a corporate attorney, there was another Black male. A Black male, not another Black female. And in fact, the entire time I was there, at the corporation that I was employed there was never another Black female the entire time I was there.

The guidance, support, and information regarding informal practices that mentoring offered these women was particularly critical. One participant talked about the high visibility opportunities that one of her mentors, who was a Black man, had provided to her:

I had written a series of memoranda for him. I didn't know that the president of the company had requested that this research be done. So I wrote the memo, turned it in. And this Black man said this was an excellent job and I want you to present it ... I mean, he got me into this room with these people who were all high muckety-mucks in the company. And he had me make a presentation to the president of the company ... He didn't have to bring me in and to give me the credit for it.

Her mentor also shared information about the informal rules operating at the meeting:

I learned a lot about White men and the informal practices that go on in the top echelons of business. Now Mr. Barnes was the president of the company. And I was making this presentation so ... I didn't know. I was one of the first people there so I went and sat to his left in the first seat. And this White guy came up to me and said, "Well why don't you sit here. This is my seat." ... What I found out is that the seats right next to the boss are the most political, the most powerful.

Although the number of Blacks, male or female, in middle and upper management is relatively small, the numbers of Black men are larger, and Black men received access to the upper echelons before Black women. Two or three of my participants vividly recalled the hand that advanced Black men in their organizations held out to them. One respondent noted in talking about her first mentor, who was a Black man, that:

Alex was very helpful in telling you what the game was. That yes, it is important to be a good attorney but also you keep your job and get your promotions based on what political work you do and your stated willingness to be political ... Alex was so insistent on bringing us, us new Black ones, into the political scheme because this was really an opportunity for all of us to be able to achieve, to make other contacts, to move on.

Another respondent noted that as her Black male mentor advanced in the corporation, he made sure that he took her with him:

Now for me later on my mentor, who was at the larger corporation where I was, became general counsel and vice president of a subsidiary of the company where I was. And a year later that person brought me on as counsel to the subsidiary. So now he was in a direct line to be my mentor. There were no if, ands, or buts about it. So when you talk about important assignments, he made sure that I was active with all of the other vice presidents. That I was on their business teams, that I went to their meetings, their staff meetings. And that was the thing. He was arranging my visibility.

However, these examples were more the exception than the rule. The same respondent from the group interview acknowledged that she was the beneficiary of a "phenomenon, a situation that is not repeated very often."

More often than not, Black women who had mentoring had White males in the mentor role. This finding is no surprise given that the number of women and minorities in high-level corporate positions who can serve as mentors is usually limited (Ibarra, 1993). For example, Thomas (1990), in his study of race and mentoring relationships, found that Blacks in upper level positions comprised less than 5% of the total number of professionals in this stratum and that White men predominated as mentors for all four race–gender groups he studied: White women, Black men, Black women, and White men.

Most participants in my study reported positive interactions with their White male mentors. For example, in response to a question about what her mentor did for her, one of the group participants talked about her White male mentor as follows:

> Well, in the first instance he saw how I was handling a situation and he made some suggestions about another approach I might take and what he was also going to do on his end. In future discussion, if something was going on that he thought it would benefit me to know about, anything like changes in the organization or the position of management on a certain thing, he would contact me behind the scenes, if you will, and make sure that I knew what was about to occur so that I would be positioned to take advantage of opportunity.

Another respondent indicated that her White male mentor had clearly taken her under his wing. In response to my question, "How did he make it clear that he was your mentor?" she responded:

> He told his manager. That was his style. I mean, he said, "I brought S.S. here. You know we are about to embark upon some changes in this organization to bring us closer together. And she's here." Of course he did what they want and that's to outline what my qualifications were for the job. And he just openly said, "I support her and I expect you to help her do this." And so that set the tone … And when things got tough though, it was great to be able to pick up the phone or send him an e-mail and tell him, "Hey, you know, things are real bad and I need some help."

It is apparent that the White male mentors were able to provide important career functions of sponsorship, which include exposure and visibility, challenging assignments, and protection (Crosby, chap. 1, this volume). Psychosocial functions, which include emotional bonding and friendship, were not as evident. One respondent noted that as a rule she didn't socialize with White males; she kept her interactions with them at a professional level. This example is consistent with research on cross-gender mentoring (Burke, McKeen, & McKenna; 1990; Kram, 1985), which suggests that psychosocial functions are not as prevalent in developmental relationships between senior men and junior women. Alternatively, it is possible that I did not probe sufficiently to tease out the intricacies or the obstacles operating in cross-gender mentoring. This is certainly an important area to consider in future research.

On the basis of sisterhood, the common frontier of gender, I expected that Black women would gain their greatest support from White women. Thus, I was surprised by the overwhelmingly negative feelings that the Black women in the group interview expressed when discussing their relationships with White women. They shared sentiments ranging from indifference to vehement anger and distrust. One respondent shared her feelings about White women as compared to White men:

> But I would have to say that I find the White female to be different from the White male ... There is that good ole boy network. And somehow even through team sports or whatever, they learn to semi look out for one another. They're more comfortable doing that. But White women have no concept whatsoever of sisterhood, I mean, from my whole experience. They can not relate to the notion of sharing, taking care of each other, never mind you ... by and large they tend to be far more cutthroat than the good ole boys are to each other. So I see them as a breed apart.

Another respondent talked about a historical difference between White and Black women:

> There are some differences there. And one of them is that White women are extremely competitive. People of color are taught to be trusting and I think that women don't have that piece of it in terms of competitiveness. So while we are competitive, we tend not to cut your legs off. But if you look at White women, there is not trust there. And they will cut your legs off.

This anger evoked two responses from me. The first was a wariness as I saw stereotypes about both Black and White women being used. I went back through the two individual interviews looking for this same theme of mistrust of White women. One respondent indicated that it was easier for her to associate with White women than with White men, but she noted a distance between her and her White female associates. Although they were able to connect on a social level, the relationship never entered her personal domain, her home life. The second respondent reported positive relationships with two White women in her office who mentored her. In talking about her relationship with these two White women, she noted:

> They were peers. I mean they were two years ahead of me but they made sure I understood what I was doing. You know, they helped me with respect to finding out what the law was. They showed me their briefs and asked me if I had any questions. If I had any questions, they made it clear that I could always ask them whatever I needed to do … what they did was they showed me what a trial brief was, they gave me my responsibilities, they helped make … they didn't smother me with it. They let me do it myself. But they encouraged me, they gave me a lot of support. I mean it was an excellent way to start the practice.

This woman also received psychosocial support from these two White women:

> We would socialize together as well … Oh, we would go to lunch together. We would go out on the weekends together, go to movies, take trips together. I think we went whitewater rafting together. That kind of thing.

Although the individual interviews did not mirror what I saw in the group interview, I was reluctant to ascribe the anger that I heard solely to group interaction dynamics. Something about the anger expressed by the group of Black women struck a resonant chord for me, a memory. Then I remembered where I had encountered this anger previously. Excerpts from Audre Lorde's (1984) essay, "The Uses of Anger: Women Responding to Racism," in which she describes her rage at the racist attitudes of White women, resonated with what my group of participants said about White women:

> I speak out of direct and particular anger at an academic conference, and a white woman says, "Tell me how you feel but don't say it too harshly or I cannot hear you." But is it my message that keeps her from hearing, or the threat of a message that her life may change?

I wheel my two-year-old daughter in a shopping cart through a supermarket in Eastchester in 1967, and a little white girl riding past in her mother's cart calls out excitedly, "Oh look, Mommy, a baby maid!" And your mother shushes you, but she does not correct you. And so fifteen years later, at a conference on racism, you can still find that story humorous. But I hear your laughter is full of terror and dis-ease.

Delving into works that documented Black women's participation in the feminist and civil rights movements (Giddings, 1984, 1988; hooks, 1981, 1989, 1990; Hurtado, 1989; King, 1988; Lerner, 1972; Rodgers-Rose, 1980; Wilson & Russell, 1996), I found a historical basis for the distrust evidenced by the women in my study. Although it is not widely acknowledged, Black women such as Mary Church Terrell, Anna Cooper, Josephine St. Pierre Ruffin, and Sojourner Truth were ardent advocates of Black women's participation in the women's rights struggle. Yet Black women faced inequity and virulent racism from White women as they worked "together" in the feminist movement. Both King (1988) and Hurtado (1989) refer to the politics of expediency, which characterized White women's actions during the debate for universal suffrage for women and Black men. hooks (1981) noted:

> In their struggle to win the vote, Black women had learned a bitter lesson. They found as they worked for suffrage that many Whites saw granting women the right to vote as yet another way to maintain the oppressive system of racial imperialism. Southern white suffragists rallied around a platform that argued women suffrage in the South would strengthen white supremacy.... In their efforts to secure the ballot, white women's rights advocates willingly betrayed the feminist belief that voting was the natural right of every woman. (pp. 170–171)

As a result of this treatment, Black women have been reluctant to participate in the contemporary women's movement. hooks (1981) eloquently summarized the position of many Black feminists:

> From our peripheral position in the movement we saw that the potential radicalism of feminist ideology was being undermined by women who, while paying lip service to revolutionary goals, were primarily concerned with gaining entrance into the capitalist patriarchal power structure. Although white feminists denounced the white male, calling him an imperialist, capitalist, sexist, racist pig, they made women's liberation synonymous with women obtaining the right to fully participate in the very system they identi-

fied as oppressive. Their anger was not merely a response to sexism. It was an expression of their jealousy and envy of white men who held positions of power in the system while they were denied access to these positions. (pp. 188–189)

Because of the historical context of their relationship, Black women are often wary of aligning themselves with White women (Hurtado, 1989; King, 1988; Wilson & Russell, 1996). The differences that emerged in the suffrage movement continue to affect contemporary relationships between White women and Black women. King (1988: 59) found that "Within organizations, most twentieth-century Black women encounter myriad experiences that deny their reality" (p. 59). This legacy of anger, mistrust, and fear of betrayal has important implications for the relationships, mentoring as well as others, in which Black and White women can engage.

Thomas' (1989) study, in which he interviewed 22 cross-racial pairs within one corporation, found that the historical race relations between Blacks and Whites does indeed affect the mentoring relationships formed within the organizational context:

> Just as a superior and subordinate can enact the unconsciously experienced dynamics of a parent and child, Whites and Blacks can enact the history of race relations, with all of its difficulty and promise, in their everyday interaction, in the microcosms of supervision and mentoring, and in career planning. (p. 280)

Thomas described female–female cross-race relationships using the Black woman house slave–White mistress relationship as the historical context. Because of the "congenial and supportive nature" of this relationship, he suggested that Black and White women are now able to interact in a manner that suppresses their racial difference to draw upon their shared womanhood. Yet the interviews in my study indicate that the bond of womanhood does not sufficiently overcome racial differences. One woman in the group interview talked about her relationship with her White female mentor:

> I play a game with her. And I'll give you a good example. I had a problem a couple of weeks ago with a Black female that I supervise. And I was pretty upset about it. The girl is on drugs and she's doing some things that are totally inappropriate. And I'm her mentor because I'm protecting her butt right now. And I couldn't … I really wanted Penelope's support in looking at this situation. But Penelope is either you do it or you don't. There's no gray area;

it's black or white. And I couldn't really ... she's a White female. She has no, absolutely no ability to relate to a Black woman caught up in the ghetto with a lot of problems. There's no ability to do that ... So, it's just very difficult because we come from two totally different worlds. It's not like having a Black mentor.

This woman has placed distance between herself and her mentor, "cooling out" their relationship (Thomas, 1989, p. 286). Because of her distrust of her mentor, she actively resists any attempts to move the career-focused relationship to a more personal realm:

I have gained a lot of insight into her personality. To the point that she confides in me about her personal life. She invites me to her home. She wants to go shopping. But I will not allow myself to get that close.

This distance between the mentor and protégé undermines the potential power that mentoring offers to both parties. Each is deprived of the psychosocial support and personal learning that make mentoring relationships so powerful.

MOVING BEYOND THE IMPASSE: LESSONS AND INSIGHTS

Where do we go from here? How do Black and White women move beyond this impasse of anger, silence, blame, and perhaps guilt? How can this work move beyond identifying a problem to offering a solution? Are there ways in which these relationships might change to replicate and extend the different kinds of benefits Black women report about their relationships with Black and White men? These are questions I have been asking since the conception of this project. It has only been with the passage of time—time to do more research, ask more questions, gain more insights, and talk informally with more women, both Black and White—that possible answers have been forthcoming. Next I offer suggestions as to what women in management, Black or White, can do to support one another. I also discuss the role of future research in moving beyond this impasse. My concluding remarks address some of the limitations of this study.

Lessons for Managers: Building Bridges

An issue of *Working Woman* (January, 1995) was dedicated to an annual salary survey of more than 200 jobs in 30 fields. Findings from the survey presented good and bad news. On a positive note, the survey indicated that professional and managerial women are leading the workforce in wage growth (Harris, 1995). In a large number of the reported fields, statistics broken out by sex indicate that women typically take home 80 to 90 cents for every dollar made by a man in the same position, which is an improvement over the situation for working women as a whole, who earn 72% of what men earn. This good news is countered by the gap between the compensation figures of men and women. Additionally, the longer a woman stays in the workforce, the wider the gap grows between her salary and a man's—even at the professional and managerial levels (Povich, 1995). Finally, in Green and Green's (1995) list of the top-paid women in corporate America, the first thing I noticed, as a Black woman, was that of the 20 faces pictured, not one looked like mine; they all looked White to me. Thus, to the limited extent that these rarified ranks have been opened to women, they appear to have been opened only to White women.

Upon reading the Green and Green article, however, I was struck by an even more startling reality. I found that at the highest echelon of the corporate sector, White women's compensation was far outpaced by White men's. Green and Green (1995) reported that the median compensation of the top 20 earners on the nearly all-male *Forbes* roster was $16.7 million. Compare this to the median income of the 20 highest paid women, which was just under $1 million. The highest earning male executive in America in 1993 made $203 million; the corresponding figure for the top female executive was $4.03 million. My focus on compensation here is not to suggest that money is the most important outcome of work. Research shows similar differences between men and women in terms of promotions and other facets of corporate life. I focus on these compensation differences to reinforce the fact that *all women face disparities in the workplace.* Rather than focusing solely on the inequities between White and Black women, which may be relatively small in the grand scheme, I suggest that we take a holistic view and generate ideas and solutions to enrich the lives of all working women.

There are a number of actions that all women can take to start the journey beyond the impasse. First among them is to release the feelings of anger, blame, and presumably guilt that Black and White women experience in their relationships with one another. Wilson and Russell (1996) suggested that the key to improving race relations in this country may lie in the interactions that women have with one another. They predicted:

By now, it is clear that as long as women of different races remain at odds, traditional, White-male-dominated corporations and institutions will change only incrementally, if at all. Conversely, society will transform itself only when women decide together to fight social inequality in all its various forms, whether based on race, gender, or class. (p. 3)

A second action we need to take is to understand, as Black and White women, our relational position of subordination to White men. Hurtado (1989) noted:

The conflicts and tensions between White feminists and feminists of Color are viewed too frequently as lying solely in woman-to-woman relationships. These relationships, however, are affected in both obvious and subtle ways by how each of these two groups of women relate to White men.... (p. 834)

Again, drawing on a sociohistorical context, Hurtado offered an intriguing analysis of the relationships that White men have with both Black and White women. She suggested that White women and women of Color occupy different positions in relation to White men, the source of privilege. As a result, White women are subordinated through seduction whereas women of Color are subordinated through rejection. Thus, although White women and women of Color are both subordinated by "gender as the marking mechanism," the different processes by which they are subordinated may explain some of the tensions evident in our interactions today. Hurtado (1989, p. 843) suggested:

This is not to say that women of Color are more oppressed than White women but, rather, that White men use different forms of enforcing oppression of White women and women of Color. As a consequence, these groups of women have different political responses and skills, and at times these differences cause the two groups to clash. (p. 843)

It is incumbent upon both Black and White women to develop mutually beneficial strategies, responses, and skills that address our relational positions of subordination to White men. Remaining stagnant, stationary, stuck is simply neither an acceptable nor a productive strategy in today's rapidly changing workplace. Black and White women each bear burdens as members of our individual groups. Yet we also bear a collective burden as women. The time has come to learn how to share and ease each other's burdens. That this is possible is illustrated by the respondent in my study who reported positive mentoring alliances with White women. The psychosocial support and career guidance she received from her White female mentors helped her to be a better attorney. In developing mentoring relationships, each person needs to assess honestly the pros and the cons of those relationships, as well as her ability to develop mutual trust and respect in them.

Thus I offer women managers two challenges. One is internally directed, whereas the other is external in nature. The first is that women examine their own individual relationships for the mutual benefits they may offer. The second challenge is for each manager to examine how she uses her influence for women. We need to move beyond the Queen Bee syndrome or the crabs-in-a-barrel mentality. Rather than viewing other women as competitors and threats, we need to engage in more advocacy for one another. Black and White women have the potential to be each other's biggest allies in the fight against corporate sexism and racism.

Lessons for Researchers: Toward a More Inclusive Agenda

In the opening of this chapter, I discussed the impetus of my research as a call to fill a void in the mentoring literature, an attempt to give voice to professional Black women's experiences. Bell, Denton, and Nkomo's (1993) study of women in management also found that much of the existing body of knowledge on women in management addressed the experiences of White women managers. They suggest that there is a strong need for "research approaches and theoretical models that fit women's own constructions of their identity and that will help us to understand the diversity of women's experiences as managers" (Bell et al., 1993, p. 116).

To that end, Bell et al. (1993, pp. 121–125) offered five ways in which research on women in management must be expanded. These five prescriptives may be beneficial to mentoring research as well. They suggest that we

1. Conduct studies that examine both intraracial and interracial relationships among women managers and relationships among women of different socioeconomic statuses (e.g., managerial women versus nonmanagerial women).

2. Move away from research that begins with a male-dominated concept of knowledge that views women managers as inadequate, incomplete, or deficient. Instead of focusing on fixing the victim, we need research that examines institutional dynamics, societal assumptions, and biases that keep groups oppressed.

3. Draw extensively from many other disciplines to do research on women in management and open theorizing to new perspectives. Feminist theory has great potential for assisting us in understanding the gendered nature of organizations.

4. Become more aware of our role as researchers in producing knowledge that is inclusive. It is important that we acknowledge that as researchers we bring particular baggage to the table (e.g., group memberships, socialization, racial identity) and that these factors have an impact on what kind of research we do and how we do it.

5. Know that the proposed research approaches have implications for the methods used. In addition to traditional quantitative data collection methods, there is a need for qualitative research approaches as well.

The mentoring experiences of women, particularly of traditionally silenced groups, are important. This research is a call to contribute, an invitation to extend the discussion because this topic has important implications. Although women hold a growing share of managerial and professional jobs (Johnston & Packer, 1987), their numbers at the executive level make a division along the lines of race particularly acute. Many scholars believe that mentoring relationships may be an important tool in increasing the number of White women and people of color in leadership positions (Burke, 1984; Davis & Rodela, 1982; Zey, 1984). But Black and White women are going to have to work together if they are to receive the full and optimal benefits of mentoring relationships.

CONCLUSION

I made the methodological decision to combine individual and group interviews because of the particular topic I was studying. The organizational mentoring experiences of Black women is a relatively new area of inquiry, requiring a flexible method of data collection, which allowed unexpected aspects of the phenomenon to surface (cf. in Kram, 1983). The benefits of the method I used, however, are countered by several limitations. Because of the small number of interviews I conducted, the generalizability of these results is questionable. The scope of the paper is limited to the mentoring experiences of some professional Black women. Women of other ethnic groups, including White women, have experiences and perspectives that I have not attempted to represent here. Nevertheless, my results point to some new directions in which such research could go.

In particular, it is important to explore how other groups of women of color experience mentoring and how White women experience themselves as mentors to women of color. The research I present here offers only the perceptions of Black women, one half of a discussion that is dual in nature. It would have been interesting, and probably very instructive, to have interviewed my participants' mentors as well to gain a deeper understanding of the dyadic relationships.

I believe that it would also be fruitful to delve further into the different relationships that Black women have with White women and White men. I found that Black women were not fully engaged in their mentoring relationships with members of either group. Although I suspect that the reasons for the distance in these relationships are different, the outcome is the same. Black women were in incomplete mentoring relationships with both White men and White women, not representative of the full range of functions these relationships can provide. In order to transform these examples of cooling out, we first need to understand more fully the differential processes by which Black women place distance between and are alienated from White men and White women.

Finally, I would be remiss if I did not include the need to consider more closely the effects of class, in addition to race and gender. In this research, I focused on the experiences of professional Black women, who have the benefit of advanced education and middle-class status. The class bias evidenced here is present within both the management and the feminist literatures. King (1988) suggested that we need to go beyond considering race and gender to consider the triple jeopardy of racism, sexism, and classism. The current research on mentoring does little to elucidate what happens in the developmental relationships of those outside the managerial ranks. Black women are often clustered in low status and low-paying jobs due to race and sex discrimination (King, 1988). The factors of race, gender, and class are each important determinants, and none can be ignored if we are to get a complete understanding of Black women's lives.

Of utmost importance is the credibility of this research. Rubin and Rubin (1995) define a credible study as "one that convinces both you and the readers that what you have concluded is accurate" (p. 85). They suggest that trying to apply the traditional measures of validity and reliability that are used to judge quantitative research "distracts rather than clarifies" our understanding of qualitative research. Rather, one must assess the value of qualitative work by the extent to which it is credible, as judged by three criteria: transparency, consistency, and communicability. Transparency is assessed by the degree to which a reader is able to see the basic processes of data collection. They state (1995) that a transparent report "allows the readers to assess the intellectual strengths and weaknesses, the biases, and the conscientiousness of the interviewer" (p. 85). To this end, they suggest that the qualitative researcher keep his or her original notes and tapes, produce and verify transcripts, and document in field notes and incorporate into the analysis his or her thoughts and feelings while doing the research. Consistency is the extent to which the researcher has considered ideas and responses that appear to be inconsistent. The purpose here is not to eliminate inconsistencies; rather, it is to understand why they occur. The final criterion of credibility is communicability, which refers to whether or not the research arena feels real to the readers of this report. One way to increase communicability is to use the first hand experiences of interviewees rather than having people act as informants on the experiences of others. In this research and in the way I have reported it here, I have attempted to meet each of these criteria. No doubt, I satisfy some criteria better than others. My intention, however, has been to report many of the details of data collection that are normally not reported, such as my iterative process of reviewing the transcripts; to remain as close to the data as possible in my analysis; and to contribute my own thoughts and feelings as a source of possible insights into the meaning of the data.

The organizational mentoring experiences of women, particularly Black women, are an important and growing area of study. Mentoring in the classical sense can be used as a beacon in the rough terrain of the corporate sector. It can serve to illuminate the path, which has been obscured by the soil of the historical relationship, between Black and White women. A mentoring relationship may provide the needed communication between Black and White women, the impetus to talk, share commonalties, and understand differences. Mentoring can serve to illuminate the rungs to the top of corporate America for both Black women and White women. Mentoring provides the necessary cues for how to climb the ladder and where the slippery spots are. Finally, mentoring can serve to illuminate the way for those who come behind us.

ACKNOWLEDGMENTS

I acknowledge and thank Mark Chesler, Arnetta McRae, and Maxine McRae for their support and guidance on this project.

REFERENCES

Beale, F. (1979). Double jeopardy: To be Black and female. In T. Cade (Ed.), *The Black woman: An anthology* (pp. 90–100). New York: New American Library.

Bell, E. L. (1990). The bicultural life experience of career-oriented Black women. *Journal of Organizational Behavior, 11*, 459–477.

Bell, E. L., Denton, T. C., & Nkomo, S. (1993). Women of color in management: Towards an inclusive analysis. In E. A. Fagenson (Ed.), *Women in management: Trends, issues, and challenges in managerial diversity* (pp. 105–130). Newbury Park, CA: Sage Publications.

Braddock, J. H., & McPartland, J. M. (1987). How minorities continue to be excluded from equal employment opportunities: Research on labor market and institutional barriers. *Journal of Social Issues, 43*, 5–39.

Burke, R. J. (1984). Mentors in organizations. *Group Organization Studies, 9*, 353–372.

Burke, R. J., & McKeen, C. (1989). Developing formal mentoring programs in organizations. *Business Quarterly, 53*(3), 76–79

Burke, R. J., McKeen, C. A., & McKenna, C. S. (1990). Sex differences and cross-sex effects on mentoring: Some preliminary data. *Psychological Reports, 67*, 1011–1023.

Chesler, M. A. (1987). Professionals' views of the "dangers" of self-help groups: Explicating a grounded theoretical approach. *Center for Research on Social Organization Working Paper Series*. University of Michigan, Ann Arbor.

Clawson, J. G., & Kram, K. E. (1984). Managing cross-gender mentoring. *Business Horizons, 27*(3), 22–32.

Collins, E. G. C., & Scott, P. (1978). Everyone who makes it has a mentor. *Harvard Business Review, 56*(2), 89–101.

Collins, N. (1983). *Professional women and their mentors*. Englewood Cliffs, NJ: Prentice-Hall.

Cox, T. H., & Nkomo, S. M. (1991). A race and gender-group analysis of the early career experience of MBA's. *Work and Occupations, 18*, 431–446.

Dalton, G., Thompson, P., & Price, R. (1977). The four stages of professional careers—A new look at performance by professionals. *Organizational Dynamics, 6*(1), 19–42.

Davis, J., & Rodela, E. S. (1982). Mentoring for the Hispanic: Mapping emotional support. In S. B. Knouse, P. Rosenfeld, & A. L. Culbertson (Eds.), *Hispanics in the workplace*. Newbury Park, CA: Sage.

Davis, G., & Watson, G. (1982). *Black life in corporate America: Swimming in the mainstream*. New York: Anchor Press/Doubleday.

Deinard, C., & Friedman, R. A. (1991). Black caucus groups at Xerox Corporation. *Harvard Business School Case No 9-491-047*. Boston, MA: Harvard Business School.

Dreher, G. F., & Ash, R. A. (1990). A comparative study of mentoring among men and women in managerial, professional, and technical positions. *Journal of Applied Psychology, 75*(5), 539–546.

DuBois, W. E. B. (1903). *The souls of Black folk*. New York: The New American Library.

Dunbar, D. (1990). Desperately seeking mentors. *Black Enterprise, 20*(8), 53–56.

Essed, P. (1991). *Understanding everyday racism: An interdisciplinary theory*. Newbury Park, CA: Safe.

Evans, K. M., & Herr, E. L. (1991). The influence of racism and sexism in the career development of African-American women. *Journal of Multicultural Counseling and Development, 19*, 130–135

Fernandez, J. P. (1981). *Racism and sexism in corporate life: Changing values in American business*. New York: Lexington Books.

Fitt, L. W., & Newton, D. A. (1981). When the mentor is a man and the protégé is a woman. *Harvard Business Review, 59*(2), 56–60.

Giddings, P. (1984). *When and where I enter: The impact of Black women on race and sex in America*. New York: Bantam.

Giddings, P. (1988). *In search of sisterhood: Delta Sigma Theta and the challenge of the Black sorority movement*. New York: William Morrow.

Glaser, B. (1987). Theoretical coding. *Theoretical sensitivity: Advances in methodology of grounded theory*. Mill Valley, CA: Sociology Press.

Glaser, B., & Strauss, A. (1967). *The discovery of grounded theory*. Chicago: Aldine.

Gould, R. (1972). The phases of adult life: A study in developmental psychology. *The American Journal of Psychiatry, 129*, 521–531.

Green, K., & Green, R. (1995, January). The 20 top-paid women in corporate America. *Working Woman*, 36–38.

Halcomb, R. (1980, February). Mentors and the successful woman. *Across the board*, 13–17.

Harris, D. (1995, January). 16th annual salary survey 1995. *Working Woman*, 25–27.

Hill, L., & Kamprath, N. (1991). Beyond the myth of the perfect mentor: Building a network of developmental relationships. *Harvard Business School Case No 9-491-096*. Boston, MA: Harvard Business School.

hooks, b. (1981). *Ain't I a woman: Black women and feminism*. Boston, MA: South End Press.

hooks, b. (1989). *Talking back: Thinking feminist, thinking Black*. Boston, MA: South End Press.

hooks, b. (1990). *Yearning: Race, gender, and cultural politics*. Boston, MA: South End Press.

Hurtado, A. (1989). Relating to privilege: Seduction and rejection in the subordination of White women and women of color. *Signs, 14*, 833–855.

Ibarra, H. (1993). Personal networks of women and minorities in management: A conceptual framework. *Academy of Management Review, 18*(1), 56–87.

Johnston, W. B., & Packer, A. H. (1987). *Workforce 2000: Work and workers of the 21st century*. Indianapolis, IN: Hudson Institute.

King, D. K. (1988). Multiple jeopardy, multiple consciousness: The context of a Black feminist ideology. *Signs, 14*(1), 42–72.

Kram, K. E. (1983). Phases of the mentor relationship. *Academy of Management Journal, 26*(4), 608–625.

Kram, K. E. (1985). Improving the mentoring process. *Training and Development Journal, April*, 40–43.

Kram, K. E., & Hall, D. (1989). Mentoring as an antidote to stress during corporate trauma. *Human Resources Management, 28*, 493–510.

Kram, K. E., & Isabella, I. (1985). Mentoring alternatives: The role of peer relationships in career development. *Academy of Management Journal, 28*, 110–132.

Lerner, G. (1972). *Black women in White America: A documentary history*. New York: Vintage.

Levinson, D. J., Darrow, C. N., Klein, E. B., Levinson, M. A., & McKee, B. (1978). *Seasons of a man's life*. New York: Knopf.

Lorde, A. (1984). The uses of anger: Women responding to racism. In *Sister outsider* (pp. 125–126). Freedom, CA: The Crossing Press.

Missrian, A. K. (1982). *The corporate connection: Why executive women need mentors to reach the top*. Englewood Cliffs, NJ: Prentice-Hall.

Nieva, V. F., & Gutek, B. A. (1981). *Women and work*. New York: Praeger.

Nkomo, S. M. (1988). Race and sex: The forgotten case of the Black female manager. In S. Rose & L. Larwood (Eds.), *Women's careers: Pathways and pitfalls* (pp. 134–150). New York: Praeger.

Noe, R. A. (1986). Women and mentoring: A review and research agenda. *Academy of Management Review, 31*(1), 65–78.

Noe, R. A. (1988). An investigation of the determinants of successful assigned mentoring relationships. *Personnel Psychology, 41*, 457–479.

Povich, L. (1995, January). Paycheck checkup. *Working Woman*, 4.

Ragins, B. R. (1989). Barriers to mentoring: The female manager's dilemma. *Human Relations, 42*(1), 1–22.

Roche, G. R. (1979). Much ado about mentors. *Harvard Business Review*, January–February, 14–28.

Rodgers-Rose, L. (Ed.) (1980). *The Black woman*. Beverly Hills, CA: Sage.

Rubin, H. J., & Rubin, I. S. (1995). *Qualitative interviewing: The art of hearing data*. Thousand Oaks, CA: Sage.

Scott, N. E. (1989). Differences in mentor relationships of non-White and White female professionals and organizational mobility: A review of the literature. *Psychology: A Journal of Human Behavior, 26*, 23–26.

Thomas, D. A. (1989). Mentoring and irrationality: The role of racial taboos. *Human Resource Management, 28*, 279–290.

Thomas, D. A. (1990). The impact of race on managers' experiences of developmental relationships (mentoring and sponsorship): An intra-organizational study. *Journal of Organizational Behavior, 11*, 479–492.

Wilson, M., & Russell, K. (1996). *Divided sisters: Bridging the gap between Black women and White women*. New York: Anchor.

Zey, M. G. (1984). *The mentor connection*. Homewood, IL: Dow Jones-Irwin.

6

Do Race and Sex Affect Employees' Access to and Help From Mentors? Insights From the Study of a Large Corporation

Gail M. McGuire
Indiana University at South Bend

Business magazines are replete with advice on the importance of having a mentor for one's career. In fact, research confirms that having a mentor enhances employees' career development, chances for advancement, earnings, and job satisfaction (Fagensen, 1989; Hunt & Michael, 1983; Whitely, Dougherty, & Dreher, 1991). Are women as likely as men, and are people of color as likely as Whites, to develop mentor relationships? Do the benefits that protégés receive from their mentors depend, in part, upon their race or sex? Do Whites, for example, obtain more help in solving work-related problems, in getting around the corporate bureaucracy, and in securing promotions from their mentors than people of color? Do women receive more psychosocial help from their mentors than men?

I explore these issues using survey data from workers employed at a large corporation. Three questions lie at the crux of my analyses. First, do protégés' race and sex influence the likelihood that they will receive instrumental and psychosocial help from a mentor? Second, how does employees' race and sex affect the type of help (i.e., instrumental or psychosocial) mentors give?

Finally, what other factors relating to the mentor or the protégé shed light on the associations found in the first two analyses?

This research makes some important contributions to our understanding of developmental relationships at work. First, this study is unusual in that it examines simultaneously race and sex. Few studies have examined race differences in mentoring and virtually none have examined race and sex differences in mentoring. Second, the respondents included in the survey represent a wider cross section of a corporation than is typical. A disproportionate number of studies have focused on managerial and professional workers (Dreher & Ash, 1990; Greenhaus, Parasuraman, & Wormley, 1990; Kram, 1985; Ragins, 1989; Whitely, Dougherty, & Dreher, 1992). The inclusion of nonmanagerial women and men in the sample increases the representation of minorities and allows a test of the hypotheses about both race and sex differences among employees at these as well as managerial levels. Finally, this study contributes to our knowledge of mentoring by examining the different types of help that protégés receive from their mentors. Past research has focused more on the issue of access to mentors than on the type of help received from mentors (an exception is Thomas, 1990).

Because of its exploratory and descriptive nature, however, this chapter is simply one step toward understanding the connections among race, sex, and developmental relationships. I conducted bivariate analyses that identify race and sex differences in certain aspects of workplace mentoring. In future studies I will present the multivariate analyses, which are needed to decipher the different mechanisms that underlie the race and sex differences reported here.

The terminology in this chapter differs slightly from the terminology used in the rest of this book. I asked my respondents about someone who had taken them under their wing and did not use the words mentor, sponsor, or role model in my questionnaire. For ease of exposition in this chapter, I sometimes refer to the person named as a mentor, even though the type of help given may have been primarily instrumental. According to Crosby (chap. 1, this volume), senior colleagues who render only instrumental help without establishing a close emotional bond ought to be called sponsors rather than mentors, but to impose such a terminology on the data at hand would be both cumbersome and inaccurate.

A STRUCTURAL APPROACH
TO DEVELOPMENTAL RELATIONSHIPS

Structuralists focus on how the positions of individuals in a social system provide various opportunities for action and also place constraints on behavior—what some scholars call the opportunity context. Although structuralists recognize that social groups have different attitudes and dispositions, they attribute these differences to broader social arrangements. For example, Kanter (1977) attributed the low work aspirations of clerical workers to the fact that their jobs tended to be unchallenging and offered few opportunities for advancement.

Opportunity contexts affect whether or not workers have mentors or sponsors. It is no doubt easier to obtain help from a mentor in job settings that encourage employees to interact with each other than in settings where employees' actions are restricted. In the company that I studied, for example, most human resource employees had to interact with other employees to perform their jobs. They were also given many freedoms because of their professional status—they did not have to punch a time clock, they could take breaks as needed, and they had little direct supervision. As a result, they had many opportunities to interact with other employees and thus form developmental relationships. In contrast, some of the nonprofessional workers at the company held jobs that restricted them to their desks and prevented them from conversing with their co-workers (e.g., their phone use was monitored). It is easy to see how job settings influence people's ability to initiate or sustain developmental relationships.

The opportunity context also influences the benefits that workers receive from their mentors. Managers are more likely than nonmanagers to interact with high-status employees. High-status employees, in turn, control lucrative corporate resources, such as budgets, projects, and information. As a result, managers probably receive more benefits than non-managers from their developmental relationships.

A structural perspective also recognizes that social contexts, such as the workplace and the family, are interdependent. People's family responsibilities may limit the amount of time they have to interact and socialize with other employees and thus decrease their chances of obtaining a mentor or sponsor. Noting that employed women spend an average of 35 hours per week doing housework, whereas employed men spend an average of 21 hours per week (Shelton, 1992), the structuralist would expect women to engage in fewer developmental relationships at work than men.

Individual-level approaches, in contrast, tend to explain workers' relationships in terms of their internal states, such as their attitudes or personality traits (Berkowitz, 1982; Ibarra, 1993; Moore, 1990). For example, assume for the moment that Blacks are less likely than Whites to have mentors. Scholars adopting an individual-level approach might explain this

finding by arguing that Blacks do not take enough initiative in seeking mentors. A structuralist, in contrast, might ask if Blacks are located in jobs that
prevent them from demonstrating their skills to mentors (e.g., jobs that are
not cross-functional) or that decrease their likelihood of interacting with
potential mentors. Thus, when structuralists find differences between
workers of different ethnicities or sexes, they compare the social contexts in
which the different groups work and live rather than examine workers' internal characteristics.

DEVELOPMENTAL RELATIONS AT U.S. FINANCE

The Sample

I studied workers employed at the home office of a large financial services
company, which I refer to as U.S. Finance. U.S. Finance began as a modest
business in the 1920s and has grown into a company with annual revenues
over 30 billion dollars. The company employs over 20,000 individuals and
has branches throughout the United States and abroad. Fifty-nine percent
of U.S. Finance employees at the home office were women, and 15% were
people of color. More specifically, 48% of U.S. Finance employees were
White women, 37% were White men, 11% were women of color, and 4%
were men of color.

Data Collection

I used a mail survey to collect data on employees' informal network members, including their mentors. I distributed surveys to a stratified random
sample of 1,756 full-time employees. I excluded contract workers, part-time
employees, independent sales agents, and subsidiary employees from the
sample. I oversampled people of color so that I could conduct statistical
comparisons across race. Once I excluded the six surveys that were unus-
able, the final response rate was 65% (1,150). Of the final sample, 57% are
women and 39% are people of color. More specifically, 31% are White
women, 30% are White men, 26% are women of color, and 13% are men of
color. The majority of people of color are African American.

One week after employees received the survey, they received a reminder
postcard. I mailed a second round of surveys to the approximately 850
non-respondents one week after the reminder postcard. I mailed surveys to
employees' work addresses through the company mail system for two rea-

sons. First, I expected that respondents' recall would be better at work than at home because the survey was about employees' work experiences. Second, I expected that employees would be more inclined to complete the survey on company time, for which they would be paid, than on personal time. Respondents mailed surveys back to the Ohio State University to increase their confidence that U.S. Finance would not have access to the data.

Measures

Following past research, the survey began by mapping employees' networks (Burt, 1992; Ibarra, 1995; Marsden, 1987). The survey asked respondents to think of employees at U.S. Finance who had "made an effort to give [them] job, career, or personal help" in the last year. The survey stated that network members could include people from various parts of the company, co-workers, supervisors, or subordinates. It also indicated that network members could be employees that respondents saw occasionally or daily.

I created a data set composed of all the dyads in the sample (6,047 dyads) in order to examine employees' relationships. A respondent with four network members in the original data set represents four dyads in this second data set.

Access to Mentors.   To identify network members who were mentors or sponsors, the survey asked respondents: "Has this person taken you 'under their wing' by showing a special interest in your career?" Respondents indicated either yes or no. I used a subset of the dyad data set including only those employees who had mentors (1,698 dyads) to analyze these relationships in particular.

Type of Support.   To measure instrumental support from mentors, the survey asked respondents to answer yes or no to five questions about each person in their network: "Has this person helped you with a work-related problem or question?" "Has this person helped you get around bureaucratic hurdles or cut through red tape?" "Has this person helped you to meet high-level employees, such as directors or officers?" "Has this person helped you gain a new position or promotion at [U. S. Finance]?" "Has this person helped you gain recognition for your work?" I summed respondents' answers to these questions to obtain an overall measure of instrumental support. This measure represents the amount of different types of instrumental help that a protégé received from a mentor.

Two questions tapped into emotional support from mentors: "Has this person given you support with a personal problem?" "Has this person given you encouragement and moral support?" I summed respondents' answers to these questions to obtain an overall measure of socioemotional (or psychosocial) help.

A single item measured the emotional intensity of the developmental relationship. The employee was asked to assess how close he or she felt to each mentor. Response options for closeness ranged from *very distant* (1) to *very close* (5).

Characteristics of the Mentor or Sponsor. Structural factors might enable some mentors and sponsors to give more help than others. To assess this, I examined several related factors that tap into the status of employees' mentors—their organizational rank and their control over corporate resources—with the idea that people in higher ranks and with more control over corporate resources might be able to provide more help than people in lower ranks and with less control over corporate resources. The organizational rank item had five response categories: non-supervisor, supervisor, manager, director, or officer and above. The survey questions to measure control over resources were: "Does this person make major purchases ($10,000 or more) without getting permission from higher up?" "Does this person have access to sensitive or confidential company information?" "Can this person make final decisions that significantly change [U.S. Finance] products, programs, or services?" Respondents indicated yes, no, or don't know for each mentor.

Protégé Characteristics. To measure protégés' organizational rank, the survey asked respondents to categorize themselves as non-supervisor, supervisor, manager, director, or officer and above. I measured protégés' job communication with the question, "How important is it for you to communicate regularly with employees *outside* of your work group in order to do your current job?" The range for this measure was *not at all important* (0) to *essential* (4).

Method of Analysis

I employed *t* tests and two-way analyses of variance to test for race and sex differences in mentoring. I also used a test of the difference between proportions when appropriate (Blalock, 1979).

FINDINGS

Who Has Developmental Relationships?

Not everyone claimed to have had developmental help: 36% of men and 34% of women said that none of the network members they listed had taken them under their wing and shown a special interest in their career. Categorizing the data by race, I found that 39% of people of color and 32% of Whites reported that no one had taken them under their wing.

As shown in Tables 6.1 and 6.2, there were no significant sex or race differences, respectively, in the number of mentors people reported, nor was there a significant interaction between race and sex.

The lack of sex effects in number of mentors is consistent with past studies (Burke, 1984; Cox & Nkomo, 1991; Dreher & Ash, 1990; Fagenson, 1989; Greenhaus et al., 1990; Ragins & Cotton, 1991; Whitely et al., 1992). The lack of race differences accords with some previous studies (e.g., Thomas, 1990) but not others (Cox & Nkomo, 1991). My results suggest that, contrary to some popular claims that White women and people of color do not network, White women and people of color were as adept at forming mentor relationships as White men.

TABLE 6.1
Average Number of Mentors by Protégés' Sex

Sex of Protégé	Average Number of Mentors
Women (N = 651)	1.52
Men (N = 481)	1.44

Note. Data in Table 6.1 are based upon the original network data set (N = 1,150).

TABLE 6.2
Average Number of Mentors by Protégés' Race

Race of Protégé	Average Number of Mentors
People of Color (N = 443)	1.44
Whites (N = 689)	1.52

Note. Data in Table 6.2 are based upon the original network data set (N = 1,150).

Why are there no sex and race effects in access to mentors at U.S. Finance? Two explanations come to mind. First, I expect that most employees realize the importance of having a mentor or sponsor for their careers and jobs. Second, U.S. Finance, like many other corporations, is working to diminish the overt exclusion of White women and people of color from informal developmental relationships. For instance, a 1992 employee poll at U.S. Finance found that 80% of employees had participated in some type of diversity activity—typically diversity awareness training. When asked on the employee poll, the majority of employees claimed that U.S. Finance is making progress in its diversity efforts. Fifty-three percent of employees in a company poll reported that the company had made progress in providing opportunities for minorities, and 52% agreed that opportunities for advancement were equally available to all employees regardless of their sex or their cultural or ethnic background.

Like some other researchers (e.g., Brass, 1985; Ibarra, 1992; Marsden 1987; Scott, 1996), I discovered homophily in the pairing of mentors and protégés. Sixty-one percent of women's mentors were women, and 66% of men's mentors were men. Similarly, people of color were more likely than Whites to list mentors who were people of color. Thirty-five percent of the mentors for people of color were themselves people of color, whereas only 7% of the mentors for White people were people of color.

My findings are consistent with the now commonplace sociological observation that the workplace is segregated by race and sex (Baron, Davis-Blake, & Bielby, 1986; King, 1992; Reskin, 1993). Bielby and Baron (1986) found almost complete sex segregation in jobs among the more than 200 California firms they studied—96% of the women or the men in their sample would have had to change jobs to equalize the sex composition of jobs. In addition, King (1992) found that approximately 32% of Black men would have to change to an occupation dominated by White men and 30% of Black women would have to switch to an occupation dominated by White women to integrate occupations by race (also see Tomaskovic-Devey, 1993). This kind of segregation likely leads workers to interact primarily with people of the same race and sex at work and therefore to form developmental relationships with others who are similar to them on these dimensions.

What Kind of Help is Given to Whom?

Looking first at sex of the employee, the findings regarding the kinds of help respondents received are clear. Men received significantly more instrumental help from their mentors than did women. Meanwhile, women received significantly more socioemotional help than did men. Tables 6.3 and 6.4 present the mean scores for amount of instrumental and socioemotional help, respectively, by sex. The largest sex differences concerned an aspect of instrumental help, getting one's work recognized: Eighty-two percent of men received help from their mentors in this regard, as did 75% of women (results not shown).

Looking next at employee race, we see parallel findings. White employees received significantly more instrumental help from their mentors than did protégés of color. Meanwhile, employees of color received significantly more socioemotional help than did White employees. Tables 6.5 and 6.6 present the mean scores for amount of instrumental and socioemotional help, respectively, by race. The largest race difference was again help in getting one's work recognized: Eighty-two percent of Whites had mentors who helped them in this way, as did 71% of people of color (results not shown).

To understand why men and Whites received the most instrumental help whereas women and people of color received the most socioemotional help, the structuralist again looks to the social context. One aspect of the social

TABLE 6.3

Average Amount of Instrumental Help Received by Women and Men

Sex of Protégé	Average Amount of Instrumental Help from Mentors
Women ($N = 927$)	3.18
Men ($N = 660$)	3.36

Note. Sex differences are significant at the .05 level.

TABLE 6.4

Average Amount of Socioemotional Help Received by Women and Men

Sex of Protégé	Average Amount of Socioemotional Help from Mentors
Women ($N = 959$)	1.62
Men ($N = 679$)	1.49

Note. Tables 6.3 through 6.10 are based upon the dyad data set ($N = 6,047$) but include only those employees who had mentors ($N = 1,698$)

Sex differences are significant at the .05 level.

TABLE 6.5

**Average Amount of Instrumental Help
Received by People of Color and Whites**

Race of Protégé	Average Amount of Instrumental Help From Mentors
People of Color (N = 573)	3.12
Whites (N = 1012)	3.34

Note. Race differences are significant at the .05 level.

TABLE 6.6

**Average Amount of Socioemotional Help
Received by People of Color and Whites**

Race of Protégé	Average Amount of Socioemotional Help from Mentors
People of Color (N = 596)	1.63
Whites (N = 1040)	1.53

Note. Race differences are significant at the .05 level.

context that seems especially relevant here is who is giving the help. Examining the sex composition of mentor–protégé relationships, one sees that both male and female protégés received more instrumental help from their male mentors than from their female mentors and more socioemotional help from their female mentors than from their male mentors. There is no evidence that male mentors differentiated between their male and female protégés either in terms of instrumental or socioemotional help. However, female protégés had fewer male mentors, on average, than male protégés. Thus, women were less likely to have male mentors, but when they did have male mentors women received as much instrumental help from them as did men. Female mentors, interestingly enough, differentiated between their protégés. As Tables 6.7 and 6.8 show, they gave less instrumental and more socioemotional help to their female protégés than to their male protégés.

Once again, the parallels between sex and race are uncanny. As Tables 6.9 and 6.10 show, White mentors gave more instrumental help than did mentors of color, and they gave the most instrumental help to Whites. The greatest amount of socioemotional help was given by mentors of color to protégés of color.

TABLE 6.7
Average Instrumental Help by Protégés' Sex and Mentors' Sex

	Male Mentor	Female Mentor
Male Protégé	3.44 (N = 431)	3.22 (N = 227)
Female Protégé	3.42 (N = 364)	3.02 (N = 553)

Note. Significant effect of mentor's sex at the .05 level. No significant effect of protégés' sex. No significant interaction between sex of protégé and sex of mentor.

TABLE 6.8
Average Socioemotional Help by Protégés' Sex and Mentors' Sex

	Male Mentor	Female Mentor
Male Protégé	1.44 (N = 447)	1.58 (N = 229)
Female Protégé	1.46 (N = 372)	1.72 (N = 580)

Note. Effect of protégés' sex significant at the .05 level. Effect of mentors' sex significant at the .05 level. Significant interaction between sex of protégé and sex of mentor at the .05 level.

TABLE 6.9
Average Instrumental Help by Protégés' Race and Mentors' Race

	White Mentor	Mentor of Color
White Protégé	3.37 (N = 904)	3.06 (N = 67)
Protégé of Color	3.21 (N = 353)	2.88 (N = 186)

Note. Significant effect of protégés' race at the .05 level. Significant effect of mentors' race at the .05 level. No significant interaction between race of protégé and race of mentor.

TABLE 6.10
Average Socioemotional Help by Protégés' Race and Mentors' Race

	White Mentor	Mentor of Color
White Protégé	1.54 (N = 929)	1.48 (N = 67)
Protégé of Color	1.58 (N = 365)	1.70 (N = 196)

Note. Effect of protégés' race significant at the .05 level. Interaction between race of protégé and race of mentor significant at the .05 level. No significant effect of protégés' race.

Closeness.   I suspected that female protégés with female mentors developed more intimate relationships than their male counterparts because of their disadvantaged status in the company. Interestingly, I found no significant differences in the closeness of same-sex and cross-sex mentor relationships. Women were as close, on average, to their male as to their female mentors (results not shown). Similarly, men were equally close to their male and female mentors.

The findings for race and closeness between mentor and protégé were not parallel to the findings for sex and closeness. People of color reported that they were significantly closer to their same-race mentors than to their cross-race mentors. For example, 30% of people of color with White mentors described their relationships as very close, compared to 40% of people of color with mentors of color. White employees, in contrast, said that their relationships with White mentors and mentors of color were equally close.

Why doesn't race mimic sex in the findings on closeness between mentors and protégés? The answer may have to do with the fact that people of color are numerical tokens at U.S. Finance. People of color may develop close bonds with each other in response to working in an environment where they may be treated as outsiders.

What Structural Factors Are Relevant?

Structuralists recognize that employees do not have a random pool of potential network members from which to choose mentors and sponsors. Rather, formal work arrangements influence with whom employees come into contact and thus influence potential networks. Race and sex segregation of jobs, furthermore, does not simply separate people according to race and sex; it also leads people to perform different types of work. White women and people of color are more likely than White men to occupy jobs with low authority, prestige, complexity, rank, chances for advancement, and earnings (England, 1992; Glass, 1990; Hodson, 1989; Jacobs, 1992; McGuire & Reskin, 1993; Reskin & Ross, 1992). White women and people of color are more likely to work with and thus form developmental ties with workers who control few corporate resources and possess little power and status.

My data confirm the structuralists' wisdom. Among my sample of employees at U.S. Finance, women and people of color occupied significantly lower organizational ranks than men and Whites. In other words, women and people of color were less likely than men and Whites to be managers and officers. Lower ranking employees also have, on average, lower ranking mentors and sponsors. In my sample, White protégés were significantly more likely than protégés of color to have mentors who were supervisors and managers; 73% of Whites' mentors occupied the rank of supervisor or higher, whereas only 56% of the mentors of persons of color did. Women's mentors were also less likely to be supervisors and managers than men's mentors. In addition, protégés of color were less likely than White protégés to have mentors who made final decisions on important corporate matters, made large purchases on their own, and had access to confidential information.

Another relevant structural factor is the degree to which employees interact with workers outside their work group. Having a job that requires a high degree of communication may increase an employee's likelihood of having a mentor who has high status and controls corporate resources because it allows a worker to interact with a range of individuals. Employees who occupy jobs requiring communication with a wide range of employees should also be able to obtain new information quickly, increasing their utility and attractiveness to potential high-status mentors. In other words, the greater the outside communication, the greater the possibility for instrumental help.

I found that women were significantly less likely than men to report that communicating with employees outside their work group was very important or essential to performing their jobs. In addition, people of color reported that communication with employees outside their work group was less essential to performing their jobs than did Whites. These race and sex differences in job communication may help to explain race and sex differences in instrumental support from mentors.

ANSWERS AND QUESTIONS

This chapter presents preliminary results on the relationship between race, sex, and mentoring and provides a structural framework with which to interpret these results. Employees' race and sex were not significantly related to the number of mentors they had, but they were crucial for the types of help they received from their mentors and sponsors.

A structural approach encourages us to ask what it is about being a woman or a person of color that makes the mentor experience different from that of a man and a White person. Consistent with the structuralist approach, I found that women and people of color occupied different organizational positions and had different amounts of authority in the company than did men and White people. These structural factors may be what really accounts for the sex and race patterns observed. Many questions remain about how and why protégés' race and sex, as well as the race and sex composition of mentor-protégé dyads, influence the types of help given. We do not know if the same mentors treat their protégés differently based upon their protégés' race and sex. For instance, does a White mentor provide more inside tips to White protégés than to protégés of color?

We also need information on the effectiveness of help provided by mentors. Although this study examined differences in the amount and type of help provided by mentors, it did not ask protégés how useful or effective their mentors' assistance was to them. For instance, a protégé may have received help from his or her mentor on a work-related problem, but did that help create more work for the protégé or less work? This study also focused on the perspective of the protégé in the mentor–protégé relationship. It is necessary to ask mentors what they have done on their protégé's behalf because protégés may not always be aware of the efforts their mentors have made to help them.

A structural perspective recognizes that mentor relationships are embedded in broader social networks, composed of mentors and non-mentors. For example, respondents in this study listed an average of five employees who gave them career, job, or emotional support. However, the average number of mentors they listed was only one. Thus, focusing solely on mentor ties does not give us a complete picture of employees' developmental relationships. For example, a study might find that women receive less career advice from their mentors than men, but what if women receive career advice from the non-mentors in their network? Similarly, if a study finds that Black and White protégés receive the same amount of information on company politics from their mentors, should we conclude that Blacks' and Whites' career socialization is equivalent? If Whites' informal networks are larger than Blacks, then surely this would be a false conclusion—Whites would have more sources of advice and would be better able to assess the quality of the advice they received than Blacks. In summary, in order to assess how workers' sex and race influence their developmental relationships, we must examine not only their mentor ties, but the entire range of developmental relationships they cultivate at work.

REFERENCES

Baron, J., Davis-Blake, A., & Bielby, W. (1986). The structure of opportunity: How promotion ladders vary within and among organizations. *Administrative Science Quarterly, 31*, 248–273.

Berkowitz, S. D. (1982). *An introduction to structural analysis: The network approach to social research*. Toronto: Butterworth.

Bielby, W. T., & Baron, J. (1986). Men and women at work: Sex segregation and statistical discrimination. *American Journal of Sociology, 91*, 759–799.

Blalock, H. (1979). *Social statistics*. (second ed.). New York: McGraw-Hill.

Brass, D. (1985). Men's and women's networks: A study of interaction patterns and influence in an organization. *Academy of Management Journal, 28*, 327–343.

Burke, R. (1984). Mentors in organizations. *Group and Organization Studies, 9*, 353–372.

Burt, R. (1992). *Structured holes*. Cambridge. MA: Harvard University Press.

Cox, T., & Nkomo, S. (1991). A race and gender-group analysis of the early career experience of MBAs. *Work and Occupations, 18*, 431–446.

Dreher, G., & Ash, R. (1990). A comparative study of mentoring among men and women in managerial, professional, and technical positions. *Journal of Applied Psychology, 75*, 539–546.

England, P. (1992). *Comparable worth: Theories and evidence*. New York: De Gruyter.

Fagenson, E. (1989). The mentor advantage: Perceived career/job experiences of protégés versus non-protégés. *Journal of Organizational Behavior, 10*, 309–320.

Glass, J. (1990). The impact of occupational segregation on working conditions. *Social Forces, 68*, 779–796.

Greenhaus, J., Parasuraman, S., & Wormley, W. (1990). Effects of race on organizational experiences, job performance evaluations, and career outcomes. *Academy of Management Journal, 33*, 64–86.

Hodson, R. (1989). Gender differences in job satisfaction: Why aren't women more dissatisfied? *The Sociological Quarterly, 30*, 385–399.

Hunt, D., & Michael, C. (1983). Mentorship: A career training and development tool. *Academy of Management Review, 8*, 475–485.

Ibarra, H. (1992). Homophily and differential returns: Sex differences in network structure and access in an advertising firm. *Administrative Science Quarterly, 37*, 422–447.

Ibarra, H. (1993). Personal networks of women and minorities in management: A conceptual framework. *Academy of Management Review*, January, 56–87.

Ibarra, H. (1995). Race, opportunity, and diversity of social circles in managerial networks. *Academy of Management Journal, 38*, 673 | nd703.

Jacobs, J. A. (1992). Women's entry into management: Trends in earnings, authority, and values among salaried managers. *Administrative Science Quarterly, 37*, 282–301.

Kanter, R. M. (1977). *Men and women of the corporation*, New York: Basic Books.

King, M. C. (1992). Occupational segregation by race and gender, 1940–1980. *Monthly Labor Review, 115*, 30–37.

Kram, K. (1985). *Mentoring at work: Developmental relationships in organizational life.* Glenview: Scott, Foresman.

Marsden, P. (1987). Core discussion networks of Americans. *American Sociological Review, 52*, 122–131.

McGuire, G., & Reskin, B. F. (1993). Authority hierarchies at work: The impacts of race and sex. *Gender and Society, 4*, 487–506.

McPherson, J. M., & Smith-Lovin, L. (1982). "Women and weak ties: Differences by sex in the size of voluntary organizations. *American Journal of Sociology, 87*, 883–904.

Moore, G. (1990). Structural determinants of men's and women's personal networks. *American Sociological Review, 55*, 726–735.

Ragins, B. (1989). Barriers to mentoring: The female managers' dilemma. *Human Relations, 42*, 1–22.

Ragins, B. R., & Cotton, J. (1991). Easier said than done: Gender differences in perceived barriers to gaining a mentor. *Academy of Management Journal, 34*, 939–951.

Reskin, B. F. (1993). Sex segregation in the workplace. *Annual Review of Sociology, 19*, 241–270.

Reskin, B., & Ross, C. (1992). Jobs, authority and earnings among managers: The continuing significance of sex. *Work and Occupations, 19,* 342–65.

Scott, D. B. (1996). Shattering the instrumental-expressive myth: The power of women's networks in corporate-government affairs. *Gender and Society, 10,* 232–247.

Shelton, B. A. (1992). *Women, men, and time: Gender differences in paid work, housework, and leisure,* New York: Greenwood.

Thomas, D. (1990). The impact of race on managers' experiences of developmental relationships: An intra-organizational study. *Journal of Organizational Behavior, 11,* 479–492.

Tomaskovic-Devey, D. (1993). The gender and race composition of jobs and the male/female, White/Black pay gaps. *Social Forces, 72,* 45–76.

Whitely, W., Dougherty, T., & Dreher, G. (1992). Correlates of career-oriented mentoring for early career managers and professionals. *Journal of Organizational Behavior, 13,* 41–154.

7

Women's and Men's Role Models: The Importance of Exemplars

Donald E. Gibson
Yale University

Diana I. Cordova
Yale University

Research has long stressed the need for women, ethnic minorities, and other disempowered groups to have role models in organizations as exemplars of achievement. Many have suggested that a lack of women in leadership positions means a paucity of role models for junior women (Ely, 1994; Gilbert, 1985; Kanter, 1977). Starting in the late 1970s researchers began to investigate issues of gender and role modeling in people's careers. The findings emanating from these early efforts have been largely inconclusive and, more important, have failed to convey what role models mean to male and female observers (Speizer, 1981). Few studies have assessed what the patterns of identification are for men and women, and thus we still know little about how men and women go about identifying role models in organizations. If White women and ethnic minorities lack exemplars of achievement, what are their strategies for identification? Do they identify with male success models or simply go it alone, using trial-and-error learning?

This chapter approaches the issue of gender and role modeling by examining men's and women's choices of role models within different organizational contexts. In addition, we examine an underexplored element in the literature: the degree to which the strategies individuals use in identifying with role models differ according to individual characteristics (such as sex) and according to contextual characteristics (such as the proportion of women and minorities in leadership positions). We aim to forge a connection between the literature on modeling in work organizations, on the one hand, and aspects of developmental psychology, on the other.

Our chapter is divided into four parts. First, we introduce the topic by offering definitions, reviewing some of the relevant developmental literature, and posing our research questions. We then describe the methodology of our research project. In the third section, we examine results from our study showing the importance of organizational context in role model identification. We conclude with the implications of our findings for women and ethnic minorities seeking guidance for individual development and organizational success through the use of role models.

BACKGROUND

Definitions

Although some overlap appears between the concept of mentor and the concept of role model, critical distinctions also exist. Some studies have assumed that junior people seek role models in hierarchically superior others who are "provided" more or less strategically by the organization in the form of supervisors, trainers, and cultural heroes (Deal & Kennedy, 1982; Javidan, Bemmels, Stratton-Devine, & Dastmalchian, 1995; Manz & Sims, 1981; Pascale, 1985). Such studies tend to assume that protégés more or less automatically accept their superiors as role models. It is in part to be consistent with current empirical findings that Crosby (chap. 1, this volume) insisted on differentiating among role models, sponsors, and mentors.

Identification theory suggests another reason for conceptually separating the constructs of role model, mentor, and sponsor. Whereas mentoring and sponsoring are generally based on interaction with and active intervention by a senior person on behalf of a protégé, role modeling assumes only *identification* on the part of an observer with a model. By identification we mean the desire of an individual observer to enhance perceived similarity to another person, to assimilate aspects of the role model's attitudes, behaviors, and values, and ultimately to occupy the role model's life situation (Bell, 1970; Kelman, 1961; Kohlberg, 1963). Because identification resides in the head of the observer, interaction may or may not be a component of a role modeling relationship: The observer *makes* another a role model by a conscious cognitive process of selectively viewing and assimilating desired attributes.

In agreement with identification theory, social learning theory suggests that observers create a verbal or visual image of how a model carries out a particular task and can generalize attributes from that image to apply to different situations. Modeling is characterized as a symbolic process of actively combining "aspects of various models into new amalgams" (Bandura, 1977, p. 48) that differ from any single source, so that the resulting behaviors may in fact be characterized by considerable novelty as well as emulation (Mischel, 1966). As Fisher (1988) noted:

> With all our hearts, we want our role model to be out there. But, even though we may find a variety of people to help us in this struggle, and even though we may adopt some of them as role models, these people and the models we make of them are not the same. (p. 218)

Drawing on identification and social learning theories, then, we define role models as cognitive constructs created by observers based on the attitudes and values, outcomes or achievements, or interpersonal or process skills of single or multiple models with whom the observer seeks to enhance similarity based on his or her ideals, goals, and needs. Thus, the nature of models may vary from actual people to fictional or mythical figures, from positive lessons of how to act to negative lessons of how not to.

Gender Development and Role Models

The notion that children, when given a choice, will predominantly model the behavior of same-sex models is simple and appealing, but systematic research does not bear this out. What researchers have found are sex differences in the tendency to imitate the behavior of same- versus cross-sex models (Bussey & Perry, 1982; Maccoby & Jacklin, 1974). Boys tend to emulate the behavior of male models to a substantially greater extent than they emulate female models and are much less inclined to adopt behavior regarded as gender inappropriate, regardless of the gender of the models displaying it (Bandura, 1986; Bussey & Bandura, 1984). Girls, on the other hand, are more inclined to emulate the behavior of both male and female models (Perry & Bussey, 1979).

Several intriguing moderators can shift these overall trends, however. First, both boys and girls are more likely to emulate same-gender behavior

to the extent that they see a higher percentage of same-gender models performing the behavior. The more consensus there is about the gender-typed
behavior, in other words, the more likely are children of both sexes to emulate actions that are associated with their own genders (Bussey & Perry,
1982). Second, as Bandura (1986, p. 97) notes, modeling tendencies are
not "oblivious to social reality"; when researchers alter the social power of
models, such that both female and male models are seen in positions of
power, substantial cross-sex modeling occurs. One study found that even in
an experimentally generated family setting, both boys and girls tended to
imitate the behaviors of the more powerful adult (Bandura, Ross, & Ross,
1963). Another found that boys were more responsive to power differences
between models than were girls (Bussey & Bandura, 1984). Specifically,
boys who observed female models enacting positions of high social power
emulated these models to the same extent that they emulated the behavior
of male models in power, but girls did not differ in their emulation of male
and female models in either the male- or female-powerful conditions.

The existing literature thus suggests that boys and girls observe and learn
extensively from models of both sexes; they know what behavior is appropriate for each sex but tend to be quite selective in what they express
behaviorally (Bandura, 1986). One potential reason that boys are more
likely than girls to change their modeling patterns in response to social
power is that dominant, aggressive actions (regardless of whether men or
women perform them) are more consistent with a masculine gender stereotype (Bussey & Bandura, 1984). If a feminine gender stereotype, such as
nurturance, were varied, girls might likely exhibit a similar pattern of
cross-sex modeling.

As might be expected from studies of childhood modeling, the effects of
role models for same-sex adolescent and young adult females are not entirely clear. Studies conducted in the 1960s and 1970s—when employed
mothers were still the exception and not the rule—showed that adolescent
daughters of employed mothers had higher career aspirations than adolescent daughters of at-home mothers (Almquist & Angrist, 1971; Tangri,
1972), suggesting that young women modeled important women in their
lives. Yet Tangri (1972) also showed that female teachers were not as important as supportive boyfriends for female undergraduates as they made career
decisions. Other research conducted in the same era has suggested that college women's educational aspirations were boosted in environments, such
as women's colleges, where there were many women on the faculty (Tidball,
1973); but methodological problems, especially self-selection, have caused

many to doubt this interpretation (Crosby et al., 1994). More recently, researchers documented the positive effects of caring and inspirational adults in the lives of struggling Hispanic teenage mothers (Rhodes, Contreras, & Mangelsdorf, 1994; Rhodes, Gingiss, & Smith, 1994). Yet again, it is unclear from the studies how much positive role models matter and how much of the salutary effect is due to simple social support. More straightforward is a finding by Gilbert (1985) showing that female graduate students with female role models invest more importance in the relationship than do male graduate students with male role models. In another study, Gilbert, Gallessich, and Evans (1983) argued that similarity, attractiveness, power, competence, and life style of the role model, as well as the personality, motivation, and life situation of the observer all moderate the influence of role models on aspirations. The match on personality variables, for many women in their study, exceeded the importance of gender.

In contrast to the data on the influence of same-sex role models, data on the choice of role models are relatively unequivocal. During the college years, women select male and female role models with approximately equal frequency, whereas men tend to avoid female role models. Basow and Howe (1980) found that women were more influenced, according to self-report, by female models than men were but were equally influenced by male models. The same pattern of results occurred in Erkut and Mokros' (1984) study of sophomores and seniors at six different colleges. Women's willingness to choose men as well as other women for their role models probably has less to do with sex-role ideology than with practical necessities (Basow and Howe, 1980). Oftentimes, senior women are scarce whereas senior men are much more in evidence. Indeed, the proposition that choice of role model may be constrained by the numbers of visible men and women has received some empirical support (Erkut & Mokros, 1984).

Changing Schemata.   Visible exemplars of women in positions of authority may be associated with an increase in women's ambitions not because the exemplars spur individual women to increase their aspirations but because, by their very presence, they change the old gender schematic visions of status and power. The existence of a Ruth Bader Ginsberg, for example, may unleash women's hopes not so much directly, by making all women want to become lawyers, as indirectly, by rearranging women's and men's thoughts on how much power a woman can have. The importance of women role models, in other words, may stem from an indirect altering of stereotypic schemata rather than from a direct causal link to career success.

By accepting women in nonstereotypical roles, such as in positions of authority and leadership, observers may be altering their schemata about gender and leadership (Fagenson & Marcus, 1991; Heilman & Martell, 1986).

A laboratory study gives support to the schema-changing line of reasoning. Geis, Boston, and Hoffman (1985) arranged discussion groups with men and women students. They demonstrated that the mere presence of visible exemplars—in this case, female authority figures on a television commercial—could have at least a temporary effect on the likelihood of women taking leadership roles in subsequent discussion group interaction.

The presence of women role models in leadership positions thus may play a role in a woman's perception of the possibility of success, but the link may be an indirect, symbolic one: The fact that a senior woman can succeed means something to the young woman observer; at the same time, the younger woman may not directly identify with the senior as a role model. This indirect relationship between the presence of women in leadership positions and the possibility of success for juniors points to a structuralist rather than developmental position—that patterns of modeling are more dependent on the gender context a woman faces than on inherent differences in modeling tendencies.

Organizational Demography. If observers consider characteristics such as gender to be important in generating their identifications in organizations, it follows that the demographic composition of organizational groups on dimensions of identity, such as gender, race, ethnicity, and age, are also important. Although age and tenure have been the traditional focus of demography studies (e.g., Wagner, Pfeffer, & O'Reilly, 1984; Zenger & Lawrence, 1989), more recent research has shown that race, ethnicity, and gender also affect perceptions and relationships in organizations (Ely, 1994; Konrad & Gutek, 1987; Tsui & O'Reilly, 1989).

In her classic work on the effect of proportions on group life, Kanter (1977) argued that proportional representation of different social types affects the dynamics of group interaction. Groups that are uniform—that is, homogenous in terms of master statuses such as sex, race, or ethnicity—will differ qualitatively from groups that are skewed (those with a 15% or less minority) or balanced (those with a 40–50% minority). Specifically, she contended that in skewed groups individuals may become tokens by virtue of being uniquely identifiable by their external characteristics, which typically carry stereotypical assumptions about what those characteristics mean. In the case of women, the term *token*, Kanter (1977, p. 968) argued, "reflects one's status as a symbol of one's kind," suggesting that women who enter male-dominated organizations are more visible to others due to their uniqueness, more likely to be viewed as different from the dominant group, and more likely to be stereotyped as "just like other women."

Kanter's (1977) proposed solution to the token problem was to turn skewed settings into more balanced ones. "Women," posited Kanter, "need to be added to total group or organization membership in sufficient proportion to counteract the effects of tokenism" (p. 968). Hence, simple math is at the heart of Kanter's analysis.

Others do not agree. Some have argued that merely increasing the number of women overall in an organization will do little to change the nature of women's lower status in organizations (Ely, 1995; Yoder, 1991). Ely (1995) pointed out that as long as women are underrepresented in positions of power "sex may persist as a salient category with negative consequences for women lower down in the organization" (p. 590), despite gender balance at those levels.

Ely (1994) tested her idea in a study of law firms with either few women in senior positions (so-called male-dominated firms) or a significant number of women in senior positions (sex-integrated firms). She found that the proportion of women in senior positions shaped both the peer and hierarchical relationships women had in their firms. Ely found, for example, that junior women in male-dominated firms were less likely than those in sex-integrated firms to view senior women as good role models. She explained this finding by arguing that in male-dominated firms junior women perceived that membership in their gender group was incompatible with membership in more powerful organizational groups. Thus, senior women in these firms present a dilemma for junior women: To reconcile the incompatibility, junior women see senior women either as not legitimately senior—they obtained their positions by illegitimate means—or as not truly women—they obtained their positions by acting like men. In either case, senior women in male-dominated firms are not attractive role models for the more junior women in those firms.

Research Questions

There is some support for a structuralist perspective that suggests that role models will be chosen to the extent that they are considered powerful by observers and that the structure of the situation—including the social identities of those who attain leadership positions—determines who is perceived as powerful. But role model studies of children suggest that boys may be more responsive to shifts in social power than girls, a tendency that has not been explored in organizational settings. Such a tendency, if replicated in organizations, could have important implications for whether or not structural changes alone will enhance the achievement of women and minorities.

The structuralist position contends that men and women have equivalent techniques for role modeling and congruent desires for role models and organizational achievement. Any sex differences in identification patterns may be due to systematic differences in the availability of role models to men and women. This notion remains speculation, however, because it has not been examined in organizational settings.

The study reported here seeks to explore these issues by addressing two research questions. First, do men and women differ in their choice and assessment of role models? Second, does the availability of same-sex role models influence whether or not men and women differ in their choice and assessment of role models?

A STUDY OF ROLE MODELS

The data we present come from two phases of a larger study of role models in organizations. The first phase consisted of 43 in-depth interviews with men and women of varied ages in two professional service organizations, one engaged in financial services, the second in management consulting. The firms were generally matched in terms of size, age, hierarchical levels, and emphasis on strong cultural values. They differed, however, in their proportional distribution of women, particularly in leadership roles: At the skewed financial services firm, women made up about 15% of the professional workforce and 7% of the partnership; at the balanced consulting firm, they represented 55% of the professional workforce and 23% of the partnership. The interviews generated rich descriptive data from which we developed a quantitative survey.

As the second phase of the study, we distributed the survey to a total of 215 respondents in these two firms and in two additional firms. The response rate was 61%, with 132 surveys returned. The two additional firms were law firms that we chose in order to explore possible differences related to women's proportional representation in settings with comparable structures but somewhat different cultural norms and tasks. More specifically, the law firms we selected were similar to the two original firms in their professional service orientation, hierarchical structure (traditional partnerships), highly selective promotion patterns, size (greater than 500) and age (more than 40 years old). Furthermore, law firms share with management consulting and financial services firms a history in which women have only recently begun to populate the upper ranks (Ely, 1994; Morrison & Von Glinow, 1990); thus, the timing of professional women's entry into these firms was comparable. Finally, the two law firms, based on information provided in the 1991 *NALP Law Directory*, were similar to the two original firms in their distributions of women. Twenty-two percent of the lawyers at the skewed law firm were women, and women comprised 8% of the partners. At the balanced law firm, 42% of the lawyers were women, as were 29% of the partners. These percentages are not significantly different from those for the financial services and consulting firms, respectively.

Respondents in the financial services and consulting firms identified on average significantly more role models overall (2.64) than did the lawyers (1.52); this difference was statistically significant ($p < .001$). However, there were no such differences in the proportions of male versus female role models they identified, and respondents in the skewed firms were more similar to one another than to respondents in the balanced firms. Therefore, we combined the data across firms in our analyses.

Respondents

We sent surveys to regional office managers of all four firms, who distributed them to professionals according to a stratified sampling scheme intended to balance the number of men and women and those under and over age 35. Respondents over 35 were frequently at the partnership level and thus busy. To keep response rates high, 19% of the survey data was gathered by telephone. Fortunately, there were no significant differences between responses in the telephone interviews and responses on the questionnaires.

Men made up 53% of the final sample; respondents over the age of 35 made up 49%. Law firm respondents made up 58% of the sample and the financial services and consulting firms the remaining 42%. One hundred percent of respondents had a college degree, and 75% had advanced degrees. The average tenure was 6.9 years. Ethnic minorities made up 5% of the sample, roughly equaling their representation in these organizations.

The Survey

We designed the survey to elicit data in two primary areas: the attributes of particular role models and the perceived availability of and satisfaction with role models in the firm. In the first section we asked respondents to identify any persons they currently considered to be role models within the firm. The exact wording of the question read:

> Of all of the people working for the firm, who do you think of as a role model for you now, personally and professionally? List the names of the persons you consider to be a role model. If you wish, use first names or initials, whatever will help you identify them in later questions.

We provided space for up to four models, with an opportunity to add more. Respondents who were over the age of 35 could indicate both current and previous models. We provided space for respondents to write role model attributes, followed by items assessing the relationship between the respondent and model, including the role model's hierarchical position, location, frequency of interaction, age, and sex. We coded and grouped the attributes into categories (organizational effectiveness, balancing personal and professional life, interpersonal skills, and personal traits and values). Two coders blind to the intent of the study assigned the attributes listed to categories; there was an overall interrater reliability of 81% based on Scott's (1955) pi procedure.

A subsequent section assessed respondents' "thoughts about role models in the firm." Included here were 20 items pertaining to perceived availability of role models and their importance. The items had been suggested by the qualitative interviews and included such statements as, "I think I have role models available to me of how I can succeed in this firm." Responses ranged on a Likert scale from 1, (*strongly disagree*) to 7 (*strongly agree*). We used one-tailed *t* tests to assess differences in means.

Findings

We explored our research questions in two parts. First, we looked at the responses of women and men. Second, we addressed the effects of women's proportional representation on men's and women's choices of role models.

Overall Gender Similarities and Differences

Presence of Role Models.　Men and women did not differ in the number of role models they identified. Men identified an average of 2.06 models and women identified 1.90; this difference was not statistically significant. Overall, 132 respondents identified 263 role models, 191 male and

71 female. Although men disagreed that it was "important to me that a role model be the same sex as I am," they overwhelmingly chose male role models: Seventy men respondents identified 144 role models, 89% of whom were men. Women, on the other hand, were much more likely to identify both male and female role models: Sixty-two women respondents identified 118 role models, 53% of whom were men and 47% women. These results are shown in Table 7.1.

Role Model Attributes. Based on both interview and survey data, respondents tended to make a primary distinction between attributes related to the job and organization (i.e., professional attributes) and attributes inherent to the models themselves (i.e., personal attributes). Further analysis revealed four general categories of attributes (see Table 7.1). The first was organizational effectiveness, which included all the professional attributes, such as technical expertise, leadership ability, and organizational and financial success. The three remaining categories were a further refinement of the personal attributes and were ability to balance personal and professional life, interpersonal skills, and personal traits and values.

As shown in Table 7.1, women and men did not differ substantially in their identification of role model attributes overall; for both groups about 50% of the attributes listed were professional and about 50% were personal. Respondents did make distinctions, however, in the attributes they ascribed to their male versus female role models. They were less likely to describe female role models as organizationally effective and more likely to describe them as balancing personal and professional life well. More specifically, they were less likely to describe female role models as leaders, teachers, managers, or coaches, and more likely to describe them as hard workers and as having a positive attitude.

Perceived Availability of Models. As shown in Table 7.2, 7 of the 13 questions about perceived availability of role models revealed differences between women and men. In contrast to the pattern of actual choices of role models, men were less likely than women to agree that it was important that a role model be the same sex as themselves. Women were less satisfied then men with their role models and more likely to agree that they would "have more role models in this firm if there were more people like me here." Women were also less likely than men to say they had specific individuals they looked to for success in their firms and more likely to perceive negative role models; that is, models of how not to behave. Finally, women were

TABLE 7.1

Role Model Attributes Identified
by Men and Women Survey Respondents

Role Model Attributes	Men Role Model Attributes Identified by Men Respondents	Women Role Model Attributes Identified by Men Respondents	Men Role Model Attributes Identified by Women Respondents	Women Role Model Attributes Identified by Women Respondents
	% Cites	% Cites	% Cites	% Cites
Organizational Effectiveness	51%[a]	46%	52%	43%
Technical expert, professional excellence	10[b]	11	11	9
Leader, teacher, manager, coach	8	3	11	3
Successful/financially productive	7	0	6	7
Hard worker ("high intensity level")	6	17	3	5
Respected, powerful	4	0	5	6
Effective with clients	5	0	3	2
Culture carrier—team player	3	3	2	4
Big Picture, strategic thinker	3	3	5	1
Miscellaneous (efficient, organized, works effectively, etc.)	5	9	6	6
Ability to Balance Personal and Professional Life	4%	6%	3%	10%
Balances personal and professional life	4	6	3	10
Interpersonal Skills	11%	11%	7%	10%
Caring/respect for others	11	11	7	10
Personal Traits and Values	35%	37%	37%	38%
Intelligent, smart	11	11	10	15
Positive attitude, funny, personable	8	11	7	9
Ethical, honest, fair, direct	5	3	7	6

Ambitious, aggressive, driven, gutsy, independent, confident, convincing	7	3	3	5
Miscellaneous (creative, down-to-earth, good image, well-rounded)	5	9	10	3
Total Number of Role Model Attributes	261	35	165	108
Number of Role Models Identified	128	16	63	55
% Role Models Identified	89%[c]	11%	53%	47%
Mean Number of Role Models	1.83	0.23	1.02	0.89

[a]Indicates 51% of total number of role model attributes were in the organizationally effective category. [b]Indicates 10% of the total number of role model attributes referred to technical expertise or professional excellence. [c]Indicates 89% of men respondent's role models were men.

more likely than men to desire a role model of how to balance work and personal life concerns.

There were no differences in men's and women's reports of the degree to which they "have role models available to me of how I can succeed in this firm." Furthermore, both men and women agreed that they were able to find role models among the male partners, although men agreed more strongly than women; and both disagreed that they were able to find role models among the female partners. Finally, men and women respondents did not differ in their tendency to create a composite role model from the traits and skills of several people.

Differences Across Demographic Settings

As shown in Figures 7.1 and 7.2, women's proportional representation in firms did not influence women's same- or cross-sex role-modeling patterns. In both settings, 54% of women's positive role models were men, and 46% were women. Women's proportional representation, however, influenced men's role-modeling patterns. In the skewed firms, only 5% of men's positive role models were women, whereas 16% were women in the balanced firms. Hence, women's proportional representation made a difference in men's but not women's cross-sex role modeling patterns. There were no sex differences in the number of role models respondents identified overall in either setting, although men in the balanced settings identified more role models than men in the skewed settings.

Consistent with these findings, men in the balanced settings were significantly more likely to state that they were able to find good role models
among the female partners compared to men in the skewed settings. Although women in both settings reported having a relatively high number of
women role models, women in balanced firms were somewhat less likely

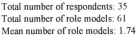

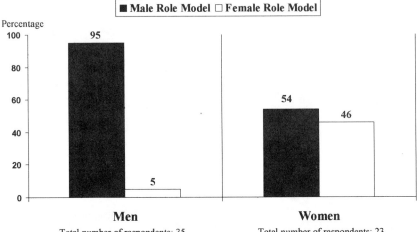

Men

Total number of respondents: 35
Total number of role models: 61
Mean number of role models: 1.74

Women

Total number of respondents: 23
Total number of role models: 37
Mean number of role models: 1.61

FIG. 7.1.   Percent positive role models—skewed firms (less than 20% female professionals
overall, less than 8% female partners).

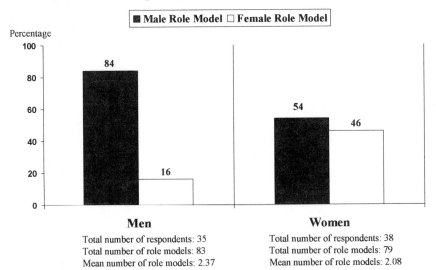

Men

Total number of respondents: 35
Total number of role models: 83
Mean number of role models: 2.37

Women

Total number of respondents: 38
Total number of role models: 79
Mean number of role models: 2.08

FIG 7.2.   Percent positive role models—balanced firms (greater than 50% female professionals overall, greater than 23% female partners).

than their counterparts in skewed firms to place importance on same-sex role models. In addition, women in both settings were equally likely to report that they were unable to find good role models among the women partners. Women in the balanced settings, however, were more likely than women in the skewed settings to say they had role models for how to treat others and marginally more likely to say they had role models for "how I can succeed in this firm" and "how I can be personally satisfied in this firm." These results are shown in Table 7.2.

Discussion

Our study contributes several new findings to the literature on men's and women's role models. First, we found that men were more likely to select women as role models in the balanced settings than in the skewed settings, whereas the setting did not influence women's selection of role models. This finding is consistent with earlier findings that boys are more responsive to changes in the social power of their models than are girls, shifting their identification in favor of female models when those models hold more social power (Bussey & Bandura, 1984). It is inconsistent, however, with the bulk of research suggesting either that men tend to avoid women as role models altogether (Erkut & Mokros, 1984) or that women role models simply do not exist for men in organizations (Kram, 1985).

Our finding that women's choice of role models was not dependent on organizational context is also at odds with the structuralist argument that balancing the number of women, particularly in positions of power, should decrease perceptions of women as tokens and expand perceptions of women as legitimate role models (Ely, 1994; Kanter, 1977). Differences in methodology and setting could contribute to these divergent findings, but the story here is clearly a more complex one than the notion that increasing the number of women, even in positions of power, will increase the number of role models for women. This is illustrated by two findings. First, women did not identify more women role models in the balanced than in the skewed setting; rather, they identified essentially the same number of women role models (and a roughly equivalent proportion of men). Second, the greater number of women partners did not lead women in the balanced setting to find more good role models among the women partners. Although women in these settings were generally more likely to say they had good role models of how to succeed available to them, their role models were not necessarily senior women. Therefore, we conclude that the shift in demographic com-

TABLE 7.2
Difference in Mean Responses Between Men and Women in Skewed versus Balanced Firms[s]

	Means						
	Men			Women			Sex Difference[d]
Items	Skewed n = 35	Balanced n = 35	t[b]	Skewed n = 23	Balanced n = 38	t[c]	
I am satisfied with the role models I have available to me.	4.74	4.67	-0.16	3.77	4.08	0.55	*
I tend to create a composite role model from the traits and skills of several people.	5.90	6.03	0.35	5.59	5.84	0.62	
I think I have positive role models available to me of how to treat others in the firm.	5.48	5.88	1.14	5.00	5.95	2.24*	
I'd have more role models in this firm if there were more people like me here.	3.84	3.55	-0.51	5.06	4.34	-1.40	*
I think I have role models available to me of how I can be personally satisfied in this firm.	4.17	4.42	0.58	3.50	4.32	1.73H	
I'd say role models are not important for me now.	2.65	2.82	0.41	3.09	3.31	0.41	
I am able to find good role models among the female partners.	2.78	4.28	2.85**	3.63	3.88	0.37	
I am able to find good role models among the male partners.	4.89	5.00	0.24	4.06	4.24	0.28	*
It's important to me that a role model be the same sex as I am.	1.94	2.53	1.69H	3.50	2.49	-1.89H	*
I wish I had more positive role models available to me of how to balance work and personal life concerns.	4.57	4.61	0.08	5.73	5.86	0.36	***

continued on next page

I see more examples of how not to behave around here than I see examples of how to behave.	3.61	-0.30	4.86	4.23	-1.24	**
I have specific individuals I look to as role models of how to succeed in this organization.	5.55	-1.36	4.22	4.92	1.42	*
I think I have role models available to me of how I can succeed in this firm.	5.11	0.15	4.53	5.23	1.60H	

[a]Based on a scale from 1 = *Strongly Disagree* to 4 = *Neutral* to 7 = *Strongly Agree*. [b]Indicates significance of t-test comparing mean responses of men respondents in skewed versus balanced firms. [c]Indicates significance of t-test comparing mean responses of women respondents in skewed versus balanced firms. [d]Indicates significance of t-test comparing mean responses of men versus women respondents. Hp<.10. *p<.05. **p<.01 ***p<.001.

position did not change women's role model identification patterns; rather, women in both settings found it critical to have both men and women as role models.

Another explanation for women's insensitivity to women's proportional representation is that women's greater representation in the balanced settings may not have been sufficient to change the cultural norms of the organization that may nevertheless have emphasized and valued work at the expense of personal life. Both the balanced law firm and the balanced consulting firm, while touting their female-friendly policies, emphasized, through norms about "face time" at work, billable hours, and part-time work arrangements, that professional concerns should come before personal ones if one is to succeed. Women partners, as among those who represent and uphold cultural norms, may therefore have been no more attractive as role models to women in these firms than they were to women in the skewed firms.

IMPLICATIONS
FOR MULTICULTURAL MENTORING

Our study suggests that women, compared to men, have a smaller pool of candidates who are similar to them on critical dimensions from which to construct role models. This finding suggests a number of consequences that make organizational life somewhat more difficult for women than for men. First, women are far more likely to identify cross-sex role models than are men. Women must adapt the kinds of behaviors that work well for their male role models into behaviors that will work well for them. For example, whereas aggressive, competitive behavior with colleagues and male bonding with clients may lead to success for men, these behaviors may not be viable options for women. Therefore, women may need to interpret more carefully and adapt more skillfully their models' actions and attitudes in order to succeed (cf. Horgan, 1989). Second, women respondents reported that they are less likely to find role models who share concerns they have about balancing personal and professional lives. Again, they must adjust the lessons they learn about success from their models to account for personal lifestyle differences. Third, although women were no more likely than men to report that they create composite models for themselves, they were less likely to have specific individuals as role models. Once again, this suggests that women's search for role models involves more interpreting and filtering than does men's. Finally, women identified more negative role models than did men. Negative role models provide lessons of how not to do it, which may distort the picture of what comprises success, requiring observers—who, in this case, are more often women than men—to translate these negative lessons into positive ones. These findings suggest that women's role modeling—as well as that of other underrepresented groups—requires greater cognitive processing. Hence, whereas White men may be able to *take* the high-achievement attributes and behaviors their organizations have recognized and rewarded in their (presumably White) male role models and add them to their own behavioral repertoire, women and minorities may have to *make* such images out of role models from more diverse and fragmented sources.

This research suggests that our current understanding of role models, which implies that all observers simply take role models provided in the form of mentors, supervisors, and charismatic heroes is too simple. Rather, men and women appear to weigh a person's sex differently in their assessments of whether or not the person could serve as a role model for them, and their levels of satisfaction with their role models differ. Our results suggest that women are more flexible in the types of information they glean and just as likely to look to male sources of inspiration as female, regardless of their relative availability. Future research should investigate further the relation between women's apparent flexibility in choosing and emulating role models and how the organizational context shapes that process.

REFERENCES

Almquist, E., & Angrist, S. (1971). Role model influences on college women's career aspirations. *Merrill-Palmer Quarterly, 17*, 263–279.

Bandura, A. (1977). *Social learning theory.* Englewood Cliffs, NJ: Prentice-Hall.

Bandura, A. (1986). *Social foundations of thought and action: A social cognitive theory.* Englewood Cliffs, NJ: Prentice-Hall.

Bandura, A., Ross, D., & Ross, S. (1963). A comparative test of the status envy, social power, and secondary reinforcement theories of identificatory learning. *Journal of Abnormal and Social Psychology, 67*, 527–534.

Basow, S. A., & Howe, K. G. (1980). Role-model influence: Effects of sex and sex-role attitude in college students. *Psychology of Women Quarterly, 4*, 558–572.

Bell, A. P. (1970). Role modelship and interaction in adolescence and young adulthood. *Developmental Psychology, 2*, 123–128.

Bussey, K., & Bandura, A. (1984). Influence of gender constancy and social power on sex-linked modeling. *Journal of Personality and Social Psychology, 47*, 1292–1302.

Bussey, K., & Perry, D. (1982). Same-sex imitation: The avoidance of cross-sex models or the acceptance of same-sex models? *Sex Roles, 8*, 773–784.

Crosby, F. J., Allen, B., Culbertson, T., Wally, C., Morith, J., Hall, R., & Nunes, B. (1994). Taking selectivity into account, how much does gender composition matter? A re-analysis of M. E. Tidball's research. *NWSA Journal, 6,* 107–118.

Deal, T., & Kennedy, A. (1982). *Corporate cultures: The rites and rituals of corporate life.* Reading, MA: Addison-Wesley.

Ely, R. J. (1994). The effects of organizational demographics and social identity on relationships among professional women. *Administrative Science Quarterly, 39,* 203–238.

Ely, R. J. (1995). The power in demography: Women's social constructions of gender identity at work. *Academy of Management Journal, 38,* 589–634.

Erkut, S., & Mokros, J. R. (1984). Professors as models and mentors for college students. *American Research Journal, 21,* 399–417.

Fagenson, E. A., & Marcus, E. C. (1991). Perceptions of the sex-role stereotypic characteristics of entrepreneurs: Women's evaluations. *Entrepreneurship: Theory and Practice,* 33–47.

Fisher, B. (1988). Wandering in the wilderness: The search for women role models. *Signs: Journal of Women in Culture and Society, 13,* 211–233.

Geis, F. L., Boston, M. B., & Hoffman, N. (1985). Sex of authority role models and achievement by men and women: Leadership performance and recognition. *Journal of Personality and Social Psychology, 49,* 636–653.

Gilbert, L. A. (1985). Dimensions of same-gender student-faculty role-model relationships. *Sex Roles, 12,* 111–123.

Gilbert, L. A., Gallessich, J. M., & Evans, S. L. (1983). Sex of faculty role model and students' self-perceptions of competency. *Sex Roles, 9,* 597–607.

Heilman, M. E., & Martell, R. F. (1986). Exposure to successful women: Antidote to sex discrimination in applicant screening decisions? *Organizational Behavior and Human Decision Processes, 37,* 376–390.

Horgan, D. D. (1989). A cognitive learning perspective on women becoming expert managers. *Journal of Business and Psychology, 3,* 299–313.

Javidan, M., Bemmels, B., Stratton-Devine, K., & Dastmalchian, A. (1995). Superior and subordinate gender and the acceptance of superiors as role models. *Human Relations, 48,* 1271–1284.

Kanter, R. M. (1977). Some effects of proportions on group life: Skewed sex ratios and responses to token women. *American Journal of Sociology, 82,* 965–990.

Kelman, H. C. (1961). Processes of opinion change. *Public Opinion Quarterly, 25,* 57–78.

Kohlberg, L. (1963). Moral development and identification. In H. W. Stevenson (Ed.), *Child psychology: The sixty-second yearbook of the national society for the study of education (Part 1)* (pp. 277–332). Chicago, IL: University of Chicago Press.

Konrad, A., & Gutek, B. A. (1987). Theory and research on group composition: Applications to the status of women and ethnic minorities. In S. Oskamp and S. Spacapan (Eds.), *Interpersonal Processes* (pp. 85–121). Newbury Park, CA: Sage.

Kram, K. E. (1985). *Mentoring at work: Developmental relationships in organizational life.* Glenview, IL: Scott, Foresman.

Maccoby, E., & Jacklin, C. (1974). *The psychology of sex differences.* Stanford, CA: Stanford University Press.

Manz, C., & Sims, H. (1981). Vicarious learning: The influence of modeling on organizational behavior. *Academy of Management Review, 6,* 105–113.

Mischel, W. (1966). A social-learning view of sex differences in behavior. In E. Maccoby (Ed.), *The development of sex differences* (pp. 56–81). Stanford, CA: Stanford University Press.

Morrison, A. M., & Von Glinow, M. (1990). Women and minorities in management. *American Psychologist, 45,* 200–208.

Pascale, R. (1985). The paradox of "corporate culture": Reconciling ourselves to socialization. *California Management Review, 27*(2), 26–41.

Perry, D., & Bussey, K. (1979). The social learning theory of sex differences: Imitation is alive and well. *Journal of Personality and Social Psychology, 37*, 1699–1712.

Rhodes, J. E., Contreras, J. M., & Mangelsdorf, S. C. (1994). Natural mentor relationships among Latina adolescent mothers: Psychological adjustment, moderating processes, and the role of early parental acceptance. *American Journal of Community Psychology, 22*, 211–227.

Rhodes, J. E., Gingiss, P. L., & Smith, P. B. (1994). Risk and protective factors for alcohol use among pregnant African-American, Hispanic, and White adolescents: The influence of peers, sexual partners, and family members and mentors. *Addictive Behaviors, 19*, 555–564.

Scott, W. A. (1955). Reliability of content analysis: The case of nominal scale coding. *Public Opinion Quarterly, 20*, 321–325.

Speizer, J. (1981). Role models, mentors, and sponsors: The elusive concepts. *Signs: Journal of Women in Culture and Society, 6*, 692–712.

Tangri, S. (1972). Determinants of occupational role innovation among college women. *Journal of Social Issues, 28*, 177–199.

Tidball, M. E. (1973). Perspective on academic women and affirmative action. *Educational Record, 54*, 130–135.

Tsui, A., & O'Reilly, C. (1989). Beyond simple demographic effects: The importance of relational demography in superior–subordinate dyads. *Academy of Management Journal, 32*, 402–423.

Wagner, W., Pfeffer, J., & O'Reilly, C. (1984). Organizational demography and turnover in top-management groups. *Administrative Science Quarterly, 29*, 74–92.

Whitaker, G., & Molstad, S. (1988). Role modeling and female athletes. *Sex Roles, 9/10*, 555–566.

Yoder, J. D. (1991). Rethinking tokenism: Looking beyond numbers. *Gender and Society, 5*, 178–192.

Zenger, T. R., & Lawrence, B. S. (1989). Organizational demography: The differential effects of age and tenure distributions on technical communication. *Academy of Management Journal, 32*, 353–376.

8

Mitigating Perceptions of Racism: The Importance of Work Group Composition and Supervisor's Race

Daria Kirby
University of Pittsburgh

James S. Jackson
The University of Michigan

In Trinity Episcopal Church of New Haven, Connecticut, when a new boy joins the choir, an old boy is assigned by the choir master to help the novice learn the rules and regulations. The system helps perpetuate the venerable traditions of America's oldest male choir. With a talent pool that is homogeneous in terms of ethnicity, affluence, and education, not to mention gender, the system works well. The essential component of Trinity Church's "old boys system" happens throughout America and the rest of the world as new members join established organizations. New employees learn how to function in their environment from their older and more senior colleagues. Sometimes the pairings are officially mandated; sometimes they evolve unofficially.

Yet the kind of homogeneity of population that marks Trinity Church is increasingly rare. Most organizations—and perhaps most notably places of business—are losing their erstwhile uniformity, especially at entry levels.

Throughout Europe and the United States, increasing percentages of the people who join companies and schools are people of color.

The growing heterogeneity of workforces makes it reasonable to wonder about the dynamics of socialization into today's organizations. What happens in a developmental relationship when the "old boy" is a White male and the new recruit is, for example, Black? What happens when the new boy is a woman? Answers to questions such as these depend in no small measure on the answers to some prior questions about the extent to which people of color face racism and sexism. We address these questions in this chapter.

We talked with a sample of Black British people to explore these issues. Like the United States, the European Union (EU) is challenged by diversity issues, including those related to race, ethnicity, and gender. Coupled with a decline in birth rates and a rapid aging of its White population as the 21st century approaches, the EU will have to find new sources of workers among its growing ethnic and racial population (Fernandez, 1993). Recruitment and retention of a diverse workforce may prove problematic given recent events documenting an escalation in rioting and open conflict with ethnic minorities and immigrant groups over the last 5 years. In addition, there has been a strong public outcry from several segments of the British population against immigrants. For example, a conservative member of the British Parliament in a recent speech called for a halt to the "relentless flow of immigrants lest the traditions of English life be lost" (Stevenson, 1993, p. A10). Similarly, a member of the Neo-Nazi party won a local council seat in London with a campaign message stating that "if Britain is to be great again it must deport all nonWhites" (Stevenson, 1993, p. A10). Certainly, these expressions of antiethnic and racial sentiment do not occur solely in England. Similar events have occurred in Germany, France, and the Netherlands.

Unlike the United States, where comprehensive antidiscrimination policies have been established, legislation prohibiting discrimination and ensuring equal employment varies widely among the EU member states. Britain, for example, has extensive legislation governing racial discrimination in employment, whereas Ireland has no domestic legislation controlling racial discrimination. A study by the British Department of Employment states that outside England legal protection against racial discrimination is nonexistent (Forbes & Meade, 1992).

Little empirical research to our knowledge has investigated the perception of discrimination among racial and ethnic group members in the EU.

We argue that the existence of racial discrimination may be a major factor generating differences in the desires and expectations of racial and ethnic minority workers in the EU. The combination of European unification, increases in racial violence, and the increasing racial diversity of the British workforce brings to the fore the question of whether Black British employees perceive racial discrimination in their work environments. More important, we are interested in the relationship between these perceptions and traditional organizational attitudes such as job satisfaction, as mediated by whether a person has a same- or other-race supervisor. We believe that insight into these questions is relevant for understanding the mentoring of people of color in the British context.

The main portion of this chapter reports on a study of Black workers conducted in spring and fall, 1994, in London, England. We asked respondents who worked for White or for Black supervisors in groups of varying racial composition about their perceptions of racism and about their job satisfaction. In this chapter we describe the method and the findings of this study. We then explore some of the implications of these findings for the developmental relationships of Britons of color.

METHODS

Two male students and one female student situated themselves in two locations in the city of London and collected information from Black Britons whom they approached on the street. The students were themselves Black, and most respondents were willing to participate in the brief interview. Altogether, 188 women and men took part, anonymously, in the study. For the purposes of this chapter, we looked at data from the 100 employed respondents who could provide data on the variables of interest to us.

In addition to gender, which we coded from physical appearance, we measured a number of demographic and attitudinal variables. More specifically, we collected data on: the respondent's job level, the race of the respondent's supervisor, the racial composition of the respondent's work group, the respondent's job satisfaction, the respondent's perception of opportunity, and the respondent's perception of racial discrimination.

To assess job level we asked respondents their occupations and then used the British Employment Office system to sort jobs into blue collar (e.g., janitor, maid, sales clerk) and white collar (e.g., proprietor, manager) positions. We assessed race of supervisor by asking, "Is your work supervisor White,

Black, or what?" We excluded from analysis people who had no supervisor and people who had a supervisor who was neither White nor Black (e.g., was Asian). We categorized the racial composition of the work group as five separate dummy variables: all Black, mostly Black, half Black and half White, mostly White, and all White except respondent. We treated the variables of sex, supervisor's race, and racial composition of the work group as antecedents to the attitudinal variables.

We measured job satisfaction with a single item: "All in all, how satisfied are you with this particular job?" Response options ranged from 1 (*very dissatisfied*) to 4 (*very satisfied*). We measured respondents' perceptions of opportunity with the question: "Are the jobs that African-Caribbean and/or East Indian people get better, worse, or the same as the jobs that White people get?" We sorted responses into two categories: those who said "worse" and those who said "same" or "better." Finally, we assessed their perceptions of discrimination with two yes—no questions: "At your work place are African-Caribbean and/or East Indian people treated unfairly or badly in any ways?" and "At the place where you work now, have you been turned down for a job that you wanted because you are African-Caribbean or East Indian?" We categorized the possible combinations of responses to these two questions in three ways, which served as our measure for this variable: both no; yes to one, no to the other; and both yes.

FINDINGS

Effects of Gender

Men and women did not differ in how satisfied they were with their jobs. The majority of both men and women were somewhat or very satisfied. Nor did men and women differ in their perceptions of opportunity. Sixty percent of the women and 73% of the men thought that the types of jobs Black people get are worse than the types of jobs White people get; this difference was not statistically significant. Women and men also by and large held the same perceptions concerning discrimination. Seventy-one percent of the women neither perceived that Black people were unfairly treated nor that they themselves had been turned down for a job because they were Black; 53% of the men reported the same. Meanwhile, 19% of the women and 16% of the men felt both that Black people were unfairly treated and that they them-

TABLE 8.1

Job Satisfaction, Perceptions of Job Opportunities, and Discrimination by Gender

		Women	Men	Chi-Square
Job satisfaction				
	Very satisfied	26%	26%	n.s.
	Somewhat satisfied	45%	50%	
	Somewhat dissatisfied	15%	9%	
	Very dissatisfied	14%	15%	
Differences in job opportunities				
	Better/Same	40%	26%	n.s.
	Worse	60%	73%	
Perceptions of discrimination				
	Both no	71%	53%	4.562 $p<.10$
	1 yes	11%	28%	
	2 yes	18%	19%	

selves had been turned down for a job due to their race. Table 8.1 presents these results.

Effects of Job Level

Dividing the sample according to job level yielded only one significant result: Blue-collar workers were significantly less satisfied with their jobs than were white-collar workers. Thirty-eight percent of the blue-collar workers reported being either very or somewhat dissatisfied, compared to only 17% of the white-collar workers. There were no significant differences by job level in respondents' perceptions of whether or not Whites have better jobs than Blacks: Nearly three-fourths of blue-collar workers and 59% of white-collar workers believed this. As for discrimination, 62% of the blue-collar and 64% of the white-collar workers thought both that Black people in general and that they in particular were as well treated as White people, whereas 38% of the blue-collar and 36% of the white-collar workers thought that neither of these was the case. These differences in perceptions of discrimination were also not statistically significant. These results are summarized in Table 8.2.

Effects of Supervisor's Race

The race of a respondent's supervisor did not affect his or her job satisfaction, but it influenced perceptions of opportunity and discrimination. Seventy-three percent of those with a White supervisor thought that the jobs Black people get are worse than the jobs White people get, whereas only 33% of those with a Black supervisor thought the same. This difference was significant. We obtained similar results for perceptions of discrimination: Only 55% of those with a White supervisor thought both that Black people in general and that they in particular were fairly treated, whereas 95% of

TABLE 8.2

**Job Satisfaction, Perceptions of Job Opportunities
and Discrimination by Job Level**

		Blue Collar	White Collar	Chi-Square
Job Satisfaction				
	Very satisfied	9%	40%	15.194 p<.00
	Somewhat satisfied	52%	43%	
	Somewhat dissatisfied	20%	7%	
	Very dissatisfied	18%	10%	
Differences in job opportunities				
	Better/Same	27%	51%	n.s.
	Worse	73%	59%	
Perceptions of discrimination				
	Both no	62%	64%	n.s.
	1 yes	19%	18%	
	2 yes	19%	18%	

TABLE 8.3
**Job Satisfaction, Perceptions of Job Opportunities,
and Discrimination by Supervisor Race**

		Black Supervisors	White Supervisors	Chi-Square
Job satisfaction				
	Very satisfied	26%	27%	n.s
	Somewhat satisfied	61%	43%	
	Somewhat dissatisfied	13%	13%	
	Very dissatisfied	0%	18%	
Differences in job opportunities				
	Better/Same	67%	27%	
	Worse	33%	73%	11.717 $p < .001$
Perceptions of discrimination				
	Both No	95%	55%	10.446 $p < .01$
	1 Yes	5%	22%	
	2 yes	0%	23%	

those with a Black supervisor thought so. None of the respondents with a Black supervisor thought both that Black people in general and that they in particular were unfairly treated, but 23% of those with a White supervisor did. Again, these differences were statistically significant. These results are presented in Table 8.3.

Effects of the Racial Composition of the Work Group

Job satisfaction depended on the racial composition of the respondent's immediate work group. Sixty-two percent of those in an all-Black group were very satisfied with their jobs, but, as Table 8.4 shows, far fewer of the other workers were. Perceptions of job opportunities did not vary according to the racial composition of the work group. As Table 8.4 shows, although the percentages of those who thought Black people and White people have the same chances of getting a good job were lower among those who worked in an all-Black or mostly Black group compared to other workers, these differences were not statistically significant. Table 8.4 shows that perceptions of discrimination did not vary systematically as a function of the racial composition of the work group.

Multiple Predictors

What happens when all the factors are considered simultaneously? We conducted regression analyses to answer this question. In the first two models, we used job satisfaction as the criterion variable and considered as predictors the number of people in the work group, occupational level of the worker, gender, the race of the supervisor, and the racial composition of the work group. These findings are presented in Table 8.5. The additive model showed that workers with Black supervisors reported higher job satisfaction

TABLE 8.4

Job Satisfaction, Perceptions of Job Opportunities and Discrimination by Work Group Racial Composition

	All Black	Mostly Black	Half Black and Half White	Mostly White	All White Except Respondent	Chi-Square
Job satisfaction						
Very Satisfied	62%	7%	17%	17%	44%	31.076 p <.01
Somewhat satisfied	12%	29%	67%	58%	33%	
Somewhat dissatisfied	0%	43%	17%	6%	11%	
Very dissatisfied	25%	21%	0%	19%	11%	
Perception of job opportunities						
Better/Same	14%	14%	50%	31%	44%	n.s.
Worse	86%	86%	50%	69%	56%	
Perceptions of discrimination						
Both no	83%	62%	78%	46%	67%	
1 yes	17%	15%	17%	29%	0%	n.s.
2 yes	0%	23%	6%	26%	33%	

TABLE 8.5

Multiple Regression Results of Job Satisfaction in the Workplace on Sociodemographic, Organizational, and Racial Saliency Variables

Predictor Variables	Standardized Beta Coefficients	
	Additive Model	Interaction Model
Number of people in work group	-.06	-.06
Occupational level[a]	-.30**	-.30**
Gender[b]	-.03	-.03
Supervisor race[c]	.21†	.29**
Mostly black work group[d]	-.29**	-.29**
Half Black half White work group[d]	-.14	-.04
Mostly White work group[d]	-.18	-.15
Supervisor race * Mostly Black work group interaction	—	-.01
Supervisor race * Half Black half White work group interaction	—	-.17
Supervisor race * Mostly White work group interaction	—	-.01
y-intercept	3.499	3.443
R-Square (adj)	.15**	.13**

[a]1 = Blue Collar, 0 = White Collar. [b]1 = Female, 0 = Male. [c]1 = Black, 0 = White. [d]Excluded group is all Black work group. The mostly White work group includes groups that were all White except for the respondent.

†$p \leq .10$. *$p \leq .05$. **$p \leq .01$. ***$p \leq .001$.

than workers with White supervisors; this difference was only marginally significant in this analysis, but it was insignificant in the previous analysis, which failed to control for the variables in this model. Consistent with the results of the simple comparisons, those in blue-collar jobs were more satisfied than those with white-collar jobs. Finally, those in mostly Black work groups were less satisfied than those in all-Black work groups; none of the other variants of work group composition significantly differed from the all-Black work group.

The interaction model further explicates the impact of supervisor race and work group racial composition on job satisfaction, showing that the impact of supervisor race depended on the racial composition of the work group. As illustrated in Figure 8.1 and evidenced in the significant b-coefficient for supervisor race in the interactive model, workers in all-Black work groups with Black supervisors were more satisfied than those in all-Black work groups with White supervisors. In addition, the significant b-coefficient for the mostly Black work group in the interaction model represents the difference, among those with White supervisors, between those in mostly Black and those in all-Black work groups: Workers with White supervisors in all-Black work groups were more satisfied than workers with White supervisors in mostly Black work groups.

In the third and fourth models, we used logistic regression to assess the impact of the same predictors as in the job satisfaction model on perceptions of job opportunities (coded either $0 = $ "Blacks better or the same as Whites" or $1 = $ "Blacks worse than Whites") and perceptions of racial discrimination.

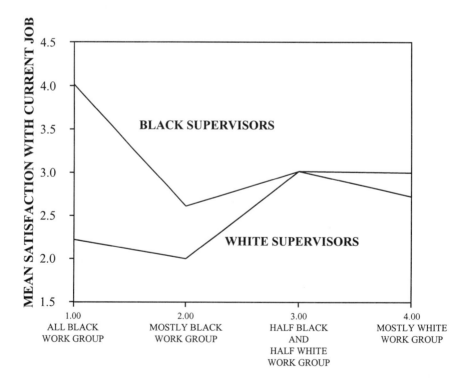

FIG. 8.1. Work group racial composition.

TABLE 8.6

Logistic Regression Results of Perceptions of Job Opportunities and Discrimination in the Workplace on Sociodemographic, Organizational, and Racial Saliency Variables

Predictor Variables	Perception of Job Opportunities	Perception of Discrimination
Number of people in workgroup	0.01	-0.11
Occupational level[a]	-0.47†	-.04
Gender[b]	-0.13	0.25
Supervisor race[c]	1.66**	4.26
All Black work group[d]	-1.60*	0.61
Mostly Black work group[d]	-1.45**	-0.22
Half Black half White work group[d]	-0.52	-.49
Constant	2.75	-4.92
Chi-Square	26.89**	21.616**

[a]1 = Blue collar, 0 = White Collar. [b]1 = Female, 0 = Male. [c]1 = Black, 0 = White. [d]Excluded group is the mostly White work group. The mostly White work group includes groups that were all White except for the respondent.

†$p \leq .10$. *$p \leq .05$. **$p \leq .01$. ***$p \leq .001$.

We recoded the racial discrimination variable for this analysis into two categories: 0 = those who answered "no" to both discrimination questions, and 1 = those who answered "yes" to one or the other. This code permitted a more simple, logistic regression analysis of the data than if we had retained the three-category system we used to present the descriptive analyses. Findings, presented in Table 8.6, were that respondents with Black supervisors were more likely than those with White supervisors to perceive that Black Britons have worse job opportunities than White Britons. In addition, respondents in all-Black work groups, as well as those in mostly Black work groups, perceived better job opportunities for Blacks than did respondents in mostly White work groups. Blue-collar workers were somewhat less likely than white-collar workers to perceive that Black Britons had worse job opportunities than Whites. Finally, there were no significant predictors in the model to explain perceptions of job discrimination.

IMPLICATIONS

Ours is a small study, but the results have important implications for how we understand the dynamics of cross-race versus same-race developmental relationships in a British setting. Overall, our findings suggest that Black Britons who work for a Black supervisor in all or predominantly Black work groups have a more positive work experience than those with White supervisors. Our findings also suggest that having White supervisors was especially problematic for Black Britons in all-Black work groups, whereas having a Black supervisor in an all-Black work group was an especially positive experience. It is interesting that among those with White supervisors, Black Britons in mostly-Black work groups were less satisfied with their jobs than were those in all-Black work groups. This result suggests an especially problematic dynamic that occurs for Blacks when the supervisor and a minority of the work group share dominant racial group status. Finally, Black Britons in all-Black or mostly Black work groups were more likely to perceive better job opportunities for Blacks than were their counterparts in mostly White work groups.

What are the implications of assuming a connection between the supervisor's race, on the one hand, and perceptions of opportunities and fairness for Black workers, on the other? One inference that we do not wish to draw is that Black supervisors are the only ones who can promote positive job experiences. After all, the presence of a Black supervisor and the perception of racial justice might both be the consequence of actual racial equity on the part of management more generally. We think it plausible, however, to consider that the presence of Black supervisors helps lessen racial injustice.

One way that Black supervisors might lessen perceptions of racism is through their developmental work. Thomas (1990) and McGuire (chap. 6, this volume) have shown that greater trust exists between senior and junior people in helping relationships when they are matched on ethnicity. Because of this trust, Black workers may well experience a sense of well-being on the job when their supervisor is Black. It is possible, for example, that Black supervisors provide the added psychosocial support vital to Black employees who are working in an environment where racial discrimination is a real possibility. Furthermore, it is likely that through such relationships Black supervisors may serve as role models who impart survival techniques that can help combat what might otherwise be a difficult environment for Black employees. Finally, for workers everywhere, it may be a reassurance and an inspiration to see others of their own race in positions of authority.

These results also have implications specific to the European setting in which we collected our data. During the past few years, the media have widely publicized the racial conflicts occurring throughout the EU, including the deportation of ethnic and racial minorities and the escalating violence of Neo-Nazi attacks against ethnic minorities. It is probable that this heightened attention has had a negative impact on the comfort level White European managers experience in their dealings with Black British employees and vice versa. As we mentioned earlier, compared to other member states, Britain has the most extensive governmental legislation prohibiting racial discrimination, yet, people still perceive—and likely experience—racial discrimination. Thus, our data suggest that national antidiscrimination policies are necessary, even if not completely sufficient, to combat racism. At the very least such efforts can provide member states with avenues for dialogue based on inclusion as opposed to exclusion.

REFERENCES

Fernandez, J. P. (1993). *The diversity advantage: How American companies can outperform Japanese and European companies in the global marketplace.* New York: Lexington Books.

Forbes, I., & Meade, G. (1992). *Measure for measure: A comparative analysis of measures to combat racial discrimination in the member countries of the European community* (Research Series No. 1). University of Southampton, UK. Equal Opportunities Studies Group.

Stevenson, R. (1993, September 19). Racial tensions in London as Neo-Nazi joins election. *New York Times,* p. A10.

Thomas, D. A. (1990). The impact of race on managers' experiences of developmental relationships (mentoring and sponsorship): An intra-organizational study. *Journal of Organizational Behavior, 11,* 479 – 491.

9

Beyond the Simple Demography–Power Hypothesis: How Blacks in Power Influence White-Mentor–Black-Protégé Developmental Relationships

David A. Thomas
Harvard University

Over the last decade, concern about the availability and effectiveness of mentoring relationships for racial minorities has increased (see Ragins, 1997, for a review of the literature). Research on mentoring, as well as that examining boss–subordinate dyads (Tsui & O'Reilly, 1989) and social networks (Ibarra, 1995), has shown that the individual's racial identity and the racial composition of the dyad influence whether or not developmental relationships form and what types of support they provide when they do form. Despite the well-documented tendency of individuals to form relationships with people from the same identity groups (see Tsui, Egan, & O'Reilly, 1992, for a review of this literature), this research has shown that racial minorities are more likely than not to engage in developmental relationships with White seniors. Indeed, in some of my own earlier research I found that Blacks formed 75% of their within-company developmental relationships with Whites, mostly White men. Hence, much of the research on race and mentoring has centered on cross-race pairings (Thomas, 1990, 1993).

Scholars have paid little attention, however, to the contextual factors that influence the formation of cross-race developmental relationships. Therefore, we know little about, for example, what moves a cross-race boss–subordinate relationship beyond the required supervisory interactions to encompass the developmental functions of mentoring. In the literature, scholars have typically offered two simple, but not unrelated explanations for this phenomenon. The first involves the logic of simple demography: Because Whites predominate in the managerial ranks of most U.S. organizations, minorities have little choice but to seek developmental relationships with White seniors. Thus, the argument goes, when constrained people will form cross-race relationships. A second explanation for the prevalence of White-mentor–Black-protégé relationships emphasizes the power dimension of them: Because Whites hold most of the power in organizations, one is at a disadvantage in the distribution of rewards and opportunities if one lacks developmental relationships with Whites (e.g., Ragins, 1997).

Both explanations have intuitive appeal and likely represent an important piece of the story. Yet both rely on an instrumental calculus that fails to consider the complexity and range of motivations that exist in the formation of any developmental relationship. Moreover, they speak to the incentives of racial minorities but say little about why White managers might also be motivated to form these relationships.

This chapter is an attempt to move beyond the simple demography–power hypothesis to understand more about the processes that underlie the formation of cross-race developmental relationships, in particular the motivations White managers have for engaging in developmental relationships with Black protégés. I draw on both theory and data to develop this understanding. The theory I use is embedded intergroup relations (Alderfer & Smith, 1982; Thomas & Alderfer, 1989) applied to career dynamics. As a source of empirical examples, I draw primarily on a thematic analysis of qualitative data from three studies in which I interviewed parties to more than 50 cross-race relationships. These included interviews with both the junior and senior members of 22 cross-race developmental relationships in a corporation, interviews with 10 Black managers about their general career evolution and experiences with White mentors and protégés, and interviews with 10 Black and 10 White partners in large law firms in New York State.

AN EMBEDDED INTERGROUP PERSPECTIVE ON RACE RELATIONS IN ORGANIZATIONS

The central proposition on which this paper rests is that the presence of minorities in positions of organizational power and authority facilitates the formation of cross-race mentor–protégé relationships between White seniors and Black juniors. This proposition flows from Alderfer's embedded intergroup theory (Alderfer & Smith, 1982; Thomas & Alderfer, 1989). According to this theory, two types of groups exist in organizations: identity groups and organization groups (Alderfer, 1987). Members of identity groups share common biological characteristics, share equivalent historical experiences, and, as a result, tend to develop similar world views. The most commonly recognized identity groups are those based on race, ethnicity, family, gender, and age. Members of organization groups are assigned similar primary tasks, participate in comparable work experiences, and tend to develop common organizational views. Most often, organizational groupings are based on task, function, and hierarchy. Although organization group membership can change as people enter and exit organizations, identity group membership remains constant or, as with age, changes as the result of natural development rather than negotiation.

The theory is that individuals and organizations are constantly attempting, consciously and unconsciously, to manage real and potential conflicts arising from the interface between identity and organization group memberships. How racial tension manifests and how organization members attend to it depend on the pattern of intergroup embeddedness in the organization. Applied to race relations, embeddedness refers to the extent to which power differences between racial groups at the suprasystem level (i.e., society) are mirrored in the relations between those groups at the system (i.e., organization) and subsystem (i.e., work group or dyad) levels. The theory distinguishes between two types of embeddedness: *congruent embeddedness*, in which power differences between racial groups are consistent across the suprasystem, system, and subsystem levels; and *incongruent embeddedness*, in which power differences between racial groups vary across levels, in particular, in which power differences at the suprasystem level are inverted at the system and/or subsystem levels. The nature of racial group embeddedness influences relationships among individuals and among groups within the organization.

Applied to the situation of the White-mentor–Black-protégé dyad, this theory points to the congruence between the power relation in the dyad in which the White person as the senior party dominates, on the one hand, and the power relation in the larger society in which Whites generally hold more power and status, on the other. In between these two levels is the organization. The organization either mirrors the dyadic and societal power relationship between Whites and Blacks, as when positions of authority are filled predominantly by Whites, producing a situation of congruent embeddedness; or fails to mirror the dyadic and societal power relationship, as when positions of authority are filled in significant measure by Blacks, producing a situation of incongruent embeddedness. Figure 9.1 graphically illustrates these two situations. In the congruent situation, the theory predicts that protégés are acutely aware of the hierarchical differentiation along race lines in their mentoring relationships and may feel more obliged to accommodate the mentor and find it more difficult to assert themselves in such relationships. In the incongruent situation, the fact that there are Blacks in senior roles breaks with the general societal pattern of White dominance, which then has significant implications for the nature and

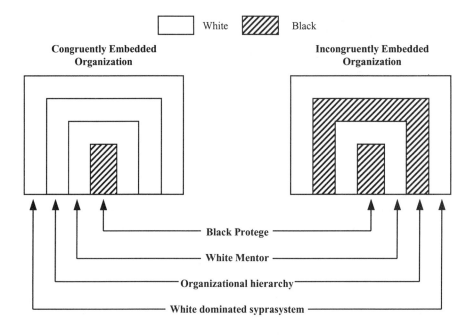

FIG. 9.1.   Racial group embeddedness for White-mentor–Black-protégé dyads.

quality of the dyadic relationship, such that Black protégés may feel freer to assert themselves in the relationships.

More generally, organizations in which race relations are congruent across subsystem, system, and suprasystem levels are likely to manage the interface between racial identity group and organizational group memberships based on an implicit and undiscussable set of values around race relations. These principles tend to reflect both the more powerful group's interests and the prevailing racial perspective of the suprasystem. In the context of U.S. race relations, the fact that Whites occupy roles of power and authority becomes a taken-for-granted aspect of the organization's culture. Assumptions of racial inferiority and performance expectations for people of color are likely to go unexamined, and people of color who exhibit outstanding performance are viewed as aberrations.

As the presence of Blacks in upper level positions of the organization increases, however, the organization becomes less congruent with the society within which it is embedded. As the correlation between racial group membership and hierarchical position in the organization diminishes, the likelihood of racial groups becoming locked into regressive projective patterns of ethnocentrism also diminishes. The presence of Blacks in legitimate positions of authority and power acts as a contextual cue that alters both Whites' and Blacks' implicit paradigms for racial group relations. This situation then becomes an important force in moderating the effects of the suprasystem on cross-race relationships in the organization.

The nature of racial group embeddedness therefore influences individuals' experiences of their own personal power positions in the system relative to members of other racial groups such that, as the system moves toward greater incongruity, more complex and less stereotypical race relations result, and people are both willing and able to engage more productively in cross-race relationships of all kinds. In the following sections I describe my observations over the course of my own research on cross-race mentorship of how increasingly incongruent embeddedness in organizations influences Whites' motivations to engage in developmental relationships with Blacks.

FINDINGS

I have organized my observations around three different organizational conditions, each reflecting a different point along a continuum of racial group embeddedness from less to more incongruent. The first condition involves Whites managing predominantly Black work groups in

White-controlled organizations, the second involves White managers in organizations in which Blacks hold significant positions of power and authority, and the third involves White managers in Black-controlled organizations.

Predominantly Black Work Groups in White-Controlled Organizations

In my research, I have encountered a number of situations in which Whites were managing or had at some point in their careers managed predominantly Black work groups in White-controlled organizations. It has been my observation that this situation, as compared to that in which Blacks comprise a minority of the work group, provides the opportunity for more and more meaningful contact between White managers and Black subordinates than is often the case when Blacks are in the minority. In addition, by virtue of their predominance in the work group, Blacks in this situation are often poised for entry into the managerial ranks, especially when the work of the group is more rather than less directly connected to the mission of the organization. As a result, feeder pools from which managers are chosen may contain numerous Black candidates. This can further enhance the quantity and quality of contact between White managers and their Black subordinates. Under these conditions, White managers' exposure to Blacks can break down the negative stereotyping of Blacks that often makes mentoring Blacks unattractive to Whites. The increased cross-racial contact in these work groups also facilitates the parties' developing a basis for identification on dimensions other than ascribed characteristics, such as race and sex. Finally, Whites who manage predominantly Black work groups may come to believe that the management structure should be more representative of the work force. Their response may be to take a personal interest in the recruitment and development of Black managers. The following case illustrates:

> After a promotion, Jack became the manager of a large unit that performed some rather routine but important functions on the operations side of the company. On arrival he found an organization with a majority of White male supervisors and a predominantly minority and female unionized work force. Most supervisors had been in the company for over 10 years, whereas many of the minorities were young. Union grievances were high, and racial tensions existed among the employees.

Jack began to think that the authority structure needed to reflect more of the unit's racial and gender composition. He set about identifying several people within the company, Blacks and women, who might be able to work in his unit as supervisors. He made sure they were competent and had good recommendations. Over time, he succeeded in bringing several of these people into his unit.

Jack took a personal interest in the career of each person he hired and developed particularly strong sponsor–protégé relations with two of his Blacks subordinates. His descriptions of these two protégés indicated that he was very open and was supportive of and critical to their promotions and selection for special developmental opportunities. On issues of race, both protégés felt he was open and noted that, when they presented problems to him that included conflicts with White peers, he probed them about whether they felt race was a significant factor.

When I interviewed Jack, he was no longer head of the department in operations and was instead heading a predominantly White male staff group. His experience with the predominantly Black unit had not moved him to articulate a need to increase the number of minorities in management throughout the company. This example suggests that context acts as a powerful cue in shaping managers' perceptions and agendas. Absent the context of a predominantly minority workforce beneath him, Jack no longer made diversity a major part of his agenda, despite his new organization's striking lack of it.

Blacks in Positions of Power and Authority in White-Controlled Organizations

When there are a number of Blacks in positions of power and authority, race relations in the organization become less congruent with race relations in the wider society. This situation has implications for both the quality and quantity of developmental relationships between White seniors and Black juniors. In particular, I have observed five ways in which Black senior managers in such organizations have directly and indirectly encouraged the formation of White-mentor–Black-protégé developmental relationships. Four relate to senior Blacks' ability to influence their White peers and subordinates to sponsor and mentor Blacks, and the fifth relates to their direct involvement with Black protégés. I detail each of these in the following sections.

Black Managers Serve as Sounding Boards for White Peers. In my data, I found numerous examples of Black managers encouraging and assisting their White peers' development of effective cross-race relations by discussing with them their interactions with their Black protégés. The value of this kind of help is significant given previous findings that majority group members frequently come to cross-race encounters with little experience in them (Thomas & Alderfer, 1989). For example, I found that parties to cross-race relationships were often uncomfortable discussing issues of race and acted to suppress such discourse (Thomas, 1993). Dealing with these issues of ignorance and discomfort can be particularly challenging in the context of a superior–subordinate dyad. Here, the pressure is often on the White senior to set the tone and boundary of the relationship. It may feel to the White senior that it is—and in fact, it may well be—inappropriate to use the time with the protégé to explore or educate him- or herself about race. In the following case example from my research, Susan, a Black manager, described an instance early in her career when Joan, a Black manager who was senior to her at the time, facilitated the development of her relationship with Deborah, her White boss—a relationship that eventually became a mentor–protégé connection.

> When Joan [senior Black woman], Deborah [senior White woman], and I [junior Black woman] were working on a project together, we became a very close-knit group. But Deborah sometimes had a tendency to misinterpret some things I said and did. Because Joan and Deborah were friends, however, and Deborah is an open type of person, she would often ask Joan, "Am I reading this right? Is this what's happening? Is this what's going on? Should I get involved here, or is this something she needs to further develop?" Likewise, I would go to Joan and say, "This is what she [Deborah] wants, and this is what I've done." Joan would go over it with me and highlight some areas I needed to work on further, and give me a direct critique.... So, I would say it was the direct interface between Joan and Deborah that helped to cultivate the relationship between Deborah and me.

White mentors told related stories of how they enlisted the assistance of Black peers to get help selecting and promoting Black protégés and figuring out approaches to various issues in working with them. Without these Black managers, these cross-race developmental relationships may not have formed or may have been of limited benefit to the protégé's career success.

Black Managers Serve as Models of Black Success for White Managers.   Senior Black managers also influenced their White peers by providing a model of Black competence and success at the executive levels. An important factor in determining how a sponsor or mentor may manage the relationship with and career of a protégé has to do with where he or she sees the protégé fitting into the organization. If a White sponsor is unable to see a Black person as a general manager or vice president of the company, then he or she may push the protégé away from the managerial track and into a more technical field, or away from line functions into staff work (Collins, 1996). The presence of Blacks in positions of authority, however, may provide models of Black success and thereby positively influence White peers' expectations for Black protégés.

The White sponsor or mentor may also associate less risk with sponsorship of a Black protégé. The importance of this modeling function as a motivator for Whites was underscored in comments by several senior-level Whites I interviewed. For example, a White corporate executive who had recently sponsored a Black protégé for promotion to a senior management level felt that the protégé's success or failure affected whether other Blacks would be sponsored by Whites to that level. Similarly, several White law partners I interviewed described how seeing Blacks in other firms successfully move up the ranks to partner convinced them that it could be done. They also realized that in order for the Black associates at their firms to succeed, partners needed to invest personally in those relationships. One described this as a change from the "prove-it-to-me" school of thought to the "investment" school. In the former, the minority had to defy the negative presumption. In the latter, the firm's partners had to invest in the individual based on a positive presumption of ability to succeed. The fact of earlier Blacks' success made the latter seem a more viable strategy.

Black Managers Encourage White Protégés to Mentor Black Subordinates.   Senior manager and executive-level Blacks also influenced the formation of cross-race developmental relationships by increasing the likelihood that their own White protégés would engage in developmental relationships with their Black subordinates. Some Black managers viewed their choices to sponsor Whites as directly related to their own roles in developing Blacks. They chose White protégés who demonstrated competence and whom they viewed as being progressive on issues of race, with the idea that these people would be more likely to serve as mentors and sponsors to Blacks below them. For example, Sidney, a Black male executive, described his philosophy in choosing White protégés and the results of his mentoring a White woman as follows:

> [When I look to sponsor Whites, I look for someone who] couples competence with a desire to be part of my agenda, and that includes the improvement of race relations. My sense is that there should be a reward for that kind of behavior. In order for that kind of behavior to be reinforced, there has to be a person or persons able to support those people. I view myself as someone with the connections and resources to do that effectively.

> She [his White protégé] has done very good work for me. She was also instrumental in getting a first-level Black woman promoted and another Black woman promoted to third level. That behavior suggests support for my agenda and begets support from me.

Sidney's strategy appeared to have worked. His protégé was instrumental in the promotion of two Black women within her department. As part of my research, I interviewed his protégé and indeed found that she exhibited behavior, articulated positions, and expressed commitments consistent with Sidney's view that he chose Whites who would actively support and contribute to the improvement of race relations in the company.

Black Managers Encourage White Subordinates to Mentor Blacks. When Blacks were well-placed in the organization's hierarchy, they influenced not only their White protégés but their White subordinates more generally to mentor and sponsor Blacks. Greg, a White mentor, described how he was at first resistant to working with David, his Black subordinate, when Bill, his Black boss, put David in his group over his objections. Bill thought Greg was a good manager and developer of people and that if he could overcome his resistance, he would provide David with the coaching, exposure, and skill development he needed. At the time of my interviews, both Greg and David felt theirs was a well-developed mentor–protégé relationship. Greg, however, still harbored negative feelings that Bill had forced David on him and felt that affirmative action held back his own career. When asked why he decided to support David's development, he gave this rationale:

> I have no control over David. He's in the high-potential program. Bill will just reach in and move him. For example, Bill called him in one day and asked where he'd like his next job to be. I mean, it's because they are both Black.

I mentor because I think mentoring is a supervisor's job. I can't hold my feelings [about what Bill did] against David.... What do I get out of [supporting David]? I'm not taking a risk. It's a success for me if I can push people like David up. His connection to Bill has already benefitted me.

Greg's statements illustrate his liberal, humanitarian ideology and his commitment as a manager. More important, Greg believed that David would advance, partly because of his connection to Bill, and that this advancement would ultimately help his own career as well.

Black Managers Serve as Early Mentors to Black Protégés.   Black protégés in the three studies I conducted frequently cited the importance of Black managers and partners as mentors. Likewise, many of the senior level Blacks I interviewed mentioned the importance they placed on developing younger Black subordinates. Most of these mentors were active in Black professional organizations, yet all had themselves benefitted from some form of White mentorship or sponsorship.

One might wonder how same-race developmental relationships between Blacks increase the likelihood of cross-race relationship formation. There are two ways in which this happens. First, these relationships can help to support a Black protégé through an initial period of transition into the organization and allow him or her the opportunity to establish a track record. Second, these relationships avail the protégé of his or her own network of mentors, sponsors, and informational contacts.

Dickens and Dickens (1982) noted that Blacks often experience a period early in their careers when they become disillusioned and even angry about the role of race as a negative drag on their career aspirations and experiences. A critical factor in successfully passing through this period so it does not lead to self-limiting behavior is support from other Blacks. Black managers often serve in the critical capacity as mentors and counselors to young protégés by offering understanding, encouragement, and a balanced perspective. For example, they provide information that makes the young protégé less vulnerable to the effects of being outside the informal networks that can prove hard to penetrate initially. By aiding Black managers through these first phases, senior Black managers can prepare them to make the best of opportunities to gain needed career support from Whites. When this form of Black-on-Black mentoring is in place, the probability increases that the Black protégé will develop a record of performance that builds confidence and makes him or her attractive to others—in particular, to Whites—as someone in whom to invest.

Developmental relationships with Black executives and senior managers can also help to reduce the alienation from the authority structure that more junior Blacks are likely to feel in predominantly White organizations. This support reduces the possibility that the Black protégé will withdraw from the organization or fail to cultivate important developmental relationships. These relationships often represent to the young protégé the possibility of successfully negotiating the challenges and complexities race brings to the pursuit of career aspirations and provide opportunities for modeling the ability to develop genuine, nonexploitative, mentoring and sponsorship relations with Whites.

Black-Controlled Organizations

Black-controlled organizations are those in which Blacks have a controlling interest and occupy the majority of the significant policy-making positions. No research to date has been done on the experiences of Whites working in such organizations. This configuration of racial group embeddedness constitutes the most incongruent condition for organizations relative to the wider society.

Interviews with Black managers in Black-dominated organizations indicate that, under these conditions, Whites are likely to engage in developmental relations with Black protégés. The case of Claudia, a Black manager, and Delores, her White mentor, illustrates how this form of racial embeddedness influences the formation of cross-race developmental relationships:

Claudia met Delores when she was hired as a teacher in the daycare center that Delores directed. Claudia answered an advertisement for the job and was hired on the spot. The center served minority children and was a project sponsored by the local Urban League [a national Black civil rights and social service organization]. Delores reported to the agency's director, a Black male.

Over time, Claudia and Delores developed a very close mentor–protégé relationship. Claudia described herself as idolizing Delores in the early years of their relationship. Delores was very much a feminist and raised Claudia's consciousness as a woman. In evaluating how Delores handled race, Claudia felt Delores was hesitant. The two of them did not discuss the influence of race on their own relationship until Claudia forced the issue.

Delores did not get along well with her Black boss, and Claudia found herself sometimes acting as an intermediary. This helped Delores manage her Black male boss, and it gave Claudia visibility and exposure in the organization. Claudia ultimately became Delores' assistant. Some of her peers, who were White, showed signs of jealousy but did not mistreat her. She sometimes wondered herself why Delores had chosen her as the "heir apparent" over her other staff.

I do not mean to suggest by this story that Delores was insincere in her relationship with Claudia. Yet it does appear that having a Black protégé served some instrumental purposes for Delores in the management of her relationship with the organization and especially with her Black male boss. Even her first act of support, hiring Claudia, appeared connected to the client and organizational context in which the program was embedded. However, this relationship was an important one both emotionally and instrumentally for Claudia as well.

SUMMARY

March and Simon (1958) noted that organizational behavior is managed not so much by constant directives from the top but rather by the organization's structure and the ways in which it shapes and restricts the behavioral choices available to managers. The theory and empirical examples I have presented here show how the organization's structure—in particular, who has power—can encourage the formation of developmental relationships between White seniors and Black juniors. In particular, I have observed that situations in which Blacks have or are poised to enter positions of power and authority: 1) decrease the White manager's sense of risk in mentoring or sponsoring a member of a different race, 2) increase the White manager's perception of the appropriateness of placing Black people in positions of greater responsibility, 3) increase the White manager's perception that some benefit to him or her will derive from engaging in the cross-race developmental relationship, and 4) increase the protégé's view that attainment of desired outcomes is possible by engaging in such relationships with Whites.

In the context of race relations in U.S. culture, the experiences of non-Whites in positions of power is the exception rather than the rule. Yet based on my research, it seems that altering the dominant pattern in organizations influences cross-race relationship formation even when the larger societal power relationships are not fully inverted. Both the possibility of inverting the dominant pattern and the actual experience of working within the new pattern can influence Whites' racial attitudes and cognitions. This provides opportunities for them to learn both cognitively and experientially about race relations and examine their own racial perspective as well as that of the organization.

REFERENCES

Alderfer, C. P. (1987). An intergroup perspective on group dynamics. In J. Lorsch (Ed.), *Handbook of organizational behavior* (pp. 190–219). Englewood Cliffs, NJ: Prentice-Hall.

Alderfer, C. P., & Smith, K.K. (1982). Studying intergroup relations embedded in organizations. *Administrative Science Quarterly, 27*, 35–65.

Collins, S. M. (1996). *Black corporate executives: The making and breaking of Black middle class.* Philadelphia, PA: Temple University Press.

Dickens, F., & Dickens, J. B. (1982). *The Black manager: Making it in the corporate world.* New York: AMACOM.

Ibarra, H. (1995). Race, opportunity, and diversity of social circles in managerial networks. *Academy of Management Journal, 38*, 673–703.

March, J., & Simon, H. (1958). *Organizations.* New York: Wiley.

Ragins, B. R. (1997). Diversified mentoring relationships in organizations: A power perspective. *Academy of Management Review, 22*, 482–521.

Thomas, D. A. (1990). The impact of race on managers' experiences of developmental relationships. *Journal of Organizational Behavior, 11*, 479–492.

Thomas, D. A. (1993). Racial dynamics in cross-race developmental relationships. *Administrative Science Quarterly, 38*, 169–194.

Thomas, D. A., & Alderfer, C. (1989). The influence of race on career dynamics theory and research on minority career experiences. In M. B. Arthur, D. T. Hall, & B. S. Lawrence (Eds.), *Handbook of career theory* (pp. 133–158). Cambridge, England: Cambridge University Press.

Tsui, A. S., Egan, T. D., & O'Reilly, C. A. (1992). Being different: Relational demography and organizational attachment. *Administrative Science Quarterly, 37*, 549–579.

Tsui, A. S., & O'Reilly, C. A. (1989). Beyond simple demographic effects: the importance of relational demography in superior-subordinate dyads. *Academy of Management Journal, 32*, 402–423.

III

Experiential Perspectives

10

Testing Theory by Practice

Ellen McCambley
Bell Atlantic Corporation

A valid theory is a thing of beauty. Over the last 10 or 15 years, social scientists have articulated some interesting theories about developmental relationships in organizations. Following the initiative of Boston University Professor Kathy Kram, they have defined developmental relationships as those in which a senior person in an organization renders help to a more junior person, and they have proposed that developmental relationships can be beneficial to the junior person, the senior person, and the organization. Even while acknowledging the costs of developmental or mentoring relationships, theorists have sent a bold and clear message to industry: Mentoring relationships can benefit everyone in the organization.

The theory sounds good, but is it valid? As the other chapters in this book make clear, many of the hypotheses social scientists have advanced have received abundant confirmation in the ways social scientists traditionally confirm or refute hypotheses. They have operationalized the concepts and quantitatively assessed the relationships among them. However, researchers have yet to explore whether formally arranged mentoring associations between junior and senior people are as beneficial as those that occur naturally.

A few years ago, Catalyst, a not-for-profit organization that works with corporate America to make positive change for women, published an informative booklet outlining concepts and describing very briefly 10 formal mentoring programs that work well (Catalyst, 1993). The news looked good, but one could not tell much about each program in the few pages allocated. Around the same time as the Catalyst publication, an in-depth study of Motorola Corporation described an experiment with a formal mentoring program that was largely unsuccessful (Caruso, 1992).

The purpose of this chapter is to chronicle another company's efforts to promote developmental relationships through formal, company-sponsored programs. The company is NYNEX (now known as Bell Atlantic). At the time of this undertaking, NYNEX provided local telephone service to New York and New England, employed about 65,000 people, and had eight levels of management, from first-line supervisor to the president of the company. Traditionally, the higher levels of management have been the domain of White males. In other parts of the company there are male and female "ghettos," such as network operations, which has been principally male, and operator and customer services, which has been principally female.

NYNEX implemented two programs between 1992 and 1997 designed to foster developmental relationships. These programs sought to open the gates of upper management to people who were not White males. One of these programs was a mentoring program, initiated by the Association of NYNEX Women (ANW), which was designed to foster networking opportunities between senior and junior women. The other program, called the Accelerated Succession Affirmative Action Pilot, or ASAP, also grew out of ANW and was designed to increase the numbers of women and people of color in the feeder pools for management succession. One of ASAP's components was designed to facilitate what Thomas (1990) and Crosby (chap. 1, this volume) call "sponsorship." Its primary purpose was to foster developmental relationships in which senior people would provide instrumental help to junior people, in particular women and minorities. Both programs began at the grass roots level and, when they proved successful, garnered corporate support. I know both programs intimately because I helped to create and administer them.

Catalyst's (1993) booklet describes both programs briefly. In this chapter, I describe them in more detail. Both programs support the hypothesis that developmental relationships help employees—junior and senior—and help the corporation.

MENTORING CIRCLES

In 1992 I became the President of the Association of NYNEX Women (ANW), a voluntary organization of dues-paying members. In 1991, we had conducted a strategic planning session to address issues concerning women in the workplace. At the top of the list was the issue of mentoring. The first problem we faced was the limited number of senior women who could provide traditional one-to-one mentoring relationships to more junior women. One member of the Executive Committee, who had had experience with consciousness-raising groups in the late 1960s and early 1970s, suggested initiating what she at first called discussion circles. These later became known as mentoring circles. In a mentoring circle, two to four senior women would join a circle, or group, with 8 to 10 junior women. ANW adopted this suggestion and assigned at least two senior women to each circle to serve as mentors. This number assured that, given the responsibilities and hectic schedules of the senior women, at least one mentor would be present at any circle meeting. Following the lessons of the 1960s and 1970s, each group was to meet on a regular basis with assigned topics and the assurance of confidentiality. We formed a pilot group of eight women: six at second level and two at fourth level. The pilot group was to meet for six months and then report back to the executive board.

When I think back on that moment, a certain movie springs to mind. In the movie was a great scene in which the hero, in search of the Holy Grail, finds himself on the edge of a deep abyss. He remembers a verse that he had read that said that he must make a leap of faith. He steps out into seeming nothingness and finds a path. This incredible scene makes me think of the diversity efforts at NYNEX. Sometimes you have to put everything that you know behind you and just take that leap of faith. When you do, incredible things happen.

Our leap was not without direction, however. We put together some initial guidelines, at the core of which were some definite rules. First, we decided that the circle would be designed to meet for a 6-month period, so the obligation was not indefinite. Second, meeting times had a regularity. They would take place before or after work or during the lunch hour. For the first five or six meetings, when trust was being established, the groups were to meet once a week. Later, they could switch to once a month. Participants would decide on the discussion topic a week in advance. Third, time boundaries were not flexible. Each meeting was to last one hour—no more, no less. Each group had a timekeeper who made sure that everyone in the circle had a chance to talk. Fourth, everything that was said was confidential because trust was at the heart of what we were doing.

We also had guidelines about group composition. We recommended that no one be in a circle with her immediate boss. We wanted the junior and the senior women to be able to let down their guards. Being in a circle with one's immediate supervisor or one's direct report would have jeopardized that. For this reason, we implemented a skip-level approach. One group might include two to four mentors from management level four and six to eight women from management level two. Another might have two mentors from level five and six to eight women from level three. We also tried to compose groups with women from different business units within NYNEX.

The final guidelines of our pilot project concerned closure. We made sure that everyone understood that the first commitment was for only 6 months and that after 6 months everything would be renegotiated. Ahead of time, we established a review procedure and developed expectations about what to do if a group got into trouble. Most groups kept strictly to the guidelines for the first four or five meetings and then made some minor modifications. Groups that ran into trouble were those that did not follow the guidelines.

Good News

The reports that came to the ANW executive committee from the pilot group after the first 6-month trial were extremely positive. Attendance was high, and the group wanted to continue to meet. So glowing were the reports that we immediately decided to create additional circles. As the months passed, and we heard reports from the groups, we realized we had a winner!

After one year, 8 of the original 10 groups were still going strong, and we had a waiting list of over 50 members seeking to join a group. Participants spoke of the support they'd received on both personal and professional levels. We found that the coaching and counseling traveled up as well as down the corporate ladder. Senior and junior women's increased contact with one another enhanced both groups' opportunities for career change and advancement.

Most exciting was what was going on inside the groups during the meeting times. After the initial two or three meetings, the barriers had broken down. Sharing was equal. I know from my own circle that after two months of being together, we became very collegial. Even though we still knew who the senior managers were, when we came together in our circle we were simply women in the workplace facing issues and working with one another to solve them.

One time, for example, the topic for my group was sexism. A senior woman shared an anecdote regarding a meeting in which she was—of course!—the only senior woman in a room full of men. She had a lovely figure, and one man was blatantly staring at her. Finally, she told us, she looked down at her blouse with some concern and said, "Did I spill something on my blouse?" Needless to say, he got the message! Hearing a story like that was instructional for everyone in the circle.

Because the circles were composed of women, it is not surprising that breasts were a topic of discussion in another group as well. One of the younger women had just had a child and was dealing with nursing issues. As there was no lounge, she had to go to the ladies' room to express her milk. Circle members were appalled that there was no adequate place, other than a ladies' room stall, for this young woman to express her milk. Someone suggested going to the people in Human Resources. The Human Resources people did a quick study and concluded that it would not be cost-effective to build a nursing room. One of woman in the circle remarked that each bathroom had a small anteroom with a counter, a mirror, and an electrical outlet. A $4.00 shower curtain and a $3.00 extension rod provided the privacy needed. We put notices up around the building to let everyone know what we were doing. Voila! The solution cost $7.00, and it was effective, cheap, and simple.

The point is that people need to articulate their problems in order to find solutions. Yet people with a vulnerability need to know that it is safe to discuss their problems. They need to know that they will be heard and not blamed.

The advice in the circles did not flow in one direction only. Gradually, as people came to trust each other, the status barriers came down. We began to mentor one another. In one circle, a participant needed to undergo a mastectomy. Someone else in the circle who was younger and less senior had been through the same ordeal and was able to provide advice and counsel. Many workplace issues arose for the senior woman with cancer, about health and appearance and even about medical appointments, and she was able to receive support and good advice in the circle.

After the first year, the mentors, all of whom were third- and fourth-level women, expressed a desire to be mentored themselves. Because we had so few women at fifth and sixth level, we decided to establish a few upper level that which would include both senior women and senior men as the mentors. This worked to everyone's benefit. Not only were the mentors mentored, but they were able to help senior management take an honest look at a lot of issues that were sensitive or uncomfortable. In most circles, for example, the third- and fourth-level mentors would ask which issues the circle would like them to bring up the ladder to the attention of senior management. Sending information upstream isn't always easy, and the trusting environment of the circles was crucial.

How the company handled flextime illustrates the benefit of upward-flowing information. At a time when the majority of the corporation's executives were White men whose wives did not go to a workplace outside the home each day and the lower level of management was composed of working parents of both sexes, the mentoring circle dialogues helped the executives understand what was going on and to re-examine their own preconceptions about, for example, face time—the time deemed required for people to be present and visible at work—which often works to the disadvantage of women who have primary responsibility for home life and children.

As it turned out, the company has benefitted from the mentoring circles in other ways as well. The breaking down of barriers and the development of friendships across units and across levels, and an understanding of one another and one another's jobs are all real corporate assets. This fact was brought home to me at our semiannual breakfast for mentors. One vice president stated that in the past, when he needed a good manager to fill a slot, he examined all the people he knew. He admitted, at his level, most people he knew were White men. Being a mentor in a circle with six women two levels lower had broadened his horizon. Now, he stated, when he learned of an opening, he had a broader, more diverse pool from which to select.

However, not everything worked perfectly from the start. We had much to learn, but we were able to do so even from the problems we encountered. Delegates from the ANW attended group meetings and gauged the temperature of the sessions. Minor modifications needed to be made in all groups. In addition, as a result of the self-reflective meetings, two circles disbanded themselves. Although members liked their circles, they felt the circles did not measure up on the index of trust. In at least one group, one mentors' inability to let down her defenses interfered with open communication. Most members of the disbanded circles joined other circles.

The success of the pilot project encouraged us to form more mentoring circles. The vice president of Human Resources hosted a breakfast twice a year for the senior participants   the mentors—to thank them for their participation and to give them the opportunity to share experiences and concerns.

When the circle concept was introduced in New England, it came under Human Resources, not the ANW. They decided to include men in the circles as well. The circles there are equally successful but with a much different dynamic.

Over the years, it has been clear that one major benefit of the mentoring circles is that they expand people's networks. In my own circle, for example, I met eight other women whom I had never met before, and we became allies. Many times I would became aware of a job opening, and I called someone from my circle to ask if she knew about the opportunity and to encourage her to submit her resume. In my circle, and perhaps in others, we circulated our resumés to one another and spent time discussing our development plans and opportunities. This exchange was especially helpful when NYNEX entered its downsizing mode.

The networks we developed from our mentoring circles also sometimes helped with personal difficulties. I once experienced some difficulty with a car dealership. I phoned one of my mentors and described the problem. She called the dealership's headquarters and got the desired result. She was really like a big sister to me in that regard.

For the first time we had an old boys' network among the girls. The networks were not just loose associations among colleagues. Rather, they generated the kind of committed friendships and close understandings that generally come only from having lived in the same neighborhoods or having gone to the same schools. One way that capable senior men and women enjoy career success is from solid years of friendship and trust. The mentoring circles enabled just such friendships.

Words of Advice

From my experiences at NYNEX, do I have any additional advice? Yes, I do. Three points may help an organization enjoy all the benefits of mentoring circles but be spared potential costs.

First, keep the circles small. Waiting lists may be long, but the company should avoid the temptation to let a group exceed 12 people. It is also important to plan for some attrition. If you aim for a group of 8 to 10, it's best to start with 12.

Second, guidelines should be as firm as they can be without being rigid. Rules should be explicit about the expected longevity of the group, confidentiality, group composition, and the timing of meetings. There must also be clarity among group members about each other's expectations for sharing the floor. If possible, an orientation session with mentors is helpful to supplement the written rules. During this orientation mentors should learn

that their role is not to fix everything or to be perfect and that they must follow the same guidelines as everyone else. They should be clear that if they
have something to offer from their own experiences, good; if not, they must-
n't feel as if they have to say anything.

Finally, although it is helpful, official corporate support is not a require-
ment. ANW initiated the circles in a grass-roots effort and conducted them
for over a year on a strictly unofficial basis. Mentoring circles involve a lot of
emotion, a lot of what social scientists call socioemotional content
(McGuire, chap. 6, this volume) or psychosocial support (Crosby, chap. 1,
this volume). Having the blessing of the organization is good, but it is important not to let the organization's bureaucracy engulf these efforts. When it
comes to emotion, people want to feel they have choices. Kathy Kram
(1985), who may be credited with making mentoring a more visible corporate strategy, cautioned against the creation of mandatory mentoring programs in corporate America. She had a good point. Dictating trust and
openness does not seem to be a successful strategy.

ACCELERATED SUCCESSION
AFFIRMATIVE ACTION PILOT

Although I caution companies about trying to institute mandatory
mentoring programs, I highly recommend that they create formal, mandatory sponsorship programs. As compared to a mentor, who provides
socioemotional support to the protégé, a sponsor is someone who provides
instrumental help (Crosby, chap. 1, this volume; Thomas, 1990).

One drawback of the mentoring circles is that they comprised almost exclusively White women, which was the composition of ANW. Women of
color belonged to the Hispanic Support Organization (HSO), the Asian Focus Group (AFG), or the Multicultural Managers' Association (MMA).
ANW recognized this shortcoming and, working in a consortium with
other voluntary associations at NYNEX and with senior management,
strove for greater inclusivity. A specific program that ANW helped nourish
was the ASAP—Accelerated Succession Affirmative Action Pilot—program, which was in place from 1992 to 1994.

ASAP contained three main phases: selection, teamwork, and sponsorship. During the first phase, a selection committee recruited and selected
for inclusion in the program ethnic minority employees and White women
employees whom committee members felt had the potential for further career growth. During phase two, which lasted 6 months, candidates joined

one of seven teams whose purpose was to work on a human resource problem and make a final report to the CEO. In phase three, candidates were assigned a senior management sponsor. ASAP candidates, who were nontraditional managers, looked different, spoke differently, laughed differently, and told different stories to illustrate points. The role of the senior management sponsor was to establish rapport with the candidate and, as a role model, to give the candidate exposure to upper management, show him or her the ropes, and demonstrate how best to negotiate the unwritten rules of the organization. Phase three lasted for one full year. Since the formal end of the pilot, Human Resources has kept track of the careers of the participants and prepared follow-up reports periodically.

ASAP, like the mentoring circles, provides concrete validation of the proposition that developmental relationships are good for both individuals and the corporation. Like the mentoring circles, ASAP demonstrated the applicability of academic wisdom in a real world setting, as the following historical highlights of the ASAP program illustrate.

Phase One: Recruitment

At the start of the pilot, I was both president of ANW and project leader for ASAP. I strongly recommended open enrollment, similar to a program initiated by the women of color employee resource group at USWest. During the recruitment phase for their program, they had put the word out to all women of color in USWest and encouraged self-nominations. They winnowed down the original 2,000 applicants to 50 final participants. I believed that NYNEX could do the same.

The Human Resources Department felt differently. They believed that the newness of the initiative meant that we needed to use procedures that felt familiar to people at NYNEX: They wanted to institute the more traditional practice of officer nominations. One problem with officer nominations was that officers were far removed from the candidates we were seeking. ASAP intended to find candidates at second level who were ready, willing, and able to assume third-level responsibilities. Third level is historically where management succession begins. Because the officers are at sixth level, however, their knowledge of people three levels below is dependent upon their managers' impressions. If their managers had been able to identify and promote a diverse mix, we wouldn't have needed ASAP. This was a real conundrum. Nevertheless, they decided to institute officer nominations as the primary method of recruitment. In addition to these nominations, however, they also solicited candidates from each employee resource groups including the ANW, in order to ensure a diverse mix.

With some gentle persuasion, I managed to convince the ANW Executive Committee that, even though the corporation as a whole would not have self-nomination, we should give this option to our members. We notified all our members that we had been asked to nominate at least five members for the Pilot and asked for self-nominations. Fifty members applied, and we created a screening board that selected the final candidates to be nominated by ANW.

Two benefits came from our insistence on self-nominations. First, we discovered some excellent candidates whom we wouldn't have seen otherwise. I recall one woman who did not look very impressive on paper. Her interview was not going very well, but when we asked her to tell us one way she had shown leadership, she told us about her community and civic work outside the company, and it was clear that she had high potential. She was selected for the program, and she did extremely well both during and after her participation in ASAP.

The second benefit of the self-nomination method was that ANW learned a lot about process. Wisdom, it is said, comes from experience, and experience comes from mistakes. We gained a lot of wisdom! When we announced our pick of six candidates to the association as a whole, turmoil ensued. Many members felt that by screening out candidates who had self-nominated, we were doing just what we had perceived the corporation to have done: deny opportunity. Under my leadership, we held a special session for all members during which the ANW selection panel explained how we had made the decisions. We gave examples of application letters written in pencil; applications with no resumé attached; and answers to the question, "how do you feel participation in this program will benefit you?" such as, "not much; too little, too late." I should note that both of my senior mentors attended this meeting to provide support. During the discussion they explained to disappointed applicants how reasonable the selection committee's stance seemed to them and asked what the group felt the next step should be. The members present concurred that some form of professional development and career counseling was needed for the membership as a whole. They suggested that ANW establish a professional development committee to provide these services. The board agreed, and this committee is still in effect today.

Using officer-, employee-resource-group-, and self-nominations, we had a final count of 300 nominees for the pilot. The selection team, of which I was a member, interviewed the nominees and from this group selected 48 final candidates to participate in the pilot: Ten White women and 38 minority men and women. When selecting the ASAP candidates, we were very clear with them that the program carried no guarantees of promotion. The point of the program was to gain exposure to more senior management and to acquire new skills. We discouraged people from applying who did not want to risk the effort without assurances of a concrete payoff. Of course, behind closed doors, I made it clear that the purpose of the pilot was to increase the numbers of White women and minorities in the feeder pool for management succession, and although I would never use the P-word around the candidates, if promotion were not a part of our strategy, I felt we were wasting our time.

Phase Two: Team Work

Several commentators have noticed a catch-22 in corporate life. Often, to apply for a position you need a certain type of experience, but the only way to get the experience, it seems, is to get the job. ASAP was designed to allow minority men and White and minority women a way out of this catch-22.

As project manager, I met with the program participants in August, 1993, and told them their assignment was to work in teams on issues of crucial interest to the company and then to make a presentation to top management. Each team was assigned a senior management sponsor. Over a 6-month period, the team members were given one Friday each month on company time to work together with each other and, for a couple of hours, with their sponsor. All other times, they had to meet on their own. In addition, an administrator was available to consult with teams and help them stay on track.

The problems to which they were assigned were not just make-work; they were critical issues affecting equal opportunity. For example, teams addressed issues such as management succession, the appraisal process, recruitment, the Americans with Disabilities Act, and work–family issues. Each team had to do its own research and devise its own presentation.

There were a couple of reasons why we decided, in effect, to throw the teams into the water and let them sink or swim. One was the company's confidence in the candidates. These people did not need motivation. They were oozing motivation; what they needed was an opportunity to develop skills and obtain exposure. The second reason was that we wanted the candidates to experience the realities of life as a district manager who is often thrown a problem with a mandate to figure out the nature of the problem and develop a solution. Like district managers, the candidates had to put in the extra time required to do the job on their own.

One objective indicator of the success of the second phase was the outstanding performance of the presenting groups. The chairman and CEO of the company declared himself very favorably impressed and asked to be included in future briefings about the career developments of ASAP participants. His sponsorship proved invaluable to the pilot's ultimate success. In addition, a host of vice presidents and other senior people also expressed enthusiasm. Many were then willing to act as one-on-one sponsors to the program participants.

Other indicators came from the testimonials of the participants. Almost all participants learned a great deal about effective group functioning. One group, for example, had a very assertive member who became the leader of the group. No one liked his style, however, and after a month the group did what many unhappy groups do: They became passive-aggressive and uncooperative. In frustration, the group leader stormed out of a meeting. The rest of the group members came to me for help. In my administrative role, I told them that they had created the problem, and it was now their responsibility to solve it. They had to cooperate to get him back and work through their conflicts. They learned how to handle their own emotions, and they learned how to deal with one another. They learned what some of their strengths and their weaknesses were, and then they began to work more effectively with one another.

Other participants undertook to improve themselves when feedback from the group indicated a problem. Most commonly, problems centered on communication. Two teams included silent members. One young woman recognized how her shyness interfered with her participation and asked her teammates for help. They made her team leader, and, of course, she not only stepped up to the bar, she surpassed it. In another case, an Asian American man was surprised by the feedback that he was too quiet. He appealed to the Asian Focus Group, and they elected him president for a year, during which he had to conduct formal meetings and represent the group at all functions. He also exceeded expectations.

Another participant, a young Black woman, related that when she had joined the company 6 years earlier, she had been told that she was bright, that she was a go-getter, that she was really going to move ahead, that she had potential. As she observed her follow ASAPers, she perceived that some of them could, in her words, "run circles around me." She adopted the more senior women of color as her role models, and set herself a rigorous course of self-improvement.

By all accounts, phase two of ASAP was a success. With very little investment in terms of time and company resources, a number of very talented people had received excellent training and gained important exposure. Their commitment to the company and to each other was strong.

Phase Three: One-on-One Sponsorship

With the final phase of the pilot came more challenges and more successes. In phase three, each candidate worked one-on-one with a senior sponsor. The goals were to consolidate the gains the candidates had made in communication skills (including self-presentation) and networking and to introduce the candidates to some political realities of life in a corporation. Both the sponsor and the candidate received administrative support for their efforts in this regard.

What happened with one of the pairs illustrates the heartache and delights of phase three of ASAP. A young ethnic minority man with long hair and a beard was assigned to a senior (White male) officer. My first clue that the arrangement was not working well came when the candidate barged into my office after his first meeting with his officer-sponsor and declared that he could not work with the senior person to whom he'd been assigned. I told the candidate I'd look into it. I met with the sponsor and, although he was a bit staid, it was my sense that he had the best interests of the candidate in mind. I went to the candidate and told him that his sponsor had a great track record of bringing along people with nontraditional backgrounds (which was true) and that he, the sponsor, would probably be very eager to work well with the candidate if only he would provide some behavioral reassurances. Once both sides made an effort, great changes began to take place. The sponsor took the young man under his wing; the young man opened himself to learning from his sponsor. Within a year of the program's ending, the young man was promoted and moved to the territory he desired in order to be close to his family.

In addition, innovative arrangements happened when, for example, some women candidates wanted more contact with their male sponsors. Because we did not have enough senior women to act as sponsors for the junior women, we made a few cross-sex pairings. One junior woman felt that a lot was happening on the golf course and that she was excluded. She believed that her sponsor did not offer to take her golfing alone because he was afraid it would not look proper. She suggested they team up with a fellow ASAPer, and with their two sponsors they made a golf foursome. All enthusiastically accepted this suggestion.

Sponsors proved to be creative too. A couple of the vice presidents were in the habit of bringing their ASAP candidates with them to meetings with the district-level managers. One of vice president realized that he could have the ASAP participant prepare reports for the meetings, thereby giving exposure to the junior person and delegating some of his own work load. One sponsor even sent his ASAP candidate to London to represent him in some meetings.

In January, 1994, when the pilot came to an official end, nearly everyone was feeling good. Good working relations had been everywhere in evidence, and some personal friendships had grown from the positive interactions as well. However, the numbers were demoralizing: Only one candidate out of 48 had been promoted to a new job by the end of the program. I was charged with presenting the wrap-up report to senior management. I did not pull any punches. I spoke aloud of how odd it was that the most powerful people in the organization appeared powerless to initiate change.

Follow Up

As it turned out, follow-up proved crucial. The final meeting of the ASAP pilot program resulted in several declarations of intentions to promote people and to help their careers. Three months later, however, official records showed no additional action. At that point I went to the man to whom several of the sponsors reported. I noted that one promotion out of 48 was not an impressive number. He replied that he was fully supportive of diversity initiatives and that promotions would be made as soon as there were openings. I produced figures that showed that 42 openings had occurred in his organization but not one of them had gone to an ASAP candidate, nor to any ethnic minority. His embarrassment was evident, and he made a very strong commitment: Within 6 months, every ASAP candidate who had a sponsor who reported to him would be promoted. He lived up to his word and became a true (and vocal) advocate.

One of the beauties of the ASAP pilot is that it is still successful. NYNEX recently hosted a leadership and diversity awards celebration. One winner was a graduate of ASAP. He was recognized not for his own career advancement but more importantly for the fact that he integrated a district that had previously included entirely White men in its management ranks. Each time someone retired, he thought of the list of qualified minorities and White women. The talent was available, and he worked to bring the talent to his district.

There is much evidence within the company that diversity remains profitable. For example, when a communication was to be sent to a Chinese community, public relations personnel knew enough to check the communication with the Asian Focus Group. It turned out that two character in the message had been reversed inadvertently. The meaning of the message would have been distorted. Fortunately, they caught the error and saved the company much embarrassment. The eventual success of the ASAP program can only serve to increase these kinds of experiences, ultimately increasing the organization's effectiveness.

Words of Advice

What additional wisdom can I share about sponsorship programs like ASAP? Three pieces of advice are worth heeding. First, the company must devote a lot of resources to recruiting and screening participants. Their success or failure will be important for years to come. Second, the company should be prepared to expend a lot of energy in the beginning of the program until it is going on its own momentum. During the initial phases, there must be support systems, not only for the protégés but also for the sponsors. Early in phase three, we noted that sponsors were behaving rather ethnocentrically: They were telling candidates to take speech classes, get haircuts, dress appropriately. It took much coaching and counseling to convince the sponsors that their way was just that—their way, and only one way to do things. They needed to look beyond cultural differences and focus on the real issues of what it took to be a leader. It is important to remember that sponsors are entering new terrain too and can benefit from sharing their concerns and receiving attention and sometimes advice. Finally, there must be numerical accountability in any follow-up assessment of the program's impact, and reports on those numbers should go directly to the head of the company.

PARTING THOUGHTS

Creating change, even through such positive vehicles as mentoring and sponsorship programs, is hard work for everyone. It is often tiring and difficult to maintain one's optimism. But it is important to resist cynicism. It's hard to move an elephant up a hill; but if you remember to thank the elephant for every step, perhaps he will be less likely than otherwise to stop and sit on you.

REFERENCES

Caruso, R. E. (1992). *Mentoring and the business environment: Asset or liability?*

Catalyst. (1993). *Mentoring: A guide to programs and practices.* New York: Catalyst.

Kram, K. (1985). *Mentoring at work: Developmental relationships in organizational life.* Glenview, IL.: Scott, Foresman.

Thomas, D. (1990). The impact of race on managers' experiences of developmental relationships (mentoring and sponsorship): An intra-organizational study. *Journal of Organizational Behavior, 1,* 497–491.

11

Mentoring With Class: Connections Between Social Class and Developmental Relationships in the Academy

Sandra K. Hoyt
Miami University

Many factors influence our actions and interactions in the social world. Issues of race and gender affect our lives greatly, but another area that influences our lives has not been looked at closely—social class. In a world that places so much importance on economics and individual achievement, the social hierarchies that accompany economic structures are the basis for most of our social interactions. We are socialized in a class system and are taught class values from the beginning. We attend schools that are segregated on the basis of class, and people from different classes receive different educations. Poor neighborhoods do not generate enough money to fully support their school systems. The children who go to these schools are poor, so the children who need it the most often do not get an adequate education.

Socialization occurs within neighborhoods, and cross-class interactions are discouraged in our society. Even in the myths of Hollywood movies, when the rich boy meets the poor girl, they do not often live happily ever after in her impoverished neighborhood. She has been magically transformed into an upper-class debutante and it seems doubtful that her poor relatives would be invited to dinner.

189

Class differences don't end with early education. Social class distinctions continue to determine people's paths in life beyond their graduation from high school. Levine and Nidiffer (1996) outlined the barriers that block the poor from getting into college. They cited data that show that attendance rates for the poor in college have dropped steadily over the last 20 years. In 1993, an individual from the bottom income quartile had 10% of the chance to attend college of an individual from the top quartile (down from 16% in 1970).

It is not always sheer economic opportunity that determines who goes to college and who does not, as evidenced by Levine and Nidiffer's (1996) study of poor students who "made it" to college. The authors reported that other factors such as few role models for poor children impact admittance to college. What the authors demonstrated through their study is that the single most important influence in the lives of poor students attending college was mentors. Almost all participants referred to an influential person who "pushed" them, who sought *them* out and encouraged them to attend college. Poor and working-class students are often overlooked when it comes to the possibilities that are automatically assumed for middle-class students, but caring mentors can change the status quo. It is vital therefore that social class issues become focal in our efforts to understand mentoring so that lower- and working-class students are better able to realize their dreams.

In keeping with other chapters in this book and with Levine and Nidiffer (1996; see also Fish, 1993), I define a mentor as more than an advisor. Mentors take a personal interest in their students, seeking to teach them, be their ally, further their careers, and provide support in other life areas. Mentors are those who will "take you under their wing." A mentor tries to help you be the best at whatever you are doing.

This chapter is about the connections between social class and academic mentoring. As a working-class woman who is attempting to complete a doctoral degree in social psychology, I have entered a world that is foreign to me, that of middle-class academia. My experiences in bridging these two worlds, in becoming class-conscious, and in having mentors who did or did not share my class background have led me to believe that social class may be one of the most overlooked issues facing society today. And I believe that as more people from diverse backgrounds enter the academy, the issue of mentoring and social class will be critical. In this chapter I present theory and research on social class, issues around mentoring and social class, as well as personal experiences to illustrate the issues. Finally, I give what I hope will be useful advice for working-class students and for middle- and upper-class academics who wish to become better mentors for lower- and working-class students.

The knowledge that social class issues intersect with and are complicated by gender, race, ethnicity, and many other characteristics will hardly be news to anyone reading this chapter. The points expressed in this chapter come mainly from the perspective of a White, working-class woman who finds herself attending a midwestern "public ivy." Working- and lower-class individuals of different ethnic backgrounds and genders may experience different issues in entering the academy (hooks, 1993). Social issues impact every aspect of the characteristics that make each of us unique, and all aspects intertwine in complex ways. Still, a starting point is needed.

WHAT IS SOCIAL CLASS?

Social class indicators differ from society to society, but they generally contain similar elements (Argyle, 1994). Objective indicators may be collectively agreed upon as indicating a person's social class (e.g., income, education, occupation, and lifestyle), whereas subjective indicators are more personal to an individual (a personal idea of one's social class and social identity). Just as people categorize themselves on the basis of social class, they also categorize others into social classes. Mazur (1993) demonstrated empirically that, when shown photos of brides from local newspapers, subjects could classify the brides by social class. This classification was significantly correlated with the social class category the researcher had determined for each bride ($r = .62, p < .01$). Indeed, when asked, most people are capable of stating what their social class is, with lower, middle, upper, and working class being the most common responses (Argyle, 1994).

Class issues are overlooked or minimized in this country much more than they are in other societies such as Britain. In the United States, we believe that all people can "make it" if they work hard enough. Abraham Lincoln and the fictional character Horatio Alger are American icons because they started with little or nothing and became successful in their endeavors. We ignore the barriers that lower-class people face, and we deny the very existence of classism. Langston (1992) made this point in her essay:

> Unlike our European allies, we in the U.S. are reluctant to recognize class differences. This denial of class divisions functions to reinforce ruling class control and domination. America is, after all, the supposed land of equal

opportunity where, if you just work hard enough, you can get ahead, pull yourself up by your bootstraps. What the old bootstraps theory overlooks is that some were born with silver shoe horns." (p. 110)

In order for the topic of social class to come to light, and for an acknowledgment of classism to take place in society, class consciousness must occur. Class consciousness is a realization not only of one's own social class, but also of class relations and classism. Interactions among individuals and within institutions are affected by issues of social class. Just as gender consciousness and race consciousness are not confined to women and people of color, neither should class consciousness be confined to the lower classes. In order for change to occur, people from all classes must realize the privileges and prejudices they face and create because of their class positions. Even before one develops a class consciousness, class is present. We are born into a social class, grow up in a social class, and may work to persevere or change our social class throughout our lifetime.

Class consciousness is an individual process that can come with a jolt or be developed over a period of time. For me, it occurred both ways. As a high school student in a poor, rural area of Ohio, I was pretty ignorant of class—I just assumed that I was middle class. After all, many people were "worse-off" than my family, and many were "better off." I had bought into the capitalist framework of our society—that middle class is the norm and the "majority," those who worked hard and led decent, moral lives, must be middle class. We did, so I must be middle class. It wasn't until a discussion of class in an undergraduate literature course that I came to the realization that I was working class. The realization came as quite a shock. The professor asked what made someone working class. No one answered. The professor began listing a few things that made her believe she was working class—her father's job, where they lived, and so on. I had not given much thought to any of these things; they seemed normal. Then the professor said that working-class people (herself as an example) did not typically have matching sets of living room furniture. You'd have thought I'd been hit by a truck. It was a simple thing, but it struck a chord. In an instant I both agreed with her and realized that my family had never had any furniture that matched. No big deal really, but it connected immediately with a whole host of other things that pointed to my social class. I had just gone down the class ladder one rung, and I somehow knew that in this world that wasn't a good thing (not my current belief, but I was young then).

Over time, I began to think about other experiences I'd had, particularly regarding education. As an undergraduate from a working-class family, I lived at home. We could not afford for me to live on campus. I commuted to school and worked part or full time during my entire undergraduate experience. Needless to say, I didn't have the typical college life and didn't make many friends in my courses. Most of my friends from that time were old high school friends or people with whom I worked. At my university, I knew from talking to other students who came from my neck of the woods, that local kids weren't looked upon favorably by elite students or professors. Local students often didn't tell others that they were from the area. There was a rumor that a professor had vowed in front of his whole class to make sure that local students would get such a hard time from him that they would want to leave. This was a combination of discrimination against Appalachians and a form of classism. If you sounded as if you were Appalachian, you probably weren't middle class.

As a people watcher, I was quick to notice that the students who were local and/or older (i.e., generally working class) were the ones that the other students did not like, particularly when the working-class students spoke in class. I remember one incident when a young mother with an Appalachian accent was verbally attacked by another student. The Appalachian student had always talked in class, and we had just received our grades on an exam on which most of us had not done well. In going over the exam the Appalachian student gave an answer to one of the questions. From the moment she opened her mouth, everyone thought she was wrong (even me—classism works best when it comes from one of your own). Much to our surprise, the professor agreed with her. Immediately, another student said that the Appalachian student must obviously be wrong, how could she be right (implying that she was not very bright). The professor said that the Appalachian student was right because she got the highest score in the class and he wanted to know if anyone had a problem with that. The entire class quite literally shrank in their seats, and I was impressed, both by the Appalachian student and the professor. I now wonder if the professor was of working-class origins.

Eventually, I began to wonder how I had gotten where I was. I realized then that classism had been working against me long before I even had an inkling about it. My junior year of high school is a prime example. In our vocational high school, during junior year you began taking specialized classes in an area you chose. Most of the middle-class kids were directed toward the college-prep courses—college was at least a possibility for them. The rest of us were pointed toward a skilled career. For the boys it was auto mechanics, welding, and electronics (coal mining was closed out a few years earlier when the mines began laying off hundreds of people). For the girls, it was cosmetology, secretarial, or accounting. My choice? Accounting.

By the end of my junior year I had made the unlikely decision that I wanted to go to college to become an accountant. I went to my guidance counselor and asked for applications to the two local universities. The thought never occurred to me to look any further than our local colleges. After all, I had always been bright and was currently ranked 7th in a class of 150. To my surprise, my guidance counselor took one look at me and, without even asking my name, told me "I can give it to you, but you won't get in." Those words are seared into my memory. The whole incident is so vivid that I can even tell you that I was wearing my dad's green sweatshirt, a pair of jeans, and tennis shoes. Thank goodness, for the sake of this chapter, that I was not easily put off. I responded, "Well, I want an application anyway." The guidance counselor gave the forms to me reluctantly. Later I was accepted in the first round of offers to the university that was my first choice. I didn't even finish sending my application to the other university.

If only that were the end of the story. In the middle of the year, my accounting teacher told me that some of the college-prep students were taking a class trip to visit the school I was interested in. (You see, our accounting class had already had our trip to two small technical/business colleges.) He asked if I wanted to go and said he would see if he could arrange it. No one ever said anything, but I always had the feeling that my participation wasn't acceptable. I felt and was treated as an outsider within the group. Although I could not have used the language of social class analysis at the time, it seemed quite a feat that the teacher got permission for me to go on the college tour.

Then there was the local scholarship that the guidance counselors tried to deflect from another female, working-class student and myself so that one of the male, middle-class athletes could get it. They conveniently said they didn't have the applications, but my step-dad made a call to a neighbor who was on the board of the scholarship committee, and the next day we had the applications (it helps to live in a small town). The other working-class student and I got the majority of the scholarship because we had better grades than the boy.

In hindsight, these experiences demonstrate that the middle-class American dream that anyone can make it, can go to college if they just work hard enough, is a myth. The barriers to social mobility, self-fulfillment, knowledge, and increased livelihood are phenomenal. You might be saying to yourself, "Ah, but you did work hard and that's why you succeeded." But you're wrong, for that implies that others didn't succeed because they didn't work hard. What if I hadn't been so stubborn in insisting that I be given an application? How many other students were turned away by that guidance counselor's classist stereotypes? Does it mean that they didn't work hard in the 12 years since our graduation? No, I have a feeling that most of them have worked much harder than you or I will ever dream of doing.

CLASSISM, STEREOTYPES, AND ATTRIBUTIONS OF SOCIAL CLASS

Devine (1989) and others have found in recent years that it is increasingly difficult to get individuals to express racist or sexist stereotypes. These researchers are not proposing that racism or sexism no longer exist, but simply that they may now be hidden. Devine proposes that this is due to the controlled processing of some stereotypes. Her experiments have demonstrated that individuals can control stereotypes they may have. In responding to her experiments, subjects process more information and instead of making immediate judgments take more relevant information into account than, say, the color of one's skin. In today's society, it is not acceptable to be openly racist or sexist—there can be negative consequences for such behavior.

Recently I have conducted studies showing that social class stereotypes are still very acceptable in today's society (Hoyt & Dietz-Uhler, 1998). This preliminary work, in which we rely heavily on the paradigm created by Devine (1989), is divided into two experiments. In the first study, we asked 77 respondents to list the common, cultural stereotypes they were aware of, for the terms lower class and middle class. Here, the respondents were not giving their own feelings toward the groups, but rather they were relating the stereotypes they were aware of in society in general. The results, which were coded by independent raters, were quite interesting. A few of the most frequently listed stereotypes of the lower class included uneducated (64.9% of respondents listed this), lazy (50.6%), dirty (42.9%), drug/alcohol users (33.8%), racial minorities (28.6%), and criminals (26.0%). Some of the most frequently listed stereotypes of the middle class included educated (50.6%), positive family lives (51.9%), hardworking (53.2%), and White (18.2%).

There were few positive stereotypes mentioned for the lower class in this study. For instance, only 5 respondents out of 77 stated that the lower class were seen as hardworking. Societal stereotypes for the middle class, on the other hand, were primarily positive; only the "negative" characteristic of having bad jobs (11.7%) was notable. We made efforts in this research to reach undergraduate students of varying social class backgrounds. It appears from this work that, regardless of their class background, the respondents were aware of many negative stereotypes of the lower class and many positive stereotypes of the middle class.

In our second study (Hoyt & Dietz-Uhler, 1998), we attempted to get respondents to give their own beliefs regarding the lower and middle classes. Here, we asked 154 respondents first to identify alternate labels for the terms *lower class* and *middle class*, and then to write down all their thoughts in response to the labels they generated. Devine (1989) developed this methodology in order to determine participants' personal beliefs about the group in question. We analyzed the thoughts our participants listed and found results that were almost identical to those we obtained in the first study: The respondents believed that the lower class possessed negative characteristics almost exclusively, such as lazy, dirty, and low in intelligence, whereas they believed that the middle class possessed mainly positive characteristics. Participants, regardless of their class background, responded with significantly more negative thoughts for the lower class than the middle class and significantly more positive thoughts for the middle class than the lower class. College students not only know that social class stereotypes exist, but also hold the stereotypes as their own beliefs. Our research suggests that classism is quite acceptable in this society, and it has been ingrained into individuals from all social class levels.

How does this connect to academic mentoring? Perhaps you have made the connection already—if people automatically think that individuals from the lower class are unintelligent, criminal, or dirty, how can lower class (and working class) students make it into universities? How can they get through a middle-class institution without being marginalized and hurt? How are they supposed to continue on to graduate school?

Other studies from the area of social psychology illustrate the connection of classism to mentoring. In one classic study, Darley and Gross (1983, and largely replicated by Baron, Albright, & Malloy, 1995) demonstrated the effect of social class on decisions about education and intelligence. In this study, participants were shown a videotape of a little girl named Hannah. In the video, she was depicted in her neighborhood and playing at her school. The neighborhood and school were either visibly middle class or lower class. Participants then saw an uninformative video of Hannah taking an academic test (in other words, it was purposely ambiguous as to her actual academic abilities). The results demonstrated that participants who were led to believe that Hannah came from a middle-class background rated her academic abilities much higher than her actual grade level (which they were told), whereas participants who thought Hannah came from lower-class origins rated her academic abilities much lower than her grade level.

Key to this discussion is the fact that the participants thought they were assisting a federal agency to study teacher evaluation methods for use in assigning students to special programs. How are admissions affected today by socioeconomic information? How are students going through interview processes evaluated? What kind of mentoring are working- and lower-class students getting if classism is pervasive and acceptable in our society?

THE IMPACT OF SOCIAL CLASS IN THE ACADEMY

Education has predominantly been connected with higher social class status. History tells us that lower-class individuals were not taught to read and write and only the wealthy were permitted to attend universities, which were created by the upper-class to educate their children. Even in today's society, poor children have few opportunities to attend universities. Some have a marginal chance to attend trade or technical schools. Those who do get accepted to a university find themselves in a place with a very different atmosphere than they are used to, and for them it may not be a friendly one. They may feel, as Donna Langston felt, like "a stranger in a strange land" (1993, p. 67).

The academy requires particular styles of communication, speech, and dress, often referred to as "cultural capital" (Granfield, 1991). These particular styles are based on middle-class norms. Students who do not come to the academy with these styles intact are at a disadvantage. Some students learn to "pass" in order to fit in, whereas others do not. These students, myself included, then find these styles of communication and conduct foreign and unfriendly. As Johnson (1993) discusses in her essay, "In graduate school I was expected to have ideas, express them, write them down, and—horrors—defend them. How does one do that? If you defend them, some hot-shot White male is there to tear your arguments to bits. What manner of discourse is this? ... We thought that tearing apart arguments was rude at best and cruel at worst" (p. 202).

My experience with defending ideas is a bit different because arguing is something that I'm fairly good at. My frustration is with everyday conversation with middle-class academics, or, I should say, the lack of everyday conversation. Even with the simplest of topics you are questioned, debated, and told that you must have evidence to back up what you are saying. It seems as though even a conversation about the weather must be concrete and contain references. This is not how I have experienced conversations in working-class environments. There, people simply talk and do not have to prove everything that they say. If one is accustomed to working-class speech, it can seem much more friendly and much less nerve-wracking than middle-class speech. However, the problem occurs when individuals from the higher status group (the middle-class) impose their speech style on those of the lower status group (the working/lower class). The outcome can be that when working-class individuals do not use middle-class speech, they are stereotyped as unintelligent, uneducated, and possibly lazy. This can result in fewer life opportunities for these individuals—in other words, class discrimination.

Granfield's (1991) ethnography of working-class students at an elite law school is another example of the impact of social class in the academy. Although these students entered school taking great pride in their class background, values, and ideals, they soon came to "define themselves as different and their backgrounds a burden" (p. 336). They described increased feelings of stress and incompetence, generally greater than those of middle-class first-year students, because of a lack of cultural necessities (i.e., speech, manners, clothing, and experiences of the middle class).

One student reported "that she was very aware of using 'proper' English, adding that 'it makes me self-conscious when I use the wrong word or tense. I feel that if I had grown up in the middle class, I wouldn't have lapses. I have difficulty expressing thoughts while most other people here don't'" (Granfield, 1991, p. 336). My own experiences with language difficulties are two-fold. I have experienced the problems with middle-class speech patterns, but I have also experienced problems because of my working-class, Appalachian accent. Mine is not the sophisticated southern drawl heard in *Gone with the Wind*, but rather the rough accent from *The Beverly Hillbillies*, *Andy Griffith*, or *The Dukes of Hazzard*. Accents, like language patterns, begin to change during college. My "passing" included learning not to say "y'all," not to speak in a "backward" style, and not to sound like Opie Taylor. More recently, with my class consciousness and my need to educate others about class issues, I have begun to slip into the accent and familiar patterns at various times. I am hopeful that hearing intelligent ideas come through in a different way will open some people's minds. Whether I am hurting myself in some way (lowering students' opinions and confidence in me) is a risk I am willing to take.

Aspects of cultural capital that must be learned by working-class students include writing style, confidence, and dress. Middle- and upper-class people do not generally think about these things: they come with privilege. Their writing comes out abstract and formal, whereas working-class people's writing is often familiar, informal, sense-based (Tokarczyk & Fay, 1993). The differences in my own writing in this chapter point out the double life of a working-class person "passing" in academia—the theoretical portions are written in "academese," and the experiential portions are written much as if I were telling them to someone back home.

The confidence that comes with privilege is something with which working- and lower-class people have little experience. Working-class students tend to second-guess their statements, decisions, and abilities in matters pertaining to their education. I know that I am quite capable of writing this chapter, but the very thought that it could be published and read by others makes no sense to me. Why would anyone want to read what I have to say? I wonder if anyone will understand what I am saying, and I perceive a large gulf between middle-class readers and myself. A little voice says that my worries don't matter because surely the chapter will get pulled from the book before it even goes to the publisher. When the editors presented the idea of a book based on our work at a Nag's Heart conference, I immediately assumed that they were only talking about the faculty members among us as contributors. It did not occur to me that the graduate students would even be considered as such. I have learned my place in society very well, and my class consciousness is not yet strong enough to keep self-doubt out.

Dress is a very important component of cultural capital. Your dress is a clear sign of your social class status. Even people in denial of social class issues (you know, the ones who say "I wouldn't know what your class background was from what you're wearing; you could be wealthy for all I know") can distinguish categories at a glance. They may not know that it's social class that they are basing their judgments on, but it is. One of the first things that Melanie Griffith's character in the movie *Working Girl* does is change her outward appearance. In order to "pass" as middle class, you have to look like you are middle class, and dress is an important part of that.

When I began college, I certainly thought about what I wore to school. Few teenage girls in America go to school without thoughts about wardrobe, but for me, it was which T-shirt to wear. I remember attending pre-college during the summer. I didn't stay the night in the dorm with the other students because I lived close by and if I remember correctly it cost extra to stay. I wore my best jeans and a good shirt. I remember that I looked nothing like most of the other students there. I remember feeling as if I didn't fit in. At lunch, one student's mother tried to hold a conversation with me about my high school, but her daughter rolled her eyes and was very embarrassed that her mother was talking to me. When I began college and my work study job, I just wore what I had worn to high school. Later, about a year later, I realized that my clothes weren't quite acceptable for this new environment, and I tried to buy clothes that fit in a little better, although I always felt that I never quite got it "right."

One interesting thing about dress and different cultures is that often the dominant culture appropriates the "look" of the marginalized culture. The same is true with working-class dress. The middle-class appropriation of lower- and working-class dress styles (e.g., the "grunge" look and L.L. Bean) are only copied in the most upscale way. Everyone wants to wear workboots and jeans, and rugged outdoor wear, even bib-overalls, are stylish. However, these clothes are not really very grungy, and the work clothes have never known years of wear, the kind that comes from working on cars, in fields, in factories, in coal mines.

Working-class students are very conscious of the ways in which they dress. Whether they choose to "pass" or not, what they wear marks them. As an example, my attendance at the Nag's Heart conference was arranged several months before it took place. The entire time, I was worried about how I would look, what I would wear. I knew that it would be summer, and that these were feminist, liberal faculty and students and that the dress would be casual. Still, I decided that I had to have new clothes to wear—what I had would not work; I would be marked, set apart. I am not, of course, asserting that anyone else at the conference saw me as dressed differently from the norm, but my own self-consciousness was nonetheless phenomenally real. Even if they didn't notice it, I would feel it.

Another experience for graduate students is that of first meeting the faculty and students at your new school. Some students are interviewed before being accepted; others, like myself, visit the school after they are accepted. I came dressed in a jacket and skirt (I was currently working as a secretary, and although that was not how I dressed on the job, I knew that I needed to look serious, and I had a great need to fit in from the beginning). The following year, a student visited wearing sweatshirt and jeans. I knew immediately that she was working class even though class issues were not in the forefront of my thinking at the time. Still rooted in hypocritical classism, I wondered why she didn't come dressed at least a little nicer. I was even a bit angry. She did not receive the warmest of welcomes, and students, myself among them, thought that she was "weird." Not long after that I realized that I was angry with her because she wasn't working to "pass" as I was. I was putting a lot of effort into it (and I wasn't sure I was doing all that good a job at it), and she just strolled in as she was, daring everyone to accept her or not. I have talked with her about this and about many other social class issues. Our discussion intensified when, the next year, another student showed up the same way (T-shirt and jeans) and also received a cool welcome. She chose to attend another school.

BETWEEN TWO WORLDS

Granfield (1991) and Gardner (1993) discussed the implications for individuals from working-class backgrounds when they begin to move out of those backgrounds. Gardner presents the feelings of marginality that result from an increased level of education and status as individuals (herself included) begin to move beyond their working class backgrounds:

> Despite our objective position in the class structure, many of us did not feel middle class or as if we really belonged in the world we inhabited. What we were keenly aware of, which many of our middle-class colleagues failed to understand, is that "education and a good job don't turn a black person white and they don't negate a white working-class person's background." As a consequence, a part of our identity was middle class while another part remained back in the working-class world of our roots. (p. 50)

Both authors discuss various strategies that working class individuals use when they are confronted with this identity conflict. They include identity management or "passing," integrating the new class identity with the old, coming out of the closet with one's class background, and taking on the identity and values of the middle-class while leaving behind their former class identity. As Granfield (1991) stated:

> In regard to social class, the ideology of meritocracy serves to legitimate devaluation of the lower classes. Because social class position is frequently seen as the outcome of individual talent and effort, the assignment of stigma to lower socioeconomic groups is not seen as being based on arbitrary evalua-

tion. Given the legitimacy of the meritocratic ideology, is it any wonder that upwardly mobile working-class students choose not to directly confront the devaluation they experience but rather to forge a new identity which effectively divorces them from the working class? (p. 348).

Many working-class students and faculty I have talked to have expressed the difficulty they experience because they do not feel that they fit, in either the world they came from (i.e., their working-class background) or the world they are now perceived to belong to (i.e., their increased status due to their education and positions). They report that family members often do not understand why they should continue their schooling to such great lengths. Parents are often supportive because they want more for their children, but sometimes they seem unsupportive because they feel that their children are changing and becoming different from them.

When I told my family that I wanted to go to college, they were mainly supportive, but my brother asked why I would want to "go and do something like that." To this day, my grandfather still asks me if I'm working or when I'll get a job (school is not seen as work). My grandfather's attitude is a problem for me because I have always held jobs even when in school, but holding a part-time job and going to school full-time wasn't the same to him as having a full-time job.

Another issue for working-class students is that family members often don't understand what the student is studying at school. It's not as if they're not intelligent enough to understand it (after all, you did come from them, and if you can understand social identity theory, they can too). For most working-class students, their family members do not have education beyond high school or technical school. The topics studied at universities are simply unfamiliar to them. This is the case with my family. It also has to do with the fact that psychology is so abstract. ("What's it got to do with the price of eggs in China?" "How can you make a living by studying psychology?" "What can you *make* with all of these degrees?" "How will what you do affect us, or anyone?") Add to that the fact that the bachelor's degree that you got is absolutely worthless by itself. ("You have to get *more* schooling to get a job? What was that first degree for?") Then, to add fuel to the fire, mention the fact that you're not studying clinical psychology, and you won't be treating the mentally ill. No, *you're* going to be a social psychologist. ("A what?") You finally end the conversation by saying that you're going to be a professor. ("Oh, a teacher!") I don't blame my family for not understanding; it still doesn't make sense to me, maybe even less so now. In fact, I'd be very worried if they did understand this world that I'm thinking of entering where you get paid to think and write about topics that may have no practical application.

When my mother finally realized that my B.A. wasn't going to get me a job and that I was miserable as a secretary, she was all for my going back to school (as a matter of fact, she was for anything that would get me out of the place I was working). That was when she began asking serious questions about what I was studying and what I would do when I was finished. She had asked them before, but I probably didn't give very good answers because I didn't know. It has only been recently, while I've been explaining my interest in social class, that it has made sense to her. Looking at how people like us are treated and discriminated against is something tangible, something real (to her and to me). She has even offered to help me gather materials for some of my studies. (Now if we could just figure out how to get me a job....)

Can a working- or lower-class person ever become middle class? Isn't the attempt to appear middle class always just "passing?" If it goes beyond "passing" has the person sold out?

> I think some working class [sic.] people may successfully assimilate into the middle class by learning to dress, talk, and act middle-class—to accept and adopt the middle-class way of doing things. It all depends on how far they're able to go. To succeed in the middle-class world means facing great pressures to abandon working-class friends and ways. (Langston, 1992, p. 113)

My own notion of the class transition is that most working- and lower-class people do not really become middle class. I believe that working- and lower-class individuals are always marked by their background. I will never feel or act comfortably in middle-class environments, and my discomfort may always show. I will never act as if the whole world were at my beck and call. I will never dress quite right. Even when I manage to buy a nice outfit, it either doesn't look quite the same as it would on a middle-class person, or it was purchased from somewhere like Fashion Bug or Wal-Mart. I feel that, at the most, I will always be "passing." To me, to have made it to the middle-class means what Langston was talking about, to have sold out.

One professor I know became very interested when I presented my research on social class and mentioned being a first-generation college graduate. Presumably this meant that he came from a working-class background, though he never said so explicitly. I would never have known it, for he had completely assimilated into the middle-class—the dress, speech, manners, attitude—everything that was foreign to me and to other working-class students. I have to admit to having had ambivalent feelings about his possible desertion of a class background.

My own class consciousness has allowed me to examine for the first time the hostility I feel toward the middle- and upper-classes. I do not want to become one of "them." I realize how I dislike the materialism, the backstabbing, and the looking down on others because they have less. Why would I want to be part of that? It is true that not everything in the working-class world is rosy, just as it is not in the middle-class world. Violence, abuse, drugs, and alcohol are a part of both worlds (not just the working class, as the stereotypes lead us to believe). But the simplicity, honesty, values, and morals, and the general concern for others that are part of my personal experiences make me proud. I do not want to sell out my White, working-class background, my family, and my friends for the chance to have a 15-room house and two-car garage in the middle of suburbia.

I do not want to minimize the concept of "passing." There is a real fear to being discovered as having working- or lower-class origins, a fear that is not paranoia. Any person who is an outsider, the other, or marginalized knows that there can be serious consequences for those who are different from the norm. Stereotypes and attributions do not stay in the theoretical for people; they are often acted upon to become discrimination and abuse. Working-class students who are "out of the closet" (Gardner, 1991, p. 55) may be seen as less intelligent. Also, in the classic double bind, working-class academics who have "made it" may be seen as extraordinary individuals (after all they did rise above their background to better themselves), and may be called upon to work harder or more than others. They may also be called upon more frequently to do the "dirty work," much as women are still asked to make the coffee or type up the meeting minutes.

So what's left? Where do academics from the working class, who refuse to lose their heritages, who refuse to "pass," end up? Are they middle class? Are they still working class? The answer is that they are probably neither, or both. I know that I am not middle class, and I don't feel that I ever will be. But I also know that already I have moved away from the working class.

MENTORING AND THE IMPLICATIONS OF CLASS IN THE ACADEMY

What has been presented previously in this chapter has not been to say that working- or lower-class students need special consideration, or that they are incapable of becoming academics without special help. You only need to look around at faculty and graduate students to see that many working- and lower-class individuals have made it there already. They are bright, hard-working individuals who have had to learn how to survive in a foreign land. In some ways that is part of the problem. Working- and lower-class students are very independent. This is something that is instilled in them by their backgrounds and their families (contrary to what our current government would have you think). These students may be so independent and hard-working that they seem to need little if any mentoring. They often slip through the cracks.

Another important aspect of working- and lower-class students' lives is that they often have greater responsibilities outside of their work at school than other students. They may have families to support (financially, physically, and emotionally). If they do not have families of their own, they often have extended families to whom they have obligations. These students are also the ones who are taking out student loans in order to help pay for school. One of my worst nightmares is that I will finish my doctoral program with about $40,000 in loans and I won't be able to find a job (and this isn't even close to the debts of some lower or working-class students). After all, I completed a bachelor's degree and was unemployable except as a secretary. I keep telling one of my professors that no matter what, I can't get this degree and not have a job. I just can't afford to do that. I realize that in this society not many people can afford to go without a pay check, but imagine signing over most of your future on the bet that you will have a job in a world where academic positions for social psychologists are few and far between. Even if I find a job, will it be worth it? For many years I will live much as I do now, because the payments on my loans promise to be substantial. My colleagues will probably be selling their starter homes and purchasing their second or third homes when I might be purchasing my first. What kind of advice do you give someone who has these concerns?

Working- and lower-class students are also the ones who are holding down part- or full-time jobs during winter and summer breaks. Many may be working during the school year just to make ends meet. These are things for mentors to consider when advising their students about choices. Does the student take on that extra research project this semester or wait until next? Do the students attend the regional or national conference in their profession? There won't be any departmental money to help them out. Should they even stay in school? Are the costs of going on for the Ph.D. greater than the benefits? These are questions that mentors should consider seriously. Mentors must be prepared to assist students with making contacts and networking, not just when to do it and with whom, but *how* to do it. Working- and lower-class students won't know how, and will probably feel very uneasy networking. They may not have previous connections to the academic world, which would give them contacts or even make them feel at ease in that world. Mentors need to act like sponsors, giving much instrumental help.

Working- and lower-class students may also have poor job-seeking skills. First, they will be pre-occupied with "finding and keeping a job" (Langston, 1993, p. 68). They may take the first job offered to them instead of waiting for the best offer. They may also not know how or where to look for jobs in their fields, or how to conduct thorough job searches. My own job-seeking skills consist of looking in the Sunday paper for secretarial jobs. You don't find many professor jobs in the newspaper.

The issues presented in this chapter bring me to one final question: Can the marginalized student get adequate mentoring in academia? Are mentors from different backgrounds (social class, race, gender) capable of understanding and giving proper guidance? Do marginalized students need to be mentored by faculty who share their background and experiences? From participating in the Feminist Friends conference, I found that these questions are being considered by others. Some feel that mentors who do not share the background and experiences of their students can still mentor them successfully. For the issue of social class (the only one I can speak to right now), I would say that cross-class mentoring would work only if the mentor has thought long and hard about his or her own class background. Middle-class mentors must recognize their privileges and realize that these privileges can come at a cost to someone else. The cost-bearing person is not always a distant unknown in some third-world country. She or he may be sitting in the mentor's office awaiting advice. There must also be an open discussion between student and mentor about the very thing(s) that make them different. The discussion will not be easy. For some it may be impossible.

I do think that all marginalized students should find a mentor who shares their background. It has meant the world to me to have found people who share my experiences in growing up working class. Particularly helpful to me have been academics from the working class. Without my mentors (my mother, the secretaries I have worked with, an English professor, and my current working-class professors), together with my working-class peers, I know that I would have gone crazy long ago. Instead, we went crazy together, trying to figure out this world that's based on money, power, and rules that make no sense to us.

RESOLUTIONS (OR TIPS FOR MENTORS
OF ALL CLASS BACKGROUNDS)

1. Become class conscious: Class doesn't mean only lower class, just as gender doesn't mean only women, or ethnicity only Blacks. Think about your own class: What does it really mean? What opportunities, privileges, knowledge do you have by virtue of where you came from? Think about the class of others around you (students, peers, the person who fixes your car or cleans your house) and what it means to them.

2. Encourage class consciousness in students. Some may be aware of class issues; others may not know why they feel alienated.

3. Don't dismiss or trivialize a student's emphasis on class (e.g., "You're focusing on class too much." "You're looking at this through a class lens."). Class affects the way all of us go through life, no matter what our class background is. If a student is emphasizing class, take the hint that is being offered: Examine class in your own life and encourage critical thinking about class issues.

4. Help your students to make contacts and to network. They may not even know how to go about it (e.g., how to introduce themselves to important figures in the field, how to remind someone that they've met before). It seems simple, but it's not. The oppressed learn their place very well; even the most independent of persons knows the line. Working- or lower-class students may not ask how to go about doing something that everyone assumes they know how to do.

5. Do something about policies regarding outside employment during school breaks at your institutions. Working- and lower-class students often have greater economic responsibilities than other students. Open and hidden policies are in place at many schools that not only hamper students' ability to work during breaks but actually punish them if they do.

6. Be prepared to talk with students about things that you assume other students know. Lower- and working-class students won't necessarily ask, because it can be humiliating to have to ask what you "should" already know, such as whether a gathering at a professor's home is semiformal or casual dress, how to make small talk with guest speakers, or how to contact a prominent psychologist to ask about his or her work.

7. Learn to recognize classist statements. Many are blatant. Classism is very acceptable in our society. Some classist statements are subtle. Above all, defend your students against others' classist statements.

ADVICE FOR WORKING-
AND LOWER-CLASS STUDENTS

1. Find a working- or lower-class mentor, even if she or he is not in your area, even if she or he is not at your institution. Levine and Nidiffer's (1996) study demonstrated that good mentors come from all places—family members, neighbors, teachers, community counselors.

2. Seek out other working- or lower-class students. As Langston (1992) noted, "How do working-class people spot each other? We have antenna" (p. 120).

3. Seek out staff members at your universities and colleges. Secretaries, custodians, and food-service workers can become some of your best allies.

4. Decide if you want to "pass" or not. If "passing," decide where you draw the line, if anywhere, and be prepared, as one mentor said to me, to have it "break your heart."

5. If not "passing," decide what route you will take for your career. Will you work in your community, or some other working or lower-class community? Will you work for social service organizations? Will you teach at a community college? Will you work in middle-class academia and try to withstand being "the other?"

6. Also, find strategies for coping with the classism you will experience if you choose not to "pass." Finding allies is the only thing I can advise. It's the only thing I have discovered so far.

7. Decide now if you want to stay in academia, and above all, if you want to become middle class.

A FINAL NOTE

The woman who began the shift in my class consciousness advised me to get out of academia. She was having a terrible time as a professor and eventually left the university, a move that I encouraged. We talked often about the struggles and, dare I say it, the disgust we felt being connected to an institution that was based on cut-throat competition and pretension. Even with my work on social class, she told me, I would feel like I had sold out my own kind.

The professor was right. Given my distrust of middle-class readers, it is inevitable that I should feel that. I have given away secrets—working-class people's secrets—in this chapter. I have acknowledged that working-class individuals in middle-class environments may have feelings of self-doubt, misgivings about their place in both worlds, and that they may lack some of the middle-class cultural capital necessary to negotiate the middle-class environment. Talking about these things can both help and hurt those working-class individuals. First, like other writing by working-class academics (Dews & Law, 1995; Ryan & Sackrey; 1984; Tokarczyk & Fay, 1993), this acknowledgment can help those from working-class backgrounds to realize they are not alone. It can also help them to consider the importance of their own mentoring of working-class students. However, it can also hurt working- and lower-class individuals because it shows a weakness that could potentially be exploited by those who have power over the working- and lower-classes, namely the middle- and upper-classes. My only hope is that those middle- and upper-class individuals will carefully consider what has been written here and realize that working-class students are already in the academy and in other middle-class environments. These students do not need special consideration; they simply need fair treatment and an exchange in cultural ideals or cultural capital. After all, there are many things that the middle-class could learn from the working-class culture as well.

REFERENCES

Argyle, M. (1994). *The psychology of social class.* London: Routledge.

Baron, R. M., Albright, L., & Malloy, T. E. (1995). Effects of behavioral and social class information on social judgment. *Personality and Social Psychology Bulletin, 21*, 308–315.

Darley, J. M., & Gross, P. H. (1983). A hypothesis-confirming bias in labeling effects. *Journal of Personality and Social Psychology, 44*, 20–33.

Devine, P. G. (1989). Stereotypes and prejudice: Their automatic and controlled components. *Journal of Personality and Social Psychology, 56*, 5–18.

Dews, C. L. B., & Law, C. L. (1995). *This fine place so far from home: Voices of academics from the working class.* Philadelphia: Temple University Press.

Fish, C. (1993). "Someone to watch over me": Politics and paradoxes in academic mentoring. In M. M. Tokarczyk & E. A. Fay (Eds.), *Working-class women in the academy: Laborers in the knowledge factory* (pp. 179–196). Amherst: The University of Massachusetts Press.

Gardner, S. (1993). What's a nice working-class girl like you doing in a place like this? In M. M. Tokarczyk & E. A. Fay (Eds.), *Working-class women in the academy: Laborers in the knowledge factory* (pp. 49–59). Amherst: The University of Massachusetts Press.

Granfield, R. (1991). Making it by faking it: Working-class students in an elite academic environment. *Journal of Contemporary Ethnography, 20*, 331–351.

hooks, b. (1993). Keeping close to home: Class and education. In M. M. Tokarczyk & E. A. Fay (Eds.), *Working-class women in the academy: Laborers in the knowledge factory* (pp. 99–111). Amherst: The University of Massachusetts Press.

Hoyt, S. K., & Dietz-Uhler, B. (1998). *The pervasiveness and acceptability of social class stereotypes.* Unpublished manuscript, Miami University.

Johnson, E. J. (1993). Working-class women as students and teachers. In M. M. Tokarczyk & E. A. Fay (Eds.), *Working-class women in the academy: Laborers in the knowledge factory* (pp. 197–207). Amherst: The University of Massachusetts Press.

Langston, D. (1992). Tired of playing monopoly? In M. L. Andersen & P. Hill Collins (Eds.), *Race, class, and gender: An anthology* (pp.110–120). Belmont, CA: Wadsworth.

Langston, D. (1993). Who am I now? The politics of class identity. In M. M. Tokarczyk & E. A. Fay (Eds.), *Working-class women in the academy: Laborers in the knowledge factory* (pp. 60–72). Amherst: The University of Massachusetts Press.

Levine, A., & Nidiffer, J. (1996). *Beating the odds: How the poor get to college.* San Francisco: Jossey-Bass.

Mazur, A. (1993). Signs of status in bridal portraits. *Sociological Forum, 8,* 273–283.

Ryan, J., & Sackrey, C. (1984). *Strangers in paradise: Academics from the working class.* Boston: South End.

Tokarczyk, M. M., & Fay, E. A. (1993). *Working-class women in the academy: Laborers in the knowledge factory.* Amherst: University of Massachusetts Press.

12

Mentoring at the Margin

Audrey J. Murrell
University of Pittsburgh

Sandra Schwartz Tangri
Howard University

On April 24, 1995, the Wall Street Journal carried an article entitled "How a Dedicated Mentor Gave Momentum to a Woman's Career." The woman in the article was Ms. Dianna Green, formerly a senior vice president at Xerox Corporation and named by the media as one of the 25 most powerful women in America. Green, an African American, had come to her top-level position at Xerox under the tutelage of her White male mentor, who had recently convinced her to resign her position at Xerox and join him in running a small Pittsburgh utility. As CEO of the utility company, he realized that Green "faces obstacles," the journalist reported, and so "he makes sure she understands her new corporate culture, sings her praises to outsiders at every turn and helps her land on several boards" (Hymowitz, 1995). He described his mentoring relationship with Green as not "a formal process," but rather as "something that happens because you have great respect for another person" (Hymowitz, 1995, pp. B1–2).

Despite the emphasis in the title of this article on the role of the dedicated mentor, what most struck the first author of this chapter—herself an African American woman—were the roles Green played, as both protégé in this relationship and as role model, sponsor, and mentor in many others. Recognizing how her relationship with the CEO played a critical role in her success, Green showed loyalty and gratitude and worked tirelessly to support him. Mentoring, Green said, "has to be a two-way street with both people giving something" (Hymowitz, 1995). Perhaps more striking was the clear fact that Green also did not hesitate to hold out a hand to those coming behind her. As the ranking African American executive at the company, Green worked hard to increase diversity at her company. She succeeded, for example, in promoting the first woman manager in the local utility plant. While stock prices and earnings per share were increasing significantly, Green was helping her organization win awards for diversity and affirmative action.

Green was extremely visible outside the company as well. At the time the article was written, she was receiving accolades for her involvement in community groups, her active leadership in the ethnic minority community, and the role she played as protector and provider in her family.

Then, in August, 1996, things changed dramatically for Dianna Green. Her mentor and boss left the Pittsburgh utility to head another utility. Unlike his predecessor, the new CEO in Pittsburgh did not include Green in his inner circle. Simultaneously, a controversy erupted over her credentials. Less than one year later, the Wall Street Journal carried another story about the extraordinary senior vice president, but in it, a tragic announcement: "Dianna Green, 51, has died of a single, self-inflicted gun shot wound to her head" (Hymowitz & Narisetti, 1997, pp. B4–5).

Although the fatal physical wound was reported as self-inflicted, we feel certain, based on the subtext of her story and on our own observations and experiences, that numerous psychological wounds along the way were not. As a prominent woman of color in a White establishment, Green had major responsibilities, not only in her roles as senior vice president, community leader, and family member but as role model, sponsor, and mentor to many younger White women and people of color, both in and outside her company, who looked to her for confidence, guidance, support, and protection. Despite her success and position of power, Green was enormously vulnerable: Many felt that she was held to a higher standard and not easily forgiven for her mistakes—or for her accomplishments.

This story of Dianna Green provided a catalyst for our examination of the costs and benefits of being a mentor while being marginalized within one's environment. What are the benefits and what are the burdens of mentoring from the margins? We attribute our interest in this question to the fact that we ourselves belong to marginalized identity groups and to the fact that we both teach and write about such experiences. To address this question, we draw heavily on our personal observations and experiences. Among the marginalized identity statuses we represent and write about in this chapter are being women (Murrell and Tangri), Black in a

White-dominated institution (Murrell), White in a Black-dominated institution (Tangri), lesbian (Tangri), and Jewish (Tangri). We are both faculty members in institutions of higher learning, working with students, some of whom are also marginalized by the identities they represent. Therefore, it is on this relationship—between marginalized faculty member and student (who is sometimes also marginalized)—that we focus our discussion.

Although our experiences have not been wholly positive, we do not mean to suggest that we wish to relinquish our developmental roles and responsibilities in relation to our students nor that we feel the same level of stress, alienation, or misery our protégénist, Dianna Green, must have felt. We offer our observations, experiences, and discussion here primarily to balance the one-sided story portrayed in the literature, which focuses on the ways in which developmental relationships benefit not only the junior person but the senior person as well. We identify with this story and describe how we are able, perhaps uniquely, to benefit from developmental relationships in which we are the senior parties. We also offer a contrasting point of view—the negative side of these relationships—which we hope will prove useful as it highlights the complexities of an experience that may seem paradoxical to many: We are in positions that make us less powerful as a result of our identity statuses and at the same time more powerful, as a result of our faculty positions.

DEFINING MARGINAL STATUS

We base our notion of marginalized status on the work of Frable (1993), who defined marginalization in a group or society as a subjective sense of not belonging, including feelings of uniqueness, isolation, and alienation from the mainstream, as well as an objective reality in which nonmarginalized members exclude, ignore, stereotype, and generally fail to understand the marginalized member. Frable defined two orthogonal dimensions on which one's identity group memberships may vary and that influence marginalization processes. The first concerns whether the identity group is valued and therefore a source of power or devalued and therefore a source of powerlessness in a group or society. Devalued group memberships increase a person's marginalization; valued group memberships increase a person's centrality. The second concerns the issue of visibility—whether one's membership in the identity group is visible (i.e., conspicuous) or invisible (i.e., concealed) to others. The visibility of one's identity group memberships shapes marginalization processes by determining the extent to which one is able to exercise choice in revealing those memberships. People often conceal devalued group memberships that are invisible in order to minimize their marginalization.

Identity group memberships that vary on these two dimensions are similar to what some have referred to as master statuses (e.g., Hughes, 1945). One's master statuses determine whether one enjoys core status or marginalized status within society. Experimental work by Frable has shown that people's master statuses have an impact on their perceptions of similarity to and fit within their environment. A master status that is marginal within the environment can, according to this research, either lead to feelings of isolation and uniqueness, especially if one's membership in the group is invisible, or create a common identity that links people together (Frable, 1993).

We also draw conceptually on Ragins' (1997, chap. 13, this volume; Ragins & Cotton, 1983; Ragins & Scandura, 1994) work, which explicates how the societal and organizational contexts within which people work can shape the nature and quality of diversified developmental relationships—those developmental relationships in which junior and senior party belong to different identity groups that are associated with differences in power. In particular, she has argued that identity groups that are more power differentiated in the larger society—i.e., master statuses—will have a different impact on developmental relationships than identity groups that are less power differentiated. In addition, she has argued that people's subjective sense of the importance or salience of their memberships in these groups varies across organizations and across individuals within organizations and that this too has implications for the role these identity group memberships play in diversified developmental relationships. Ragins has pointed out that in diversified developmental relationships parties may be dissimilar in some of their group memberships and similar in others. Shared membership in identity groups can provide but does not guarantee shared experience or insights. A mentor who is a White lesbian, for example, may not fully comprehend the experiences of her straight African American woman protégé despite their common identity as women and the fact that they are both members of other marginalized groups.

Finally, we found Alderfer's (Alderfer & Smith, 1982; Thomas & Alderfer, 1989) theory of embedded intergroup relations useful in helping us to think further about the ways in which our different organizational affiliations have influenced our experiences. We were struck, for example, by the complementarity between us: Murrell is a Black woman in a predominantly White institution, whereas Tangri is a White woman in a predominantly Black institution. As Thomas (chap. 9, this volume; Thomas, 1990) explains, these two situations, and our roles as mentors in them, represent different degrees of congruence with power relations between the races in the larger society within which our institutions are embedded. Murrell's position, as an African American faculty member in a predominantly White institution, is incongruent with the racial distribution of power both in the institution and in the larger society within which the institution is embedded. Tangri's position, as a White faculty member in a predominantly Black institution is incongruent with the racial distribution of power in her institution, but congruent with the racial distribution of power in society. These two situations have different implications for the roles we play as mentors, sponsors, and role models in our respective institutions.

In the next two sections, each of us in turn describes some of our experiences as mentors, sponsors, and role models to illustrate the dynamics of diversified developmental relationships in the different marginalizing contexts in which we work. We focus specifically on our experiences as the senior party in those relationships.

BEING A BLACK WOMAN FACULTY MEMBER IN A PREDOMINANTLY WHITE MALE INSTITUTION

It is often difficult for me to isolate my experiences and reflections about being an African American woman in a predominately White and male environment. Recently, a student posed this question to me: "In your profession, how often are you the only one?" My response was simply, "Always." It is difficult therefore to imagine what it would be like not to have solo status, how my perspective or professional development might be different if my status as African American and female did not carry with it the possibility of being marginalized. Perhaps my difficulty in being able to isolate times and situations in which solo status and the potential for marginalization have not affected me is, in itself, the most profound effect of all. Yet while not exclusively positive, my experiences have nevertheless given me a unique opportunity to be creative in the ways I approach my career. Although my experiences as a mentor have sometimes been a source of stress, these experiences have also been a source of great insight and inspiration. In this section, I outline these challenges and opportunities in the context of my career in the academy.

Much of my experience, I believe, has been shaped by my visibility based on my frequent solo status as an African American woman. Visibility is a key part of survival and advancement within the academic profession: Having one's work recognized and cited is a key criterion for advancement and is often what attracts students to seek mentoring relationships with faculty. Hence, my visibility is a good thing, isn't it? The answer for me, and therefore for my protégés, is both yes and no. I have found my visibility to have both positive and negative consequences in several ways.

Although my visibility within the environment may provide some benefits to the students who work with me, I am told by some of these students that this visibility carries with it some costs. For example, some students have told me that they suspect that their work is more closely scrutinized and questioned by others and that their status among other students (which, they say, is tied to their mentor's status) is low. Other students have expressed concern that although I may be an excellent source of social support, my ability to provide career support as an advocate and protector is limited. This limitation makes students feel vulnerable and places them at risk within the university and the profession more generally.

In addition, as an African American woman scholar investigating the role of race and gender in organizations, I am visible in my work in the sense that I literally both see myself and can be seen in my work. Many presume, however, that legitimate and productive scholarship demands objectivity and impartiality. Objectivity, it is argued, requires a nonpartisan, color-blind, and gender-neutral approach to research, teaching, and other scholarly activities. If I do research on Black women, for example, I am presumed unable to adhere in that work to these principles of good research. However, I believe that I have the advantage of being clear about the ways in which my race and gender can provide invaluable insights into my work. Moreover, this experience convinces me that a successful and meaningful career can simultaneously support good scholarship, the need for diversity, and the goal of a more inclusive society; they are neither separate nor divergent but rather interdependent. Finally, these are all important insights that as a mentor—especially to other women and people of color—I am able to pass on.

I also have the paradoxical experience of having a visible status yet serving in roles that have an invisible impact in some situations. For example, students who recognize that I am a willing and understanding source of support sometimes ask me to provide advice and input, whether it be my perspective on a dissertation committee or other research projects. In this sense I am visible. Yet no matter how important these roles may be, they are often roles that remain behind the scenes and sometimes hidden from formal recognition. Informally I am told that students see my contributions as a source of support, strength, and influence, and in this, I feel gratified. I like the fact that even as an informal advisor to these students I have helped to shape their perspective on their work, the questions they ask, the research they do. Formally, however, these interactions do not enhance my status and, perhaps, ultimately detract from it.

Over the years, I have been counseled by colleagues to avoid the trap that seems to derail the careers of women, faculty of color, and especially women of color—the trap, that is, of responding to these kinds of requests for support and assistance. Many fear that the burden of having responsibility for students, especially marginalized students, places marginalized faculty at risk by diverting their attention away from research and teaching. Many times I have been advised to focus on my research agenda and to avoid being distracted and overburdened by dealing with issues such as diversity, gender equity, and minority student recruitment and retention.

More difficult than trying to balance the demands of being a scholar and a role model in the African American community has been finding a way to convince others that the roles they suggest I choose between are inextricably tied: My success in one depends on and cannot be separated from my success in the other. What others do not fundamentally understand is that my sense of interest and commitment to issues of diversity and inclusion demands that I function effectively in both roles. To manage their concerns, however, I find I must keep my role as mentor (especially to students of color) out of direct scrutiny within the institution. This effort, although burdensome, seems to work: A senior colleague once congratulated me on how successful I had been at avoiding the trap. I take this so-called success, however, as evidence for the notion that a commitment to scholarship and a commitment to diversity are compatible goals within our profession. I have avoided the trap not because I have chosen scholarship over mentorship but because I have used my mentoring experiences, both positive and negative, as valuable learning experiences. I believe, therefore, that my efforts and those of many women and people of color within our profession provide a model of how one need not choose between a successful career and a personal dedication to change.

Thus, as a mentor who is sometimes marginalized, the situation is complex and constantly producing new and difficult challenges. Some students of color need me as a mentor; others feel at risk with me as a mentor. There are typically few formal rewards and little recognition for mentoring either of these groups of students. A friend outside of the academy once asked me, "Why take all of this on?" My response to her was that my own experience as a protégé, together with my belief in the value of diversified mentoring relationships, has reinforced for me the need to continue playing this role, despite its down side. I have learned, however, to seek support from other mentors in similar situations and to take what I often call mentoring breaks to help focus and recharge my energies and reduce the stress of this complex status.

This need to protect myself from the stress and its impact is a lesson I have learned from the tragic story of Dianna Green and the many conversations I have had with friends and colleagues about the meaning of her situation and its implications for our own vulnerability. I have found that social support and effective coping tools are invaluable for me to continue to play a role that I fundamentally value and believe is important to the success of my students, my own career, and the larger academic and professional community.

BEING A WHITE WOMAN FACULTY MEMBER IN A PREDOMINANTLY BLACK MALE INSTITUTION

Although I emphasize the racial and gender components of my experience, I also discuss other aspects of my identity as they enter into the experience of marginalization: I am Jewish and a lesbian in a historically Black college that is situated in a White-dominant culture and society, whose faculty and student body are predominantly Christian and heterosexual, and whose leadership is predominantly male (as is the faculty in my department). Of these, my sexual orientation is least visible, my Jewishness somewhat more so, and my gender and race most visible. Of these, gender and race have, thus far, clearly played the largest role in defining my status as marginal.

I begin my story with what I feel is perhaps the greatest benefit I have received as a White faculty member in a predominantly Black institution: I have learned a lot about African American culture, perspectives, and experiences of discrimination that have put flesh on the bones of my "understanding" of racism. Jewish history and my own experiences of anti-Semitism paved the way for my openness to this learning (Tangri, 1996). Marginalization on any basis should heighten our sensitivity to the costs of marginalization experienced by others. Yet this does not always happen. Other important benefits of being where I am is the appreciation from some of my African American students for the mere fact that I have put my-self in this situation and the extent to which I can and do identify with or ap-preciate an African American perspective. I think it is a source of some small measure of hope for African American students to experience White people as being on their side. This situation also gives me the opportunity to model the role of ally. Depending on their experiences, African Americans may have difficulty trusting Whites to do the right thing. I hope that by be-ing one of those Whites, my students will understand the importance of be-ing allies to other minorities (Jews, Asian Americans, etc.).

I also have the occasional benefit of being able to be a uniquely situated ally for them. As an ally, my outsider status allows me to hear about certain of my students' experiences of race or gender issues that they would not feel comfortable divulging to most other faculty. For example, women students, both African American and White, have confided in me about their experi-ences of sexual harassment. Male and female students, both African Ameri-can and White, have confided in me about their unhappiness with certain pedagogical practices of other faculty. Although the latter experience is probably not unique to marginalized faculty members, I think it is signifi-cant that some of these complaints concerned racially based remarks made by faculty. For instance, one student said that his complaints to his instruc-tor about the course coverage were attributed by that instructor to the stu-dent being White, and that his race was why he did not appreciate the importance of the material being presented. Unfortunately, a Black student had the same complaint. In this case, I find it difficult to address the issue in a productive way that will not penalize the student. My societally dominant status as White gives me no currency within a Black institution on an issue that pits a Black perspective against a White perspective.

In the case of complaints about sexual harassment, however, I have been able to use my status as both a woman and an expert on sexual harassment to get the Department to provide training for faculty (first) and students (next) to minimize and deal with the problem of sexual harassment. It was the first issue around which my female colleagues (Black and White) and I coalesced. On the other hand, I am sure that if any of my male colleagues had wanted, they could have achieved the same thing. Nevertheless, it was very gratifying to be this kind of ally to the students.

Another benefit that is supposed to accrue to faculty mentors is the pride that comes with being a role model to others, but knowing that one is a role model can also be a burden. One cannot be a role model unless one is visi-ble, and it is hard to be visible to one's admirers without also being visible to one's detractors. With visibility, then, comes enhanced vulnerability. Visibility also limits one's flexibility to effect behind-the-scene changes (Catalyst, 1993; Kram, 1985). A powerful person perhaps need not worry about the vulnerability, but marginalized people lack a power base. Probably Dianna Green experienced the burden of visibility. She refused to give her picture to the Wall Street Journal and said that she was already overexposed (Hymowitz & Narisettie, 1997). Each of us has also felt first hand the special burden as well as the pride of knowing that we are role models for others within an organization.

As I have moved through the stages of my life, I know that at times, various individuals have admired certain aspects of how I do in the context of who I am: An older woman aging well; a Jewish woman knowledgeable about her culture; a White person making a contribution in a Black institution. Any of these labels carrys the risk of not living up to expectations. The most worrisome risk I have faced is the possible negative effect on my protégés of guilt by association when I decided I wanted to be out as a lesbian at work. This risk was significant, and I felt it necessary to check it out with them before doing it. Thus, increasing my visibility in this way is also a source of vulnerability for me and potentially for my students. Being marginalized on so many dimensions keeps me from being able to build the kind of stable power base one needs in order to risk being vulnerable. Unlike my heterosexual counterparts, I must be careful about bringing this aspect of who I am into work, as it adds to my stress and makes me feel more marginalized.

Direct interference is another cost experienced by marginalized persons who do not have the power to protect themselves or their students from such incursions. For example, I sought to involve a student in research that had the potential of bringing credit to both myself and the student. The student hesitated and then confessed that others had challenged her and set up obstacles by asking, "Well, what do you want to work with that White woman for, anyway?" and, "You'll never finish if you work on that project." After she changed mentors, I was unable to protect her from a very unhappy experience with another faculty member, which had the effect of derailing her academic progress for at least a semester. I heard why she had left after she returned to finish her work with me.

Complicating the issue is the tendency of those not marginalized to pass on to us students who, like us, are marginalized. Students who are deemed to be desirable are sometimes funneled away from us as would-be sponsors who devalue the type of work we do (as in the previous example). Sometimes students are sent to us who are deemed a risk by those who sit at the switch. Whereas popularity among prestigious students may adduce to faculty's perceived power within a department (Aisenberg & Harrington, 1988), popularity among low-prestige students does not.

Nevertheless, if others perceive a student to be high risk or undesirable for reasons of prejudice (e.g., they are foreign students, are gay, have disabilities, or have weak academic backgrounds), then I may benefit because these students may have other qualities that make them a pleasure to work with, such as strong motivation, a steep learning curve, delight in finding a gay faculty member to sponsor them or shared areas of interest. The funneling of marginalized students to marginalized faculty can therefore result in some happy and productive unions, but it may also produce some bizarre combinations, such as the traditional Moslem male student from Iran who ended up working, unhappily, with me, the Jewish female feminist sponsor! Without any overt signs of conflict, he quietly left me to do his work with someone else—after I had spent months working with him. Yet demographics alone do not predict either productive or unproductive relationships. I also formed a comfortable and productive working relationship with a Palestinian male student whose politics and intelligence I admired. Pairing with marginalized sponsors may provide students with more psychosocial as well as instrumental support compared to other pairings in developmental relationships. For instance, protégés expect that I will stick by them through extended periods of absence and lack of contact, which may last as long as a year. I believe other mentors would consider these serious enough breaches of etiquette to warrant termination of the special relationship. Indeed, there is the significant negative cost for both myself and my protégé because work, degrees, presentations, and publications may be delayed or abandoned.

SUMMARY

We have explored the particular challenges and obstacles that can occur in diversified mentoring relationships when the mentor has marginalized or solo status within the environment. One consistent aspect across our experiences was the issue of visibility. If a mentor's or sponsor's visible identity group memberships are valued within the environment, they can enhance developmental relationships. If they are devalued within the environment, however, they can create obstacles to the power and influence a sponsor or mentor can wield on her protégé's behalf. The experiences we have de-

scribed here illustrate many of the challenges that are present when the senior person's status is devalued because of race, ethnicity, gender, or sexual
orientation. They also provide models for success in overcoming obstacles
and creating productive diversified mentoring relationships.

Clearly, one impact of marginalized status is to render the mentor less
powerful, less able to protect the protégé, and less able to access the informal networks that provide opportunity for the mentor as well as the
protégé. Some have labeled this effect the *stratification of mentoring* (see
Grant & Atkinson, 1997, or Dreher & Cox, 1996), which refers to the benefits and costs, both intrinsic and extrinsic, of functioning as a high-status
versus a low-status mentor within the environment. This stratification was
evident in our stories here.

In addition, a common theme in our experiences is the more demanding
nature of the mentoring roles we have played within our respective environments. White women and ethnic minorities may be called upon more often than White men to provide mentoring that is broad, intensive, and
self-involving. Protégés may seek us out because they see us as more likely to
provide psychosocial or spiritual as well as instrumental support. These demands require us to develop a broad range of skills and expertise in
mentoring relationships that may be unique to women and people of color
who are marginalized within their environments. These skills and expertise
have provided a foundation for our efforts to create incremental change
within our institutions by influencing the research, perspectives, content,
and values of this generation of students in the academy.

Nevertheless, we have had to manage at least two kinds of problems in
our diversified developmental relationships: internal and external
(Clawson & Kram, 1984; Kram, 1985). Problems that are internal to the relationship include the protégé becoming too demanding or the mentor losing professional distance. Problems that are external to the relationship
include fears, jealousies, or other negative opinions about the mentoring
dyad that outsiders to the relationship may feel if they perceive that the
mentor and protégé have become too close. Although these situations were
always potential problems in our developmental relationships with students, we both developed a variety of strategies for overcoming them, as
well as the other challenges we faced.

Hence, although mentoring at the margin is not always easy, we feel it
has provided us with a unique set of opportunities and skills that we will, no
doubt, pass on to the students we mentor. This kind of creative adjustment

and coping within a marginalized environment is perhaps one aspect of diversified developmental relationships that deserves further study.

CONCLUDING THOUGHTS

Our chapter began with the story of Dianna Green as one dramatic illustration of the potential costs associated with being a role model, sponsor, and mentor from a marginalized position. Her untimely death reminds us of the vulnerability and isolation many people feel as they attempt to help others achieve the kind of success they have achieved—a success that nevertheless can, for some, prove ultimately to be empty, lonely, and joyless. Clearly there are benefits to being a visible individual, as a person of color or as a woman within an organization. Our own stories illustrate that along with these potential benefits, there are often great risks. We have written about our own experiences not to suggest that we share the extent of vulnerability and isolation Dianna Green must have felt, nor to suggest that such experiences in developmental relationships routinely lead to such drastic consequences as suicide. Rather, we feel it is crucial that people recognize these experiences as some of the many sources of added stress with which marginalized people in positions of authority must cope. The story of Dianna Green is tragic yet illuminating. Her story focuses us on the need to strike a balance between visibility and vulnerability, between uniqueness and isolation, between attachment and avoidance. Finally, we hope that with this recognition might come the impetus for changes in our institutions that could help to alleviate some of that stress, ensuring that diversified developmental relationships produce positive outcomes for both the protégés and mentors who support and encourage them.

ACKNOWLEDGMENT

I (Sandra Tangri) would like to thank Kimya Lee for her help in researching this article.

RFERENCES

Aisenberg, N., & Harrington, M. (1988). Women of academe: Outsiders in the sacred grove. Amherst: University of Massachusetts Press.
Alderfer, C., & Smith, K. K. (1992). Studying intergroup relations embedded in organizations. *Administrative Science Quarterly, 27,* 35–65.
Catalyst. (1993). *Mentoring: A guide to corporate programs and practices.* New York: Catalyst.

Clawson, J. G. and Kram, K. E. (1984). Managing cross-gender mentoring. *Business Horizons, 27*(3), 22–32.

Dreher, G. F., & Cox, T. H. (1996). Race, gender, and opportunity: A study of compensation attainment and the establishment of mentoring relationships. *Journal of Applied Psychology, 81*, 297–308.

Frable, D. S. (1993). Dimensions of marginality: Distinctions among those who are different. *Personality and Social Psychology Bulletin, 19*, 370–380.

Grant, T. S., & Atkinson, D. R. (1995). Cross-cultural mentor effectiveness and African-American male students. *Journal of Black Psychology, 23*(3), 120–134.

Hughes, E. C. (1945). Dilemmas and contradictions of status. *American Journal of Sociology, 50*, 353–359.

Hymowitz, C., & Narisetti, R. (1997). A promising career comes to a tragic end and a city asks why. *Wall Street Journal*, pp. B4–5.

Kram, K. E. (1985). *Mentoring at work: Developmental relationship in organizational* life. Glenview, IL: Scott, Foresman.

Ragins, B. R. (1997). Diversified mentoring relationships in organizations: A power perspective. *Academy of Management Review, 22*, 482–521.

Ragins, B. R., & Cotton, J. L. (1993). Gender and willingness to mentor in organizations. *Journal of Management, 19*, 97–111.

Ragins, B. R., & Scandura, T. A. (1994). Gender differences in expected outcomes of mentoring relationships. *Academy of Management Journal, 37*, 957–971.

Tangri, S. (1996). Living with anomalies: Sojourns of a White-American Jew. In, K. F. Wyche & F. J. Crosby (Eds.), *Women's ethnicities: Journeys through psychology.* (pp. 142–158) Boulder, CO: Westview Press.

Thomas, D. A. (1990). The impact of race on mangers' experiences of developmental relationships (mentoring and sponsorship): An intra-organizational study. *Journal of Organizational Behavior, 11*, 479–492.

Thomas, D. A., & Alderfer, C. (1989). The influences of race on career dynamics theory and research on minority career experiences. In M. B. Arthur, D. T. Hall, & B. S. Lawrence (Eds.), *Handbook of career theory* (pp. 133–!58). Cambridge, England: Cambridge University Press.

IV

Conclusions

13

Where Do We Go From Here, and How Do We Get There? Methodological Issues in Conducting Research on Diversity and Mentoring Relationships

Belle Rose Ragins
University of Wisconsin–Milwaukee

As the millennium approaches and the workforce becomes increasingly diverse, more research will be conducted on diversity and mentoring relationships in organizations. We hope that this book will help chart new directions for future research on diversity and mentoring relationships and will ignite a stream of research in this exciting new area. Through the course of this book we have made some inroads into exploring the relationship between diversity and mentoring relationships. However, we also know that the answer to one question usually means the beginning of another. Because diversity and mentoring are both relatively new constructs and it is clear that we have more questions than answers, at this juncture we can provide only a rudimentary road map for future research on diversity and mentoring relationships in organizations.

The purpose of this chapter is to highlight methodological issues that will confront researchers attempting to navigate through this new terrain of diversity and mentoring relationships. This chapter is pragmatic and admittedly prescriptive and focuses primarily on practical issues involved with conducting survey research in this area. I first delve into the thorny issues regarding measurement and operationalization of the constructs of mentoring and diversity. Then I explore special considerations in designing research to study diversity and mentoring relationships. Finally, I present a brief research map for pathing the new frontier of diversity and mentoring relationships.

MEASUREMENT AND OPERATIONALIZATION OF CONSTRUCTS

Defining and Measuring Mentoring

As discussed in Faye Crosby's comprehensive introductory chapter (chap. 1, this volume), practitioners and academics have defined mentoring somewhat differently. Although a mentor is often viewed as being different from a sponsor in corporate settings and this distinction has been made in some practitioner journals, most recent empirical and theoretical research published in academic journals does not distinguish between a sponsor and mentor.[1] This research adheres to Kram's (1985) traditional definition of a mentor as someone who may provide a host of career development and psychosocial functions, which may include role modeling and sponsoring behaviors. The construct of mentor in this chapter also adheres to this traditional definition of a mentor and does not make the distinction between mentor and sponsor.

Whatever the term used, it is important that the definition be provided to survey respondents. Early survey research avoided using the word *mentor* or defining the term because of a lack of consensus in the literature on the definition. In some cases respondents were asked to consider someone who had helped them in their careers and were then asked to complete questions regarding the functions and nature of the relationship. Today, this approach may be confusing for the respondent; the word *mentor* is now a household word, and by *not* using that word on the survey, respondents may wonder if the researcher is asking about a relationship *different* from that of the mentor. Along those same lines, in early studies of mentoring respondents were

---

[1]See, for example, research by Dreher and Ash (1990), Dreher and Cox, (1996), Fagenson (1989), Scandura (1992), and Ragins and Scandura (1997). See also the special mentoring issue of the *Journal of Vocational Behavior* (Russell, 1997).

asked first to consider in a general sense *relationships* with senior managers who were instrumental in helping their careers and then to complete questions regarding the specific functions and nature of a relationship. This technique may have created confusion for the respondents and jeopardized the validity of the study; respondent were not clear on which relationship to consider when completing the survey. A key lesson to be learned from these early studies is that it is important to provide a clear definition of mentor for respondents and to make sure that they focus on a *specific relationship* as they complete the survey.

When conducting research in this area, it is advantageous to remember that a respondent may have more than one mentor at a single point in time (cf. Kram & Hall, 1996), particularly with the advent of formal mentoring programs, as discussed later in this chapter. The survey should allow respondents to indicate if they have more than one mentor, and the instructions should provide guidance as to which mentor the respondent should consider when completing the survey. Depending on the topic of research, respondents with multiple mentors may be deleted from the final analysis. Alternatively, it would be interesting to assess the career and organizational outcomes associated with having more than one mentor at the same time, as compared to a single mentor.

Along those same lines, some individuals may be both a protégé and a mentor at a given point in time. Although we do not know the frequency of this situation, it is likely to occur for two reasons. First, an individual's experience as a protégé has been found to be a significant predictor in the decision to become a mentor (Ragins & Cotton, 1993; Ragins & Scandura, in press). Individuals who are protégés see the value in the relationship and are likely to enter the relationship again as mentors, perhaps even before they are finished as protégé. Second, as discussed later, there is an increase in the use of mentoring programs in organizations. Some mentoring programs assign entry-level protégés to first-line supervisors who are in early career stages and are also likely to be informal protégés (Murray, 1991).

Mentoring relationships may take a variety of forms (cf. Eby, 1997; Kram & Hall, 1996), so it is important to ask respondents about the type of mentoring relationships they have. The first consideration is the specific position of the mentor. Mentors who are supervisors provide different functions from mentors who hold other positions in organizations (Burke, McKenna, & McKeen, 1991; Fagenson-Eland, Marks, & Amendola, 1997; Ragins & McFarlin, 1990). Mentors who are at higher ranks than protégés may also differ from mentors who are senior in experience but hold a lateral or peer position (Kram & Isabella, 1985). Mentors who are senior in experience but hold positions lateral to protégés may provide different mentoring functions than mentors at higher ranks (Kram & Isabella, 1985). These issues are particularly relevant with respect to gender and race (cf. Ragins, 1997a). Because women face greater barriers to mentoring relationships than men (Ragins & Cotton, 1991), they may be more likely to develop relationships with their immediate supervisors and senior peers, particularly when they are seeking same-gender relationships. A different scenario may occur for other minority[2] groups who are in the numerical minority in organizations. In cases with few minority members in a work group, minority employees may need to go outside their departments, or even their organizations to find a same-race mentor (cf. Thomas & Higgins, 1996). In support of this idea, David Thomas (1990) found that African American protégés were more likely than European American protégés to go outside their departments and formal lines of authority to develop mentoring relationships with higher ranking mentors of the same race.

In addition to the hierarchical position of the mentor, it is beneficial to ascertain whether the mentor is employed in the same organization as the protégé. *Internal* mentors are those employed in the same organization, whereas *external* mentors are employed in other organizations (Ragins, 1997b). This question becomes increasingly relevant as employees engage in more lateral career paths that span organizational boundaries (cf. Arthur & Rousseau, 1996; Hall & Mirvis, 1996). With increased mobility and boundaryless careers more mentoring relationships are likely to span organizational boundaries, and more relationships are likely to become long-distance relationships. It is reasonable to assume that external relationships may provide different functions and career outcomes than internal mentoring relationships (Ragins, 1997b). Similarly, long-distance relationships may be less effective in some ways than proximal relationships. These distinctions have particular relevance for women and other minorities in organizations who, when faced with a glass ceiling and barriers to advancement, may advance by making lateral moves between organizations. Women and minority managers in organizations may therefore have a special need for external mentoring relationships, and this type of relationship needs to be measured and assessed in research on diversity and mentoring.

---

[2]The term *minority* refers to group power rather than numerical status and may include race, ethnicity, gender, physical abilities and characteristics, age, class, religion, and sexual orientation.

A third consideration is whether the mentoring relationship is part of a formal mentoring program. One key difference between formal and informal mentoring relationships is that informal relationships develop spontaneously, whereas formal mentoring relationships develop with organizational assistance or intervention, usually in the form of voluntary assignment. A second distinction is that formal relationships are usually of much shorter duration than informal relationships (Douglas, 1997); most formal mentoring relationships last a year or less. It is estimated that a third of the nation's major companies have formal mentoring programs (Bragg, 1989), and this figure is expected to increase (Murray, 1991). Existing research indicates not only that formal relationships are less effective than informal relationships but that formal relationships are less effective for women than for men (Ragins & Cotton, in press). This issue has particular relevance for women and other minority employees in organizations, as they are often targeted for mentoring programs as part of diversity initiatives. This practice may be especially harmful if formal relationships are presented as substitutes for the more effective informal relationships (Keele, Buckner, & Bushnell, 1987; Kram & Bragar, 1992).

I hope it is clear from this discussion that it is important to measure the specific type of mentoring relationships when conducting research on mentoring in general, and it is even more important to consider this issue when conducting research on diversity and mentoring. By asking respondents about mentoring relationships without specifying the nature of these relationships, researchers may be mixing apples and oranges, and the mix may differ for majority and minority groups in organizations. In the next section I explore operationalization and measurement issues involved with investigating diversity as it applies to mentoring relationships.

DEFINING AND MEASURING DIVERSITY WITHIN THE MENTORING RELATIONSHIP

Diversity is a new and evolving area of research. There are a number of different perspectives for operationalizing and measuring the construct of diversity, and most of the existing theory and research relates to work teams or dyadic relationships involving supervisors and subordinates (cf. Jackson & Ruderman, 1995). Most researchers agree that diversity extends to a variety of group characteristics, including but not limited to race, ethnicity, gender, sexual orientation, physical ability and appearance, mental ability, age, class, education, and religion (Loden & Rosener, 1991). Some researchers include a host of other demographic and personality variables, including knowledge, skills, abilities, values, beliefs, attitudes, personality attributes, cognitive and behavioral styles, and organizational variables relating to position, rank, department, and tenure (McGrath, Berdahl, & Arrow, 1995; Milliken & Martins, 1996).

A number of theories have been applied to the area of diversity.[3] The major ones include social identity theory (Brewer, 1995; Tajfel, 1978), which investigates the impact of group membership on self-concept, relational demography theory (Tsui, Egan, & O'Reilly, 1992; Tsui, Egan, & Xin, 1995; Tsui, Xin, & Egan, 1995; Tsui & O'Reilly, 1989), which investigates the causes and consequences of the composition of specific demographic attributes of employees on the dyad or group; and group proportions theory (Tolbert, Andrews, & Simons, 1995), which explores how changes in the relative sizes of subgroups affects the relationships between groups. Other perspectives include the effects of group and societal culture (Ferdman, 1995; Triandis, 1995) and organizational structure and climate (Cox, 1993) on individuals and teams in organizations.

Although these approaches help explain processes involving diversity in the workplace, they are somewhat limited in explaining diversity in mentoring relationships. This limitation stems from the fact that most perspectives on diversity do not incorporate power as a contextual variable. As illustrated so poignantly by Murrell and Tangri (chap. 2, this volume) and discussed at length here, power is a critical factor in the development and outcomes of mentoring relationships, especially in mentoring relationships involving minority members.

Some authors define diversity within the context of power and privilege in organizations (Ely, 1995a, 1995b; McGrath et al., 1995; Ragins, 1995, 1997b), and others (Nkomo, 1995; Sessa & Jackson, 1995) observe that many existing theories and models of diversity ignore group differences by assuming that different types of diversity are more or less equal in their consequences: Gender and race differences, for example, are equated with demographic differences in age, education, and occupation. As a point in fact, all demographic groups are not created equal: Some groups face discrimination in society, in the organization, and in the work group. These group differences in discrimination reciprocally affect group differences in power,

---

[3]See, for example, edited books by Chemers, Oskamp, and Costanzo (1995), Jackson and Ruderman (1995), and the special diversity issue of the *Academy of Management Review* (Jackson, 1996).

which in turn spill over to individuals (Blalock, 1967; Schermerhorn, 1956) and their work relationships (Ragins, 1997a; Ragins & Sundstrom, 1989).

Discrimination based on group membership creates a world experience that is shared among members of a group, and this experience may have more of an impact than simply having a specific demographic characteristic. For example, according to relational demography theory, the more similar an individual's demographic characteristics are to those of the group or supervisor, the greater the attraction and the more positive the outcome (Tsui et al., 1992). However, a power perspective predicts that similarity in such social identities as age, education, and organizational tenure should not have as strong an effect on attraction as similarity on the basis of race, gender, or sexual orientation. For example, the sole African American supervisor in an all-White department should feel greater alliance and similarity to her same-race subordinate than the sole Ph.D. in a department would feel toward a subordinate with the same educational background. This experience reflects more than shared social identity; it reflects a shared world and organizational experience characterized by lack of power and marginalization.

A power perspective also questions the assumption of symmetrical effects of group membership. Many existing models of diversity assume that the effects of shared social identities are the same for people in the majority and in the minority. For example, theoretically, gender as social identity is held to have the same effect for men and women. What this belief means in practice is that a sole woman in an all-men group would have the equivalent experience as a sole man in an all-women group. This view does not take into account the facts that men have more status and power in our society than women and that gender differences in societal power and status spill over into the workplace. Recent research supports the perspective that group differences are asymmetrical. Riordan and Shore's (1997) study on relational demography and group attitudes, for example, found that demographic similarity to work groups had a different effect for African Americans than for White group members. Along those same lines, Ragins and Cotton (1996) found that numerical proportions had different effects on men's and women's organizational and career attitudes; the experience of being in the numerical minority differed for men and women. These studies suggest that the experience of being an "O" in an "all-X" work group varies on the basis of group membership and the power associated with that group. This issue becomes even more complex when multiple group memberships are considered, in that these effects may be multiplicative, rather than additive, and when group memberships that are often not easily observable are considered (e.g., sexual orientation, class, some forms of disability and religion).

These issues all come into play when investigating diversity in mentoring relationships. I view diversity from a power perspective, which ties quite neatly with mentoring, which is also grounded in power relations (Ragins, 1997b). Mentoring is related to the protégé's development of resources for power within organizations; existing research indicates that protégés report more positional power (Fagenson, 1988) and receive more promotions and compensation (Dreher & Ash, 1990) than nonprotégés. Mentoring is also a source of power for mentors, as protégés affect the mentors' status and credibility in the organization and can provide a loyal base of support and expertise from which to build power (Ragins & Scandura, 1994).

A central premise promoted here, which is grounded in power and intergroup relations theory (Blalock, 1967; Lenski, 1966; Schermerhorn, 1956; Wilson, 1973), is that mentoring does not occur in a vacuum, it occurs within an organizational context composed of groups and power relationships among groups. This perspective also provides insight into the distinction between mentoring and leadership relationships. Although mentoring relationships differ from leader–member relationships in many ways, from a power perspective the salient difference between these relationships is that the central purpose of mentoring relationships is to provide resources for power for the protégé and, more indirectly, for the mentor. In contrast, leader–member relationships are concerned primarily with the effective completion of job and work group functions. Mentoring relationships also differ from leader–member relationships in that mentors usually reach beyond the work group to capture power resources for their protégés. The outcomes of mentoring relationships are therefore affected by other individuals in the organization and often those in other organizations. The mentoring relationship essentially extends beyond the dyad into the organization. This situation has direct implications for unit of analysis issues, as discussed later in this chapter.

Diversified mentoring relationships are composed of mentors and protégés, who differ on one or more group memberships associated with power in organizations (Ragins, 1995, 1997b). This definition employs a power framework for defining diversity in organizations and presents diversity in terms of power differences between groups in organizations. Diversified mentoring relationships are unique from other types of mentoring relationships because of the differences in power brought to the relationships by virtue of group membership. As an aside, it should be noted that these differences vary by country and culture. For example, whereas most group differences in religion are not associated with substantial power differences in the United States, membership in different religious groups is associated with discrimination and differences in group power in other parts of the world, such as Israel, Northern Ireland, India, and Bosnia. It is therefore important that researchers have a clear understanding of the particular power dynamics among groups in their populations of study.

The diversified mentoring construct is described at length in an earlier article, along with specific recommendations regarding the measurement and operationalization of the construct (Ragins, 1997b). Briefly, researchers can measure both the presence of diversified mentoring relationships and the degree of diversity in these relationships. The degree of diversity in mentoring relationships is viewed as a continuous variable that takes into account group memberships of the mentor and protégé, the number of groups in which the mentor and protégé differ, the power differences associated with those groups, and the importance attached to those differences by the dyad as well as others in the organization. This concept addresses unit of analysis issues and is elaborated upon in the next section.

DESIGN AND ANALYSIS ISSUES

Unit of Analysis

The study of diversified mentoring relationship requires special attention to certain unit of analysis and other design issues. First, as gleaned from the previous discussion, it is advantageous to obtain data from both the mentor and the protégé as well as from others in the organization who can affect the relationship and its outcomes. This information provides clarity as to the degree of diversity in the relationship. Getting "360-degree" information on the dyad also illuminates the degree of congruency in perceptions of the relationship's processes and outcomes. For example, investigations of behaviors and functions in the relationship could be more fully understood if the protégé, the mentor, and others involved with the dyad gave their views on the relationship. The degree of congruency among these dyadic and network perceptions is an interesting topic of study, as is the issue of the moderators that affect the congruency of these perceptions (e.g., the degree of diversity in the relationship, the length of the relationship, and the structure of the relationship).

Second, investigating the effects of multiple group memberships on the mentoring relationship is important for assessing the degree of diversity in mentoring relationships as well as for studying the effects of diversified relationships on mentoring processes and outcomes. As illustrated by Blake (chap. 10, this volume) and other authors (Bell, 1990; Bell, Denton & Nkomo, 1993), it is reasonable to expect that race and gender interact in a synergistic fashion in mentoring relationships.

Finally, it is important to consider if these differences really matter to the members of the relationship or to other relevant members of the organization. A researcher may assess a given relationship as being quite diverse, but what if the differences are of no consequence to the members? Two relationships with identical composition are not identical in practice if the members in one relationship do not perceive the differences or view the differences as inconsequential. These issues have important implications for measuring the degree of diversity in mentoring relationships in that they call for perceptual measures and a dyadic or organizational unit of analysis.

An example helps illustrate the complexity of these issues. Consider mentoring relationship A, which involves a straight working-class female mentor and a gay middle-class male protégé. In terms of diversity, this relationship clearly differs from a relationship that varies only on the basis of gender (mentoring relationship B). To what degree do these two relationships differ? The mentor and protégé in relationship A differ on at least three group memberships that may relate to power in their organization: sexual orientation, class, and gender. Using a power perspective, the members of the relationship bring different power resources to the relationship by virtue of their group membership, and each group provides different amounts of power. It is therefore important to consider not only the number of groups in which the mentor and protégé differ but also the differences in power between majority and minority members of each group. The researcher may argue that because most gay persons in this country are not legally protected from workplace discrimination on the basis of their group membership (National Gay and Lesbian Task Force, 1996), differences in power on the basis of sexual orientation may be greater than differences based on class or gender. However, what if the organization is owned by a gay person or has policies prohibiting workplace discrimination on the basis of sexual orientation? This example illustrates the importance of asking the mentor, protégé, and other relevant members of the organization about the intergroup power differences in their organizations. To continue the example, the researcher may find significant power differences between straight and gay employees in the organization and may discover that gay employees are frequently discriminated against in hiring and promotion decisions. However, does this affect mentoring relationship A? Perhaps members of relationship A do not care a whit about their differences on the sexual orientation dimension, but these differences are very important to the network of individuals in the organization who need to work with the mentor in helping the protégé obtain career goals. This example illustrates the importance of collecting perceptual data from multiple sources.

Data Analysis

Analyzing data from diversified mentoring relationships requires special decisions and considerations. The first decision involves the inclusion of interaction terms in the analysis. Reviews of the literature on race and gender main effects in mentoring relationships reveal that the effects of race and gender on mentoring relationships are often inconsistent (Noe, 1988; O'Neil, Horton, & Crosby, chap. 7, this volume; Ragins, 1989). One reason is that many studies investigate the main effects of race or gender without testing the interaction of these variables. The interaction term is key because it represents the composition of the mentoring relationship.

Focusing only on the main effects of protégé or mentor group memberships is not only insufficient; it also has the potential to bias the findings of the study. For example, a researcher may investigate the effects of protégé gender on mentor functions in a male-dominated organization and find that female protégés report less social involvement with their mentors than male protégés report. The researcher may conclude that female protégés impose more social distance from their mentors than male protégés do. However, an inspection of the gender composition of the relationships may likely reveal that female protégés in male-dominated organizations are primarily in cross-gender relationships, whereas their male counterparts have mentors of the same gender. If a sufficient sample of male protégés with female mentors were available, the researcher may discover that male protégés in cross-gender relationships report restricted socialization as well, which in fact we found in one of our earlier studies (Ragins & McFarlin, 1990). Other research reported in this volume also points to the criticality of investigating the effect of composition of mentoring relationships on mentoring functions and outcomes (Kirby & Jackson, chap. 6; McGuire, chap. 11). Investigating only main effects assumes that the gender or racial composition of the relationship is the same for minority and majority members of organizations, which is usually not the case.

Investigating same versus cross-membership relationships may also be insufficient for capturing the true nature of diversified mentoring relationships. For example, lumping men and women in cross-gender mentoring relationships in one group does not take into account the asymmetrical nature of group differences that was discussed earlier in this chapter. A relationship involving a male protégé with a female mentor may differ dramatically from a relationship composed of a female protégé with a male mentor. In fact, we examined the separate effects of all four possible gender combinations of mentoring relationships and discovered that although same-gender and cross-gender relationships did not differ significantly in terms of mentoring functions, the specific gender composition of the mentoring relationship had a significant effect on mentoring functions and career outcomes (Ragins & Cotton, in press).

Control Variables

Another consideration related to analysis is the use of control variables. It is important to control for variables that affect processes and outcomes of mentoring relationships yet also vary by group membership. For example, the mentor's position and rank in the organization influence mentor functions (Fagenson-Eland et al., 1997; Ragins & McFarlin, 1990) and may also influence the protégé's career and developmental outcomes. Experienced mentors at higher ranks may have a greater ability to help their protégés' careers than novice mentors at lower ranks. However, group differences in these variables may confound the research: middle management women are less likely to be mentors than are their male counterparts (Ragins & Cotton, 1993), African Americans are more likely to have nonsupervisory mentors than Europeans Americans (Thomas, 1990), and minority groups tend to be in lower organizational ranks than majority groups are (Brown & Ford, 1977; DeFreitas, 1991; Korn/Ferry, 1993). As pointed out by McGuire (chap. 11, this volume), these are structural variables that may account for findings of race and gender differences in mentoring relationships. These variables may also confound research on diversified mentoring relationships.

Other demographic variables need to be considered as control variables in studies of diversified mentoring relationships. Age, career stage, organizational tenure, socioeconomic class, and education may influence mentor functions and protégé outcomes, and they may also vary by group membership (Knouse, 1992; Paludi, Meyers, Kindermann, Speicher, & Haring-Hidore, 1990; Ragins & McFarlin, 1990). In agreement with some of the ideas articulated by Hoyt (chap. 3, this volume), Whitely, Dougherty, and Dreher (1991) found that protégés from higher socioeconomic backgrounds received more career development functions from their mentors than did protégés from lower socioeconomic backgrounds. Paludi and her associates (Paludi et al., 1990) observed that gender differences in career stages may affect the mentoring relationship. Because of interrupted careers, female protégés may be older than their male counterparts, resulting possibly in constrained role modeling in their mentoring relationships. Older female protégés may also be viewed as mother figures in their mentoring relationships and may experience reversed psychosocial functions and more limited career development support. Finally, Knouse (1992) observed that language issues may result in Latino employees having different career stages and requiring different functions from their mentors than Anglo employees.

Mentoring history variables may also need to be included as control variables in diversified mentoring research. Existing research indicates that mentoring functions are related to the number of prior mentoring relationships, the length of the relationships, and the mentor's position as supervisor or formal mentor (Chao, Walz & Gardner, 1992; Ragins & McFarlin, 1990).

Researchers need to check for group differences in these potential control variables. If minority and majority group members differ on these variables, they need to be included as covariates in the analysis. Use of covariate variables uses up degrees of freedom and depletes the statistical power of analyses. It may therefore be advisable to use a matched-pairs research design to control for some structural variables (cf. Lyness & Thompson, 1997). We used a matched-pairs research design in many of our studies—we matched men and women on structural variables such as rank, department, and specialization (cf. Ragins & Cotton, 1991, 1993; Ragins & Scandura, 1994, 1997, in press). This matching strategy also eliminated gender differences in related variables such as compensation, tenure, employment status, and even age.

Sampling Issues in Diversified Mentoring Research

A dominant issue when conducting research on diversity and diversified mentoring relationships is obtaining balanced groups of minority and majority respondents. Diversity researchers struggle to obtain adequate samples of minority respondents and often end up comparing small samples of minority respondents with large samples of majority respondents. From a methodological standpoint, using small minority group samples increases the probability of skewed samples and depletes the statistical power needed to find significant effects. Using small minority group samples also raises issues regarding generalizability of samples and nonresponse bias. Finally, small minority samples prevent subgroup analysis of the effects of other dimensions of diversity (e.g., gender, sexual orientation, race, ethnicity, age, class, disability, and religion).

Some researchers combine different minority groups into one group in order to increase the size of minority group samples. For example, Latino Americans, Asian Americans, and African Americans are frequently combined into one group, labeled minority, and are compared with European American groups. Gender differences and other dimensions of diversity are essentially ignored, assumed to be held constant across both minority and majority groups. This practice create three problems. First, it limits the generalizability of findings of the study. Intergroup differences are lost when groups are combined, and it may be inaccurate to generalize the findings of the study to a specific group. This limitation is further aggravated by the fact that different studies combine different minority groups into one minority category.

Second, this practice limits the ability of the study to serve as a basis for future theory development. How can we develop adequate theory on the effects of different group memberships on mentoring relationships when we lack empirical research that distinguishes among different groups? Lack of theory, in turn, promotes research that combines groups, thus perpetuating the cycle.

Third, this practice calls to question the validity of the findings of the study. The researcher makes two assumptions when comparing minority and majority groups on one dimension of diversity (i.e., ethnicity) while ignoring differences on other dimensions of diversity (e.g., sexual orientation, gender, class). The first assumption is that differences on other dimensions of diversity are equally likely to occur in the minority group and the majority group. This is clearly not the case when a research is comparing groups on the basis of race and ethnicity while assuming no group differences in socioeconomic class. The second assumption is that dimensions of diversity are additive rather than interactive; that is, the effect of being a member of more than one group is the same for individuals in the minority and those in the majority. For example, given this assumption, the cumulative effects of race and gender are viewed as the same for African Americans and European Americans. The researcher would therefore compare an African American group and a European American group of men and women and not investigate whether gender mediates the relationship between race and the dependent variable of interest.

In order to avoid this assumption and the problems associated with it, we must have a relatively large sample of minority respondents in order to assess the interactions between group memberships in the majority and minority groups. The standard practice of conducting random surveys of employees is unlikely to produce the sample needed to conduct these analyses. Instead it may be necessary when studying a specific minority group to oversample the group or use professional associations or other organizations with minority group members.

FUTURE RESEARCH:
A ROUGH ROAD BUT WORTH THE JOURNEY

The outlook for future research on diversity and mentoring is absolutely bright, in spite of the special challenges and considerations involved with conducting research in this emerging new area. There is an absolute abundance of topics for future research, more than I can even begin to cover in the remainder of this chapter. However, I highlight a few areas that have special promise, many of which have a theoretical foundation (cf. Kram, & Hall, 1996; Ragins, 1989, 1997a, 1997b; Thomas & Alderfer, 1989; Thomas & Higgins, 1996)

First, there is a need to understand how the specific composition of the mentoring relationship affects the initiation and development of the relationship, the processes in the relationship, the stages of the relationship (Kram, 1983), and the career and organizational outcomes for both the mentor and the protégé. Additionally, future research can also explore the relationship between diversified mentoring relationships and other members of the organization, such as supervisors, work groups and informal networks (cf. Ibarra, 1993). For example, what is the relationship between mentoring and networking for minority members of organizations, and does this differ from that of their majority counterparts? How do diversified mentoring relationships affect work group interactions and relationships with supervisors? Research efforts such as these need to investigate not just race, ethnicity, and gender but also the interactive effects of these group memberships with other group memberships relating to sexual orientation, class, religion, and physical and mental abilities and characteristics.

Because the concept of career and career stages may vary for many of these groups, future research on diversified mentoring relationships can use a longitudinal design to ascertain the mentoring functions most effective for specific career stages for these different groups. The fact that career paths increasingly extend beyond organizational boundaries and span different organizations (Arthur & Rousseau, 1996; Hall & Mirvis, 1996) calls for a special consideration of the relationship between the boundaryless career and diversified mentoring relationships (cf. Thomas & Higgins, 1996). It is useful to assess how diversity in mentoring relationships affects the prevalence and form of inter-organizational and long-distance mentoring. Under what conditions do minority groups seek mentors in other organizations? What are the functions and outcomes of these relationships, and how do they differ from relationships involving members of majority groups in organizations?

Many organizations are jumping on the formal mentoring bandwagon without adequate information on whether the outcomes of formal relationships differ for majority and minority members of organizations. Although initial research indicates that the gender composition of the mentoring relationship affects mentoring functions and outcomes associated with having a formal mentor (Ragins & Cotton, in press), much work remains to be done in this area.

As illustrated by Hoyt (chap. 3, this volume), there has been a lack of research on the relationship between class and mentoring. Moreover, most of our research has focused on managers and white-collar samples. We need to look at the effects of occupation and class on functions and outcomes of mentoring relationships. Do blue-collar mentoring relationships differ from white-collar relationships? What is the effect of other dimensions of diversity on these relationships? Along those same lines, most research on gender and mentoring has been conducted in male-dominated organizations and occupations. It is important to extend this research and compare mentoring relationships in male-typed, female-typed, and gender-integrated occupations and organizations.

Finally, future research may disentangle the effects of gender and structure on mentoring relationships. As emphasized in this chapter, it is important to control for structural effects, such as rank, when comparing mentoring relationships among minority and majority groups. However, it would be interesting to compare the effects of structure and diversity on mentoring relationships. In other words, how much of the variance in mentoring outcomes is accounted for by structural variables rather than gender? One way to assess this issue is to compare two matched samples of men and women, one at a high rank and one at a low rank in an organization. Differences between the high- and low-ranking groups would be a function of structure, whereas between-group differences in gender would reflect pure gender effects. The interesting variable of course is the potential interaction between rank and gender, which may indicate that rank has different implications for men and women.

In conclusion, Workforce 2000 is here (Johnston & Packer, 1987), and so are diversified mentoring relationships. In this chapter I attempted to provide a rudimentary road map for studying diversified mentoring relationships. Researchers attempting to study these complex and challenging relationships will certainly have their hands full but will also garnish the rewards associated with breaking new grounds and frontiers.

REFERENCES

Arthur, M. B., & Rousseau, D. M. (Eds.). (1996). *The boundaryless career: A new employment principle for a new organizational era*. New York: Oxford University Press.

Bell, E. L. (1990). The bicultural life experiences of career oriented black women. *Journal of Organizational Behavior, 11*, 459–477.

Bell, E. L., Denton, T. C., & Nkomo, S. (1993). Women of color in management: Toward an inclusive analysis. In E. Fagenson (Ed.), *Women in management: Trends, issues, and challenges in managerial diversity* (Vol. 4: Women and Work Series, pp. 105–130). Newbury Park: Sage.

Blalock, H. M. (1967). *Toward a theory of minority-group relations*. New York: Wiley.

Bragg, A. (1989). Is a mentor program in your future? *Sales and Marketing Management, 141*, 54–59.

Brewer, M. B. (1995). Managing diversity: The role of social identities. In S. E. Jackson & M. N. Ruderman (Eds.), *Diversity in work teams: Research paradigms for a changing workplace* (pp. 47–68). Washington, DC: American Psychological Association.

Brown, H. A., & Ford, D. L., Jr. (1977). An exploratory analysis of discrimination in the employment of Black MBA graduates. *Journal of Applied Psychology, 62*, 50–56.

Burke, R. J., McKenna, C. S., & McKeen, C. A. (1991). How do mentorships differ from typical supervisory relationships? *Psychological Reports, 68*, 459–466.

Chao, G. T., Walz, P. M., & Gardner, P. D. (1992). Formal and informal mentorships: A comparison on mentoring functions and contrast with nonmentored counterparts. *Personnel Psychology, 45*, 619–636.

Chemers, M. M., Oskamp, S., & Costanzo, M. A. (Eds.). (1995). *Diversity in organizations: New perspectives for a changing workplace*. Thousand Oaks, CA: Sage.

Cox, T. (1993). *Cultural diversity in organizations: Theory, research, and practice*. San Francisco: Berret-Koehler.

DeFreitas, G. (1991). *Inequality at work: Hispanics in the U.S. labor force*. New York: Oxford University Press.

Douglas, C. A. (1997). *Formal mentoring programs in organizations: An annotated bibliography.* Greensboro, NC: Center for Creative Leadership.

Dreher, G. F., & Ash, R. A. (1990). A comparative study of mentoring among men and women in managerial, professional and technical positions. *Journal of Applied Psychology, 75,* 539–546.

Dreher, G. F., & Cox, T. H., Jr. (1996). Race, gender, and opportunity: A study of compensation attainment and the establishment of mentoring relationships. *Journal of Applied Psychology, 81,* 297–308.

Eby, L. T. (1997). Alternative forms of mentoring in changing organizational environments: A conceptual extension of the mentoring literature. *Journal of Vocational Behavior, 51,* 125–144.

Ely, R. J. (1995a). The power in demography: Women's social construction of gender identity at work. *Academy of Management Journal, 38,* 589–634.

Ely, R. J. (1995b). The role of dominant identity and experience in organizational work on diversity. In S. E. Jackson, & M. N. Ruderman (Eds.), *Diversity in work teams: Research paradigms for a changing workplace* (pp. 161–186). Washington, DC: American Psychological Association.

Fagenson, E. A. (1988). The power of a mentor: Protégés and nonprotégés perceptions of their own power in organizations. *Group and Organization Studies, 13,* 182–192.

Fagenson, E. A. (1989). The mentor advantage: Perceived career/job experiences of protégés vs. nonprotégés. *Journal of Organizational Behavior, 10,* 309–320.

Fagenson-Eland, E. A., Marks, M. A., & Amendola, K. L. (1997). Perceptions of mentoring relationships. *Journal of Vocational Behavior, 51,* 29–42.

Ferdman, B. M. (1995). Cultural identity and diversity in organizations: Bridging the gap between group differences and individual uniqueness. In M. M. Chemers, M. A. Costanzo, & S. Oskamp (Eds.), *Diversity in organizations: New perspectives for a changing workplace* (pp. 37–616). Newbury Park, CA: Sage.

Hall, D. T., & Mirvis, P. H. (1996). The new protean career: Psychological success and the path with a heart. In D. T. Hall (Ed.), *The career is dead—Long live the career: A relational approach to careers* (pp. 15–45). San Francisco: Jossey-Bass.

Ibarra, H. (1993). Personal networks of women and minorities in management: A conceptual framework. *Academy of Management Review, 18,* 56–87.

Jackson, S. (Ed.). (1996). Special topic forum on diversity within and among organizations. *Academy of Management Review, 21.*

Jackson, S. E., & Ruderman, M. N. (Eds.). (1995). *Diversity in work teams: Research paradigms for a changing workplace.* Washington, DC: American Psychological Association.

Johnston, W. B. & Packer, A. E. (1987). *Workforce 2000: Work and workers for the 21st century.* Indianapolis, IN: Hudson Institute.

Keele, R. L., Buckner, K., & Bushnell, S. J. (1987). Formal mentoring programs are no panacea. *Management Review, 76,* 67–68.

Korn/Ferry International & UCLA Anderson Graduate School of Management. (1993). *Decade of the executive woman.* New York: Korn/Ferry International.

Knouse, S. B. (1992). The mentoring process for Hispanics. In S. B. Knouse, P. Rosenfeld, & A. L. Culbertson (Eds.), *Hispanics in the workplace* (pp. 137–150). Newbury Park, CA: Sage.

Kram, K. E. (1985). *Mentoring at work.* Glenview, IL: Scott, Foresman.

Kram, K. E., & Bragar, M. C. (1992). Development through mentoring: A strategic approach. In D. Montross & C. Shinkmn (Eds.), *Career development: Theory and practice* (pp. 221–254). Chicago: Charles C. Thomas Press.

Kram, K. E., & Hall, D. T. (1996). Mentoring in a context of diversity and turbulence. In E. E. Kossek & S. A. Lobel (Eds.), *Managing diversity: Human resource strategies for transforming the workplace* (pp. 108–136). Cambridge, MA: Blackwell.

Kram, K. E., & Isabella, L. A. (1985). Mentoring alternatives: The role of peer relationships in career development. *Academy of Management Journal, 28*, 110–132.

Lenski, G. E. (1966). *Power and privilege: A theory of social stratification.* New York: McGraw-Hill.

Loden, M., & Rosener, J. B. (1991). *Workforce America! Managing employee diversity as a vital resource.* Homewood, IL: Business One Irwin.

Lyness, K. S., & Thompson, D. E. (1997). Above the glass ceiling? A comparison of matched samples of female and male executives. *Journal of Applied Psychology, 82*, 359–375.

McGrath, J., Berdahl, J. L., & Arrow, H. (1995). Traits, expectations, culture, and clout: The dynamics of diversity in work groups. In S. E. Jackson & M. N. Ruderman (Eds.), *Diversity in work teams: Research paradigms for a changing workplace* (pp. 17–46) Washington, DC: American Psychological Association.

Murray, M. (1991). *Beyond the myths and magic of mentoring: How to facilitate an effective mentoring program.* San Francisco, CA: Jossey-Bass.

National Gay and Lesbian Task Force (NGLTF). (1996). *Capital gains and losses: A state by state review of gay-related legislation.* Washington, DC: NGLTF.

Nkomo, S. M. (1995). Identities and the complexity of diversity. In S. E. Jackson & M. N. Ruderman (Eds.), *Diversity in work teams: Research paradigms for a changing workplace* (pp. 247–254) Washington, DC: American Psychological Association.

Noe, R. A. (1988). Women and mentoring: A review and research agenda. *Academy of Management Review, 13*, 65–78.

Paludi, M. A., Meyers, D., Kindermann, J., Speicher, H., & Haring-Hidore, M. (1990). Mentoring and being mentored: Issues of sex, power, and politics for older women. *Journal of Women and Aging, 2*, 81–92.

Ragins, B. R. (1989). Barriers to mentoring: The female manager's dilemma. *Human Relations, 42*, 1–22.

Ragins, B. R. (1995). Diversity, power, and mentorship in organizations: A cultural, structural, and behavioral perspective. In M. M. Chemers, M. A. Costanzo, & S. Oskamp (Eds.) *Diversity in organizations: New perspectives for a changing workplace* (pp. 91–132). Newbury Park, CA: Sage.

Ragins, B. R. (1997a). Antecedents to diversified mentoring relationships. *Journal of Vocational Behavior, 51*, 90–109.

Ragins, B. R. (1997b). Diversified mentoring relationships in organizations: A power perspective. *Academy of Management Review, 22*, 482–521.

Ragins, B. R., & Cotton, J. L. (1991). Easier said than done: Gender differences in perceived barriers to gaining a mentor. *Academy of Management Journal, 34*, 939–951.

Ragins, B. R., & Cotton, J. L. (1993). Gender and willingness to mentor in organizations. *Journal of Management, 19*, 97–111.

Ragins, B. R., & Cotton, J. L. (1996, April). *The influence of gender ratios on organizational attitudes and outcomes.* Poster session presented at the annual meeting for the Society for Industrial-Organizational Psychology, San Diego, CA.

Ragins, B. R. & Cotton, J. L. (in press). Mentor functions and outcomes: A comparison of men and women in formal and informal mentoring relationships. *Journal of Applied Psychology.*

Ragins, B. R., & McFarlin, D. (1990). Perceptions of mentor roles in cross-gender mentoring relationships. *Journal of Vocational Behavior, 37*, 321–339.

Ragins, B. R., & Scandura, T. A. (1994). Gender differences in expected outcomes of mentoring relationships. *Academy of Management Journal, 37*, 957–971.

Ragins, B. R., & Scandura, T. A. (1997). The way we were: Gender and the termination of mentoring relationships. *Journal of Applied Psychology, 82*, 945–953.

Ragins, B. R., & Scandura, T. A. (in press). Burden or blessing? Expected costs and benefits of being a mentor. *Journal of Organizational Behavior.*

Ragins, B. R., & Sundstrom, E. (1989). Gender and power in organizations: A longitudinal perspective. *Psychological Bulletin, 105*, 51–88.

Russell, J. E. A. (Ed.). (1997). Special issue on mentoring in organizations. *Journal of Vocational Behavior, 51.*

Riordan, C. M., & Shore, L. M. (1997). Demographic diversity and employee attitudes: An empirical examination of relational demography within work units. *Journal of Applied Psychology, 82*, 342–358.

Scandura, T. A. (1992). Mentorship and career mobility: An empirical investigation. *Journal of Organizational Behavior, 13*, 169–174.

Schermerhorn, R. A. (1956). Power as a primary concept in the study of minorities. *Social Forces, 35*, 53–56.

Sessa, V. I., & Jackson, S. E. (1995). Diversity in decision-making teams: All differences are not created equal. In M. M. Chemers, M. A. Costanzo, & S. Oskamp (Eds.). *Diversity in organizations: New perspectives for a changing workplace* (pp. 133–156). Newbury Park, CA: Sage.

Tajfel, H. (1978). The achievement of group differentiation. In H. Tajfel (Ed.) *Differentiation between social groups: Studies in the social psychology of intergroup relations* (pp. 77–98). London: Academic Press.

Thomas, D. A. (1990). The impact of race on managers' experiences of developmental relationships (mentoring and sponsorship): An intra-organizational study. *Journal of Organizational Behavior, 11*, 479–492.

Thomas, D. A., & Alderfer, C. P. (1989). The influence of race on career dynamics: Theory and research on minority career experiences. In M. B. Arthur, D. T. Hall, & B. S. Lawrence (Eds.), *Handbook of career theory* (pp. 133–158). Cambridge, MA: Cambridge University Press.

Thomas, D., & Higgins, M. (1996). Mentoring and the boundaryless career: Lessons from minority experience. In M. B. Arthur & D. M. Rousseau (Eds.), *Boundaryless careers: Work, mobility and learning in the new organizational era* (pp. 268–281). New York: Oxford University Press.

Tolbert, P. S., Andrews, A. O., & Simons, T. (1995). The effects of group proportion and group dynamics. In S. E. Jackson & M. N. Ruderman (Eds.), *Diversity in work teams: Research paradigms for a changing workplace* (pp. 131–160). Washington, DC: American Psychological Association.

Triandis, H. C. (1995). A theoretical framework for the study of diversity. In M. M. Chemers, M. A. Costanzo, & S. Oskamp (Eds.), *Diversity in organizations: New perspectives for a changing workplace* (pp. 11–36). Newbury Park, CA: Sage.

Tsui, A., Egan, T. D., & O'Reilly, C. A. (1992). Being different: Relational demography and organizational attachment. *Administrative Science Quarterly, 37*, 549–579.

Tsui, A., Egan, T. D., & Xin, K. R. (1995). Diversity in organizations: Lessons from demography research. In M. M. Chemers, M. A. Costanzo, & S. Oskamp (Eds.), *Diversity in organizations: New perspectives for a changing workplace* (pp. 191–219). Newbury Park, CA: Sage.

Tsui, A. S., & O'Reilly, C. A. (1989). Beyond simple demographic effects: The importance of relational demography in superior–subordinate dyads. *Academy of Management Journal, 32*, 402–423.

Tsui, A. S., Xin, K. R., & Egan, T. D. (1995). Relational demography: The missing link in vertical dyad linkage. In S. E. Jackson & M. N. Ruderman (Eds.). *Diversity in work teams: Research paradigms for a changing workplace* (pp. 131–160). Washington, DC: American Psychological Association.

Whitely, W., Dougherty, T. W., & Dreher, G. F. (1991). Relationship of career mentoring and socioeconomic origin to managers' and professionals' early career progress. *Academy of Management Journal, 34,* 331–351.

Wilson, W. J. (1973). *Power, racism, and privilege: Race relations in theoretical and sociohistorical perspectives.* New York: Macmillan.

Author Index

A

Adams, J., 36, 46
Ainslie, R. C., 9, 17
Aisenberg, N., 221, 223
Ajzen, I., 56, 61
Albright, L., 196, 209
Alderfer, C., 158, 159, 160, 164, 170, 214, 223, 224
Allen, B., 22, 24, 33, 43, 125, 140
Almquist, E., 124, 139
Amato, I., 69, 77
Amendola, K. L., 229, 238, 244
American Association of University Women, 65, 77
Andrews, A. O., 232, 246
Andrews, S., 76, 79
Angrist, S., 124, 139
Argyle, M., 191, 209
Aronson, J., 26, 46
Arrow, H., 232, 245
Arthur, M. B., 230, 242, 243
Asai, M., 51, 62
Ash, R. A., 66, 78, 85, 102, 106, 111, 119, 228, 234, 244
Ashton-Jones, E., 9, 10, 19, 76, 80
Astin, H. S., 21, 43
Atkinson, D. L., 8, 9, 13, 17
Atkinson, D. R., 33, 35, 43, 222, 224
Auster, D., 65, 77
Ayabe, H., 60, 61

B

Bahniuk, M. H., 8, 9, 12, 17, 18, 66, 67, 77, 79
Bai, M., 55, 61
Bandura, A., 123, 124, 135, 139
Barcelo, R., 65, 79
Bardon, J. I., 8, 12, 20, 66, 67, 80
Baron, J., 112, 118, 119
Baron, R. M., 196, 209
Basow, S., 8, 9, 17, 68, 77
Basow, S. A., 125, 139
Baugh, S. G., 66, 75, 77
Baumeister, R. F., 21, 43
Beale, F., 84, 102
Bell, A. P., 122, 139
Bell, E. L., 84, 85, 98, 102, 236, 243
Bemmels, B., 8, 9, 19, 68, 79, 122, 140
Berdahl, J. L., 232, 245
Berkowitz, S. D., 107, 118
Bettencourt, B. A., 9, 17, 32, 43
Bielby, W., 112, 118, 119
Blackwell, J. E., 9, 17
Blakemore, J. E., 28, 29, 43
Blake, S. D., 5, 10, 17, 236
Blalock, H. M., 110, 119, 233, 234, 243
Blank, R., 50, 59, 60, 61
Bol, L., 9, 17, 32, 43
Bontempo, R., 51, 52, 62
Boston, M. B., 126, 140
Bowen, D. D., 9, 17, 65, 77

Bowman, S. R., 10, 21, 22, 23, 24, 25, 26, 27, 28, 29, 30, 31, 32, 33, 34, 35, 36, 37, 38, 39, 40, 41, 42, 43, 44, 45, 46
Boyd, P., 27, 46
Boyer, E. L., 27, 43
Boykin, A. W., 24, 43
Braddock, J. H., 84, 102
Bragar, M. C., 231, 244
Bragg, A., 231, 243
Branscombe, N. R., 10, 21, 22, 23, 24, 25, 26, 27, 28, 29, 30, 31, 32, 33, 34, 35, 36, 37, 38, 39, 40, 41, 42, 43, 44, 45, 46
Brass, D., 112, 119
Brett, J., 65, 77
Brewer, M. B., 232, 243
Brinson, J., 9, 17, 23, 34, 35, 36, 37, 40, 41, 42, 43
Bronfenbrenner, U., 22, 43
Brown, B. B., 24, 46
Brown, D., 21, 43
Brown, H. A., 238, 243
Buckner, K., 231, 244
Buntzman, G. F., 8, 13, 18, 66, 75, 78
Burke, R. J., 8, 9, 13, 17, 65, 70, 77, 85, 91, 99, 102, 111, 119, 229, 243
Burt, R., 109, 119
Busch, E. T., 8, 13, 18, 66, 67, 75, 78
Busch, J. W., 66, 77
Bushnell, S. J., 231, 244
Bussey, K., 123, 124, 135, 139, 141
Byrne, D. E., 29, 43

C

Campbell, B. M., 16, 17
Caplan, P. J., 34, 43
Carrington, M. R., 9, 17
Carter, H., 65, 74, 76, 79
Caruso, R. E., 8, 10, 17, 174, 188

Casas, A., 8, 9, 13, 17, 33, 35, 43
Catalyst, 10, 17, 64, 65, 69, 76, 77, 173, 174, 188, 220, 223
Caudill, D. W., 9, 17
Ceci, S. J., 22, 43
Chan, B., 28, 35, 45
Chao, G. T., 8, 13, 18, 66, 75, 77, 239, 243
Chemers, M. M., 232, 243
Chesler, M. A., 87, 102
Clark, S. M., 69, 77
Clawson, J. G., 7, 18, 65, 72, 73, 78, 85, 102, 222, 224
Clayton, S. D., 65, 78
Coleman, H., 27, 45
Collins, E. G. C., 5, 18, 65, 78, 85, 102
Collins, N. W., 4, 6, 10, 18, 65, 68, 73, 78, 85, 102
Collins, S. M., 165, 170
Contreras, J. M., 125, 141
Conway, J. J., 67, 78
Cook, M. F., 6, 18, 65, 78
Cook, T. D., 24, 43
Corcoran, M., 69, 77
Cordova, D. I., 121, 122, 123, 124, 125, 126, 127, 128, 129, 130, 131, 132, 133, 134, 135, 136, 137, 138, 139, 140, 141
Corzine, J. B., 8, 13, 18, 66, 75, 78
Costanzo, M. A., 232, 243
Cotton, J. L., 8, 9, 12, 19, 63, 66, 68, 69, 73, 80, 111, 119, 214, 224, 229, 230, 231, 233, 238, 239, 242, 245
Cox, T. H., 8, 9, 13, 14, 18, 66, 75, 76, 78, 84, 86, 102, 111, 119, 222, 224, 228, 232, 243, 244
Craithwaite, J., 28, 35, 45
Crawford, M. E., 33, 46
Cronan-Hillix, T., 69, 78
Cronan-Hillix, W. A., 69, 78

Crosby, F. J., 3, 4, 5, 6, 7, 8, 9, 10, 11, 12, 13, 14, 15, 16, *17*, 18, 19, 20, 49, *62*, 63, 64, 65, 66, 67, 68, *69*, 70, 71, 72, 73, 74, 75, 76, 77, *78*, *79*, 80, 86, 91, 106, 122, 125, *140*, 174, 180, 228, 237
Crowley, M., 64, *78*
Culbertson, T., 125, *140*
Cullota, E., 23, *43*
Curtin, T. R., 24, *43*

D

Dalton, G., 85, *102*
Darley, J. M., 196, *209*
Darrow, C. M., 3, 6, *19*, 85, *103*
Dastmalchian, A., 8, 9, *19*, 68, *79*, 122, *140*
Davidson, W. S., 31, 46, 69, *78*
Davies, A. B., 9, 12, *19*, 34
Davies, S., 34, *44*
Davis, G., 84, 86, *102*
Davis, J., 99, *102*
Davis-Blake, A., 112, *118*
Deal, T., 122, *140*
DeFour, D. C., 28, 29, 31, 35, *44*, 45
DeFreitas, G., 238, *243*
Deinard, C., 86, *102*
Denton, T. C., 98, *102*, 236, *243*
Der, H., 49, *61*
Devine, I., 73, *78*
Devine, K. S., 8, 9, *19*, 68, *79*
Devine, P. G., 195, 196, *209*
Dews, C. L. B., *209*, 209
Dickens, F., 167, *170*
Dickens, J. B., 167, *170*
Dietz-Uhler, B., 195, *209*
DiLorio, J. A., 28, 29, *43*
Dobos, J., 8, 9, 12, *17*, *18*, 66, 67, *77*, *79*
Doosje, B., 39, *44*
Dornbusch, S. M., 24, *46*

Dougherty, T. W., 8, 13, 14, *20*, 66, 74, 80, 105, 106, 111, *120*, 239, *247*
Douglas, C. A., 231, *244*
Dreher, G. F., 8, 9, 13, 14, *18*, *20*, 66, 74, 75, 76, *78*, 80, 85, *102*, 105, 106, 111, *119*, *120*, 222, *224*, 228, 234, 239, *244*, *247*
DuBois, W. E. B., 83, *102*
Dunbar, D., 85, *102*

E

Eagly, A. H., 64, *78*
Eby, L. T., 229, *244*
Eckardt, A., 33, *44*
Edmunds, G. J., 27, *44*
Egan, T. D., 157, *170*, 232, 233, 246, *247*
Ellemers, N., 28, *43*
Elman, N. S., 9, *20*
Ely, R. J., *20*, 121, 126, 127, 129, *140*, 232, *244*
England, P., 116, *119*
Epps, E. G., 33, *44*
Erkut, S., 8, 9, *18*, 68, *78*, 125, 135, *140*
Essed, P., 85, *102*
Etcoff, N. L., 36, *46*
Evans, K. M., 85, *102*
Evans, S. L., 28, 33, 35, *44*, 125, *140*

F

Fagenson, E. A., 8, 12, *18*, 65, 66, 74, *78*, 105, 111, *119*, 126, *140*, 228, 234, *244*
Fagenson-Eland, E. A., 229, 238, *244*
Fairchild, D. L., 28, 29, *43*
Farylo, B., 65, 68, *78*
Fay, E. A., 199, *209*, *210*
Ferdman, B. M., 232, *244*
Fernandez, J. P., 84, *102*, 144, *155*

Fishbein, M., 56, *61*
Fish, C., 190, *209*
Fisher, B., 123, *140*
Fiske, S. T., 36, 38, *44*
Fitt, L. W., 6, *18*, 65, 73, 78, 85, *102*
Fitzgerald, L., *73, 78*
Fleming, C., 24, *45*
Forbes, I., 144, *155*
Ford, D. L., 9, *18*
Ford, D. L., Jr., 238, *243*
Fordham, S., 24, *44*
Frable, D. S., 213, 214, *224*
Fraser, S. C., 9, *17, 32, 43*
Friedman, R. A., 86, *102*
Frierson, H. T., Jr., 16, *18*, 57, *61*, 71, *78*
Fukuyama, M. A., 60, *61*
Fulcher, R., 69, *80*
Fullilove, R. E., 25, *44*

G

Gallessich, J. M., 28, 33, 35, *44*, 125, *140*
Gardner, P. D., 8, 13, *18*, 66, 75, *77*, 239, *243*
Gardner, S., 201, 204, *209*
Garibaldi, A. M., 23, *44*
Garvey, C., 28, 35, *45*
Gaskill, L. R., 8, 12, *18*, 71, *78*
Geis, F. L., 126, *140*
Gensheimer, L. K., 69, *78*
Gerton, J., 27, *45*
Gibbons, A., 23, *43*
Gibson, D. E., 121, 122, 123, 124, 125, 126, 127, 128, 129, 130, 131, 132, 133, 134, 135, 136, 137, 138, 139, *140, 141*
Giddings, P., 93, *103*
Gilbert, L. A., 9, *18*, 28, 33, 35, *44*, 65, 68, 70, *79*, 121, 125, *140*
Gingiss, P. L., 125, *141*
Ginsburg, R. B., 65, *79*, 125

Glaser, B., 87, 88, *103*
Glass, J., 116, *119*
Goh, S. C., 8, 12, *18*, 66, *79*
Golden, M., 65, 74, 76, *79*
Goldstein, E., 6, *18*, 74, *79*
Gold, Y., *73, 78*
Goto, S. G., 10, 47, 48, 49, 50, 51, 52, 53, 54, 55, 56, 57, 58, 59, 60, *61, 62*
Gould, R., 85, *103*
Gould, S. J., 24, *44*
Granfield, R., 197, 198, 201, *209*
Grant, T. S., 222, *224*
Greenfield, T. K., 60, 61
Greenhaus, J., 106, 111, *119*
Green, K., 96, *103*
Green, R., 96, *103*
Gross, P. H., 196, *209*
Grove, S., 36, *46*
Gutek, B. A., 85, *103*, 126, *140*

H

Halcomb, R., 6, 7, *18*, 85, *103*
Hale, M. M., 9, *18*, 68, *79*
Hall, D. T., 85, *103*, 229, 230, 241, 242, 244, *245*
Hall, R., 125, *140*
Hargrove, B. K., 16, *18*, 57, *61*, 71, *78*
Haring-Hidore, M., 28, 35, *45*, 65, *80*, 239, *245*
Harrington, M., 221, *223*
Harris, D., 96, *103*
Haseltine, F. P., 6, *20*
Haslett, B. B., 29, 31, *44*
Hee, S. J., 49, *62*
Heilman, M. E., 126, *140*
Heinrich, K. T., 72, *79*
Helms, J., 38, *44*
Henning, M. M., 5, *18*
Henry, M., 22, 42, *44*
Herr, E. L., 85, *102*

Herrnstein, R. J., 24, *44*
Herzberger, S., 49, *62*, 65, *80*
Hetherington, C., 65, *79*
Higgins, M., 230, 242, *246*
Hill, L., 85, 86, *103*
Hill, S. E. K., 8, *9*, 12, *17*, *18*, 66, 67,
  77, *79*
Hodson, R., 116, *119*
Hoffman, N., 126, *140*
Hofstede, G., 51, 52, *61*
hooks, b., 93, *103*, 191, *209*
Horgan, D. D., 138, *140*
Horton, S., 9, 63, 64, 65, 66, 67, 68, 69,
  70, 71, 72, 73, 74, 75, 76, *77*,
  78, *79*, *80*
Howe, K. G., 8, *9*, *17*, 68, *77*, *125*, *139*
Hoyt, S. K., 76, 189, 190, 191, 192, 193,
  194, 195, 196, 197, 198, 199,
  200, 201, 202, 203, 204, 205,
  206, 207, 208, 209, 210, 239,
  242
Hughes, E. C., 214, *224*
Hu, L.-T., 60, *62*
Hunt, D. M., 7, *19*, 105, *119*
Huratado, A., 93, 94, 97, *103*
Hymowitz, C., 211, 212, 220, *224*

I

Ibarra, H., 10, *19*, 41, *44*, 76, *79*, 86, 90,
  103, 107, 109, 112, *119*,
  157, *170*, 241, *244*
Ickes, W., 36, *44*
Ino, S., 60, *62*
Isabella, L. A., 7, *19*, 85, *103*, 230, *245*

J

Jacklin, C., 123, *140*
Jackson, C. H., 29, 30, 35, *44*
Jackson, J. S., 10, 143, 144, 145, 146,
  147, 148, 149, 150, 151, 152,
  153, 154, 155, 237

Jackson, S. E., 231, 232, *244*, *246*
Jacobi, M., 33, *44*
Jacobs, J. A., 116, *119*
Jacobson, L., 24, *45*
Janis, I., 17, *19*
Jardim, A., 5, *18*
Jaret, C., 8, *199*, 66, 75, *79*
Javidan, M., 8, 9, *19*, 68, *79*, 122, *140*
Jensen, A. R., 24, *44*
Jespen, D. A., 21, *43*
Johnson, E. J., 197, *209*
Johnston, W. B., 99, *103*, 243, *244*
Jones, J. M., 39, *44*
Jussim, L. J., 24, 38, *44*, *45*
Justiz, M., 42, *46*

K

Kahn, W., 65, *79*
Kalbfleisch, P. J., 9, 12, *19*
Kamprath, N., 85, 86, *103*
Kanter, R. M., 5, *19*, 107, *119*, 121, 126,
  127, 135, *140*
Katz, M., 77, *79*
Katz, P., 77, *79*
Keele, R. L., 231, *244*
Keith, B., 67, *79*
Kelman, H. C., 122, *140*
Kennedy, A., 122, *140*
Kim, C., 55, *61*
Kim, T., 55, *61*
Kindermann, J., 65, *80*, 239, *245*
King, D. K., 85, 93, 94, 100, *103*
King, M. C., 112, *119*
Kirby, D., 10, 143, 144, 145, 146, 147,
  148, 149, 150, 151, 152, 153,
  154, 155, 237
Kite, M. E., 10, 21, 22, 23, 24, 25, 26,
  27, 28, 29, 30, 31, 32, 33, 34,
  35, 36, 37, 38, 39, 40, 41, 42,
  43, *44*, *45*, 46
Klaw, E. L., 8, 9, 13, *19*

Klein, E. B., 3, 6, *19*, 85, *103*
Knouse, S. B., 239, *244*
Kohatsu, E. L., 31, *45*
Kohlberg, L., 122, *140*
Konrad, A., 126, *140*
Korn/Ferry International, 238, *244*
Kottler, J., 9, *17*, 23, 34, 35, 36, 37, 40, 41, 42, *43*
Kramer, N., 28, 35, *45*
Kram, K. E., 7, 8, 11, 14, 15, 16, *18*, *19*, 58, *61*, 65, 71, 72, 73, 74, 76, *78*, *79*, 85, 86, 91, 99, *102*, *103*, 106, *119*, 135, *140*, 180, *188*, 220, 222, 224, 228, 229, 230, 231, 241, *244*, *245*
Kwon, J.-H., 60, *62*

L

LaFromboise, T., 27, *45*
Lang, M., 23, *45*
Langston, D., 191, 197, 203, 206, 208, *210*
Lankau, M. J., 66, 75, *77*
Law, C. L., 209, *209*
Lawrence, B. S., 126, *141*
Lawrence, D., 28, 45, *45*
Lee, Y., 38, *45*
Lenski, G. E., 234, *245*
Leong, F. T. L., 51, *61*
Lerner, G., 93, *103*
Leung, K., 51, *61*
Levine, A., 190, 208, *210*
Levinson, D. J., 3, 6, *19*, 85, *103*
Levinson, M. A., 85, *103*
Levinson, M. H., 3, 6, *19*
Lewis, N. R., 16, *18*, 57, *61*, 71, *78*
Lim, Y. Y., 8, 9, *19*, 66, 75, *79*
Lipman, S., 29, 31, *44*
Locke, D. C., 57, *62*
Loden, M., 232, *245*

Lord, C. G., 37, *45*
Lorde, A., 92, *103*
Lott, B., 64, *79*
Lubelska, C., 34, *44*
Lucca, N., 51, *62*
Lunt, N., 9, *19*
Lykes, M. B., 41, *45*
Lyness, K. S., 239, *245*

M

Maack, M. N., 9, 13, *19*, 65, *79*
Maccoby, E., 123, *140*
Major, B., 22, *45*
Malloy, T. E., 196, *209*
Mangelsdorf, S. C., 125, *141*
Manstead, A. S. R., 39, *44*
Manz, C., 122, *140*
March, J., 8, *19*, 169, *170*
Marcus, E. C., 126, *140*
Markiewicz, D., 73, *78*
Marks, M. A., 229, 238, *244*
Marsden, P., 109, 112, *119*
Marsh, J., 9, *19*
Marsh, K., 66, 75, *79*
Martell, R. F., 126, *140*
Martin, J., 28, 46, *232*
Mathews, A. L., 9, *19*
Matt, G. E., 57, *62*
Mazur, A., 191, *210*
McArthur, L. Z., 36, *45*
McCambley, E., 10, 70, 76, 173, 174, 175, 176, 177, 178, 179, 180, 181, 182, 183, 184, 185, 186, 187, 188
McCauley, C. R., 38, *45*
McClelland, P., 22, *43*
McFarlin, D. B., 8, 11, 12, 20, 63, 67, 69, 70, 71, 72, 73, 80, 229, 237, 238, 239, *245*
McGrath, J., 232, *245*

McGuire, G., 72, 105, 106, 107, 108, 109, 110, 111, 112, 113, 114, 115, 116, 117, 118, *119*, 120, 154, 180, 237, 238

McKee, B., 3, 6, *19*, 85, *103*

McKeen, C. A., 8, 9, 13, *17*, 65, 70, *77*, 85, 91, *102*, 229, *243*

McKenna, C. S., 8, 9, 13, *17*, 70, *77*, 91, *102*, 229, *243*

McPartland, J. M., 84, *102*

McPherson, J. M., *119*

Meade, G., 144, *155*

Merriam, S., 7, *19*

Meyers, D., 65, 80, 239, *245*

Michael, C., 7, *19*, 105, *119*

Miller, B., 196

Miller, F. S., 39, *46*

Milliken, F., 232

Minor, C. W., 21, *43*

Mirvis, P. H., 230, 242, *244*

Mischel, W., 123, *140*

Missrian, A. K., 85, *103*

Mobley, M., 8, 9, *19*, 66, 75, *79*

Moen, P., 22, *43*

Mokros, J. R., 8, 9, *18*, 68, *78*, 125, 135, *140*

Molstad, S., *141*

Monaghan, J., 9, *19*

Moore, G., 107, *119*

Moore, H. A., 67, *79*

Morith, J., 125, *140*

Morrison, A. M., 129, *140*

Moses, Y. T., 28, *45*

Murray, C., 24, *44*

Murray, M., 229, 231, *245*

Murrell, A. J., 211, 212, 213, 214, 215, 216, 217, 218, 219, 220, 221, 222, 223, 224, 232

N

Narisetti, R., 212, 220, *224*

National Gay and Lesbian Task Force, 236, *245*

Nelson, C. E., 25, *45*

Neuberg, S. L., 38, *44*

Neville, H., 8, 9, 13, *17*, 33, 35, *43*

Newton, D. A., 6, *18*, 65, 73, *78*, 85, *102*

Nichols, I., 65, 74, 76, *79*

Nidiffer, J., 190, 208, *210*

Nieva, V. F., 85, *103*

Nkomo, S. M., 10, 16, *19*, 66, 76, 78, 79, 84, 85, 86, 98, *102*, *103*, *111*, *119*, 232, 236, *243*, *245*

Noe, R. A., 9, 10, *19*, 65, 71, *79*, 85, *103*, 237, *245*

Nunes, B., 125, *140*

O

O'Connell, A. N., 42, *45*

Ogbu, J. U., *44*, *45*

Olmedo, E. L., 69, *80*

Olson, G. A., 9, 10, *19*, 76, *80*

O'Neill, R. M., 9, 63, 64, 65, 66, 67, 68, 69, 70, 71, 72, 73, 74, 75, 76, 77, 78, 79, 80, 237

Ong, P., 49, *62*

O'Reilly, C. A., 126, *141*, *157*, *170*, 233, *246*

Ormerod, M., 73, *78*

Oskamp, S., 232, *243*

P

Packer, A. E., 99, *103*, *243*, *244*

Paludi, M. A., 28, 35, *45*, 65, 68, *78*, 80, 239, *245*

Parasuraman, S., 106, 111, *119*

Parham, T. A., 23, *46*

Pascale, R., 122, *141*

Passet, J. E., 9, 13, *19*, 65, *79*

Pena, E., 9, *17*

Perry, D., 123, 124, *139, 141*
Pfeffer, J., 126, *141*
Phillips-Jones, L., 6, 7, 15, *19*
Povich, L., 96, *104*
Price, R., 85, *102*
Priest, R. F., 36, *46*

Q

Quinn, J., 34, *44*

R

Ragins, B. R., 8, 9, 10, 11, 12, *19, 20,*
    63, 65, 66, 67, 68, 69, 70, 71,
    72, 73, 76, 80, 85, *104,* 106,
    111, *119,* 157, 158, *170,* 214,
    224, 227, 228, 229, 230, 231,
    232, 233, 234, 235, 236, 237,
    238, 239, 240, 241, 242, 243,
    244, *245, 246,* 247
Redmond, S. P., 9, 20
Reschly, D. J., 67, 80
Reskin, B. F., 112, 116, *119, 120*
Rhodes, J. E., 8, 9, 13, *19,* 125, *141*
Riley, S., 9, *20,* 33, 42, *45*
Riordan, C. M., 233, *246*
Roche, G. R., *20,* 85, *104*
Rodela, E. S., 99, *102*
Rodgers-Rose, L., 93, *104*
Rosener, J. B., 232, *245*
Rosenthal, R., 24, *45*
Ross, C., *120*
Ross, D., 124, *139*
Ross, S., 124, *139*
Rossman, K. W., 9, *18,* 65, *79*
Rouner, D., 67, *79*
Rousseau, D. M., 230, 242, *243*
Rowe, M. P., 6, *20*
Rubin, H. J., 100, 101, *104*
Rubin, I. S., 100, 101, *104*
Ruderman, A. J., 36, *46*

Ruderman, M. N., 231, 232, *244*
Russel, C., 23, *45*
Russell, J. E. A., *246*
Russell, K., 94, 96, *104*
Russo, N. F., 42, *45,* 69, *80*
Ryan, C. S., 38, *45,* 209
Ryan, J., *210*

S

Sackrey, C., 209, *210*
Saenz, D. S., 37, *45*
Sanders, D. W., 28, *45*
Sandler, B. R., 9, *20*
Scandura, T. A., 8, 9, 11, 14, *20,* 63, 66,
    69, 75, *77,* 80, 214, 224, 228,
    229, 234, 239, *246*
Schermerhorn, R. A., 233, 234, *246*
Schiffhauer, K., 39, *43*
Schmader, T., 22, *45*
Scott, D. B., 112, *120*
Scott, M. E., 35, *45*
Scott, N. E., 85, *104*
Scott, P., 5, *18,* 65, *78, 102*
Scott, W. A., 130, *141*
Sessa, V. I., 232, *246*
Shaffer, B. C., 8, 13, 14, *20,* 71, *80*
Shapiro, E. C., 6, *20*
Sheehy, G., 5, *20*
Shelton, B. A., 107, *120*
Shore, L. M., 233, *246*
Sibley, L. R., 8, *18*
Sigelman, L., 23, 24, *46*
Simon, H., 169, *170*
Simons, T., 232, *246*
Sims, H., 122, *140*
Sinnett, L. M., 36, *46*
Slipp, S., 50, 59, 60, *61*
Smith, E. P., 31, *46*
Smith, K. K., 158, 159, *170,* 214, *223*
Smith, P. B., 125, *141*
Smitherman-Donaldson, G., 22, *46*

Smith-Lovin, L., *119*
Spears, R., 39, *44*
Speicher, H., 65, 80, 239, *245*
Speizer, J., 121, *141*
Stanulis, R. N., 9, *20*
Stapp, J., 69, *80*
Steele, C. M., 22, 23, 25, 26, 30, *46*
Steele, S., 38, *46*
Steffen, V. J., 64, *78*
Steinberg, L., 24, *46*
Stevenson, R., 144, *155*
Stewart, A., 14, *20*
Stratton-Devine, K., 122, *140*
Strauss, A., 87, *103*
Stroh, L., 65, *77*
Struthers, N. J., 8, 9, 16, 20, 71, 72, *80*
Sue, D., 48, 60, *62*
Sue, S., 48, 60, *62*
Sundstrom, E., 63, 80, 233, *246*
Suzuki, L. A., *46*
Swerdlik, M. E., 8, 12, 20, 66, 67, *80*
Switzer, J. Y., 28, 29, *43*

T

Tajfel, H., 232, *246*
Tangri, S., 124, *141*, 211, 212, 213, 214,
       215, 216, 217, 218, 219, 220,
       221, 222, 223, 224, 232
Taylor, D. A., 22, *46*
Taylor, S. E., 28, 36, *46*
Tepper, B. J., 8, 13, 14, 20, 71, *80*
Tepper, K., 8, 13, 14, 20, 71, *80*
Terrell, F., 39, *46*
Terrell, S. L., 39, *46*
Thile, E. L., 57, *62*
Thomas, D. A., 9, 10, 12, 15, 20, 37, *46*,
       66, 70, 80, 85, 86, 90, 94, 95,
       104, 106, 111, *120*, 154, *155*,
       157, 158, 159, 160, 161, 162,
       163, 164, *170*, 174, 180, *188*,

       214, 215, *224*, 230, 238, 241,
       242, *246*
Thomas, R. R., Jr., 47, *62*
Thompson, D. E., 239, *245*
Thompson, P., 85, *102*
Tidball, M. E., 67, 80, *141*
Tokarczyk, M. M., 199, 209, *210*
Tolbert, P. S., 232, *246*
Tomaskovic-Devey, D., 112, *120*
Tomasson, R. F., 49, 62, 65, *80*
Treisman, P. U., 25, *44*
Triandis, H. C., 51, 52, 62, 232, *246*
Trujillo, C. M., 25, *46*
Tsui, A. S., 126, *141*, 157, *170*, 232,
       233, *246*, *247*
Turban, D. B., 66, *80*

U

Uba, L., 52, *62*
UCLA Anderson Graduate School of
       Management, 238, *244*
Unger, R. K., 33, *46*

V

Vaillant, G., 5, *20*
Valencia, L., 39, *43*
Valencia, R. R., *46*
Villareal, M. J., 51, *62*
Von Glinow, M., 129, *140*

W

Wagner, G., 126, *141*
Wally, C., 125, *140*
Walz, P. M., 8, 13, *18*, 66, 75, 77, 239,
       243
Watkins, C. E., 39, *46*
Watson, G., 84, 86, *102*
Weitzman, L., 73, *78*

Welch, S., 23, 24, *46*
Wells, L., 9, *18*
Wesley, A. L., 27, *46*
Wethington, E., *43*
Whitaker, G., *141*
White, J. L., 23, *46*
Whitely, W., 8, 13, 14, *20*, 66, 74, *80*, 105, 106, 111, *120*, 239, *247*
Williams, S., 10, 21, 22, 23, 24, 25, 26, 27, 28, 29, 30, 31, 32, 33, 34, 35, 36, 37, 38, 39, 40, 41, 42, 43, 44, 45, 46
Wilson, J. A., 9, *20*, 42
Wilson, M. S., 67, *80*, 93, 94, 96, *104*
Wilson, R., 23, 24, *46*
Wilson, W. J., 234, *247*
Wong, E., 55, *61*

Woo, D., 48, 50, *62*
Wormley, W., 106, 111, *119*
Wrench, D., 9, *20*, 33, 42, 45

X

Xin, K. R., 232, *246*, 247

Y

Yoder, J. D., 36, 37, *46*, 127, *141*

Z

Zane, N. W. S., 48, 60, *62*
Zenger, T. R., 126, *141*
Zey, M. G., 6, 7, 16, *20*, 76, *80*, 85, 99, *104*
Zimmerman, N. A., 57, *62*

Subject Index

A

Accelerated Succession Affirmative Action Pilot, 174, 180–187, *see also* Association of NYNEX Women

Adaptation to Life (Vaillant), 5

Affirmative action, 84

Allocentrism, 52–53

American Psychological Association, 32

Americans with Disabilities Act, 183

Antidiscrimination policies, 144

ANW, *see* Association of NYNEX Women

ASAP, *see* Accelerated Succession Affirmative Action Pilot

Asian Americans
  and absence of mentors, 48–54
  and allocentrism, 52–53
  collectivism vs. individualism, 51–52
  cultural incongruency, 51–54
  data from a mentoring study, 54–60
  and developmental relationships, 47–62
  diversity of population, 49–50
  and family, 51
  mentoring models, 53–54
  myth of model minority, 48–50, 58
  and occupations, 48–49

Association of NYNEX Women, 174–182
  and Accelerated Succession Affirmative Action Pilot, 174, 180–187

and mentoring circles, 174–180

Athena (in Greek mythology), 63

B

Balanced groups, 126–127

Beliefs, 56–57

Bell Atlantic Corporation (NYNEX), 173–180

Biculturalism, 84

Black American managers, 157–170, 163–169, *see also* Black Americans
  in Black-controlled organizations, 168–169
  encouraging White protégés to mentor Black subordinates, 165–166
  encouraging White subordinates to mentor Blacks, 166–167
  intergroup perspective, 159–161
  as mentors to Black protégés, 167–168
  as role models to White managers, 165
  as sounding boards for White peers, 164
  in White-controlled organizations, 163–168

Black Americans, *see also* Black American managers; Black American women
  in the academy, 21–46
  achievement affects, 24–25
  college statistics, 23

dropout rate of, 23
experience in America, 83–84
in faculty developmental relationships, 32–42
faculty positions, 23–24
graduate students and developmental relationships, 30–32
graduation rates of, 23
influences over cross–race relationships, 157–170
role models, 29–30
scholars, 22
undergraduates and developmental relationships, 27–30
in White American institutions, 26–27
work groups in White-controlled organizations, 162–163
Black American women, *see also* Black Americans
animosity between White and Black women, 88, 91–98
and the labor market, 84
mentoring, 83–104
protégés and Black men mentors, 88–90
protégés and White men mentors, 90–91
protégés and White women mentors, 91–95
psychosocial support, 92, 95, 98
in woman's movement, 93–94
Black British workers study, 144–155
Black-controlled organizations, 168–169
British Department of Employment, 144
Brothers and Sisters (Campbell), 16

C

Capitalist patriarchal power struggle, 93
Career Experience Questionnaire, 70–71
Challenge vs. remediation, 30
Civil Rights Movement, 5
Classism, 191–193, *see also* Social class
Class, *see* Social class
Collectivism, 51–52

Communicability (in qualitative research), 100–101
Compensation disparities, 96
Consistency (in qualitative research), 100–101
Constant comparison, 87
Control variables (of diversity research), 238–239
Cooper, Anna, 93
Corporate sex and race issues, 105–120
Cross-class developmental relationships, 189–210
Cross-gender developmental relationships, 5, 7–8, 185–186, *see also* Gender
consequences of, 73–76
Cross-race developmental relationships, 28–30, 50, 71, 185, *see also* Developmental relationships
between women, 91–95
with Blacks in power, 157–170
difficulties of, 34
Culbertson Industries Defense Application Laboratory, 47
Cultural capital, 197–201
Cultural sensitivity, 41–42

D

Data analysis (of diversity research), 237–238
Design and analysis (of diversity reasearch), 235–241
Devaluation, 30
Developmental functions, 6–7
Developmental relationships, *see also* Empirical studies; Gender; Mentoring; Social class; Sponsoring
of Asian Americans, 47–62
of Black Americans in the academy, 21–46
and ethnicity, 10, 16–17

history of, 5–10
literature on, 3–20
multicultural mentoring, 10–17
in practice, 173–188
qualitative studies, 9, 65, 86,
        100–101, 158
quantitative studies, 8–9, 65–66, 72,
        100–101
viewpoints of protégés and seniors, 9
Diversity, *see also* Research on diversity
        and mentoring
in mentoring, 227–247
and power perspective, 232–234
theories of, 232
Double consciousness, 84
Double jeopardy, 84
Dropout rate of Black Americans, 23
DuBois, W. E. B., 83–84

E

Embedded intergroup relations,
        214–215
Empirical studies
Black women's mentoring relation-
        ships, 83–104
cross-race developmental relation-
        ships, 157–170
developmental relationships at a
        large corporation, 105–120
gender and role modeling, 121–141
racial composition, 143–155
Ethnicity, 4
Ethnic stereotypes, 24–26
Ethnocentricity, 56
European Union (EU), 144–145
"Everyone Who Makes It Has a Men-
        tor," *Harvard Business Review*, 5
Expectations
for Asian Americans, 53–54
for Black Americans, 24–25, 37
for gender differences, 65

F

Feminine stereotype, 64

Feminist ideology, 93–94
First-generation business women, 88
Forbes, 96

G

Gay persons, 218, 220, 236
Gender issues, 35, 63–80
benefits to men vs. women, 74–75
cross-gender consequences, 73–76
differences in genders, 71–72
in different occupations, 68–70
equality, 65
frequency of developmental relation-
        ships, 64–70
gendered racism, 85
the mentoring experience, 70–73
same gender incidences, 67–68
sexual relations in mentoring, 73–74
women vs. men as mentors, 68–70
women vs. men as protégés, 65–67
Gender and role modeling study,
        121–141
attributes of role models, 131–133
balanced vs. skewed settings,
        133–138
differences across demographic set-
        tings, 133–138
implications for multicultural
        mentoring, 138–139
perceived availability of role models,
        131, 133
presence of role models, 130–131
research questions, 127–128
respondents, 129
similarities and differences, 130–135
Ginsberg, Ruth Bader, 125
Graduate Record Exam, 26
Graduate teaching assistants (TAs), 27
Green, Dianna, 211–213, 223
Groups
balanced, 126–127
homogenous, 126
skewed, 126–127
Group study, 25
Groupthink, 17

H

Harvard, 5
Heterogeneity, 144
Hierarchy, 6–7, 76
Hierarchy in Asian culture (power distance), 52
Homogeneity, 143–144
Homogenous groups, 126
"How a Dedicated Mentor Gave Momentum to a Woman's Career," *Wall Street Journal*, 211–213
Human resources, 4, 107

I

Identification, 122–123
Idiocentrism, 52
Individualism, 51–52
Individual-level approaches, 107–108
Instrumental support, 15–16, 86, 109–110, 113–115, 221–222, *see also* Psychosocial support
Instrumental vs. psychosocial support, 7, 10-11, 64, 70–73
Interdependence of workplace and family, 107
Intergroup relations, 158

L

Lesbians, 218, 220
Lewinsky, Monica, 5

M

Macro orientation vs. micro perspective, 88
Management literature, 85
Managerial Woman (Henning & Jardim), 5
Marginalized culture, 200
Marginalized identity groups, 211–224

Black woman faculty member in a predominantly White male institution, 215–218
Black woman protégé and White man mentor, 211–213
defining marginal status, 213–215
White woman faculty member in a predominantly Black male institution, 218–221
Masculine stereotype, 64
Mentor Connection, The (Zey), 6
Mentor in Greek mythology, 3–4, 63
Mentoring, *see also* Developmental relationships; Sponsoring
definitions of, 12–13, 85–86, 228–231
establishment of, 8
experiences of Black managers, 86
formal and informal, 231
forms of, 229–231
and geographic proximity, 32
incomplete relationships, 10
relationship phases, 8
and research on diversity, 227–247
and social classes, 14
Mentoring circles, 76
Mentoring literature, 87
Mentoring program, 54–60
Mentoring scale, 11
Mentoring at Work (Kram), 7–8, 11
Mentor Role Instrument (MRI), 70
Mentors, 15, 27–28
characteristics of, 110
definitions of, 70, 75, 123–124
internal and external, 230
Mentors and Protégés (Phillips-Jones), 6
Men and Women of the Corporation (Kanter), 5
Meritocracy, 201–202
Micro perspective vs. macro orientation, 88
Model minority myth, 48–50, 58
MRI, *see* Mentor Role Instrument
Multicultural organizations, 16
Multicultural sponsorships and mentorships, 16–17

N

Neo-Nazi party, 144
Nonmanagerial jobs, 106
NYNEX, see Bell Atlantic Corporation

O

Odysseus (in Greek mythology), 4, 63
Organizational behavior, 4

P

Passages (Sheehy), 5
"Passing," 198–201, 203, 208
Power distance, 52, 59, see also Asian
    Americans
Professional Women and Their Mentors
    (Collins), 6
Protégés, 110–111, 115, 117
Psychosocial support, 15, 86, 109–110,
    113–115, 221–222, see also In-
    strumental support
Psychosocial vs. instrumental support, 7,
    10–11, 14, 64, 70–73

Q

Qualitative studies, see Developmental
    relationships
Quantitative studies, see Developmental
    relationships

R

Race relations in organizations,
    159–161
Racial composition and supervisor's
    race study, 143–155
    gender, 146–147
    implications of, 154–155
    job level, 147–148
    multiple predictors, 150–153

racial composition of the work group,
    149–150
supervisor's race, 148–149
Racial group embeddedness, 159–161
    Black-controlled organizations,
        168–169
    Black managers in White-controlled
        organizations, 163–168
    Black work groups in
        White-controlled organiza-
        tions, 163–163
Racial group identification, 38–39
Racism
    effects of, 84
    in women's movement, 93–94
Reference groups, 57
Reference technique, 86
Remediation vs. challenge, 30
Research on diversity and mentoring,
    227–247
    defining and measuring diversity,
        231–235
    defining and measuring mentoring,
        228–231
    design and analysis, 235–241
    and future research, 241–243
    measurement and operationalization
        of constructs, 228–231
    sampling issues, 239–241
Role models, 15, 121–141, see also Gen-
    der and role modeling study
    background, 122–128
    Black American, 29–30
    childhood modeling, 123–124
    college years modeling, 125
    organizational demography, 126–127
    stereotypic schemata, 125–126
    young adult modeling, 124–125
Role playing, 60
Ruffin, Josephine St. Pierre, 93

S

Same-race developmental relationships,
    28–29, 71
Sampling (in diversity research),
    239–241

Scholarship, 5
Seasons of a Man's Life (Levinson, Darrow, Klein, Levinson, & McKee), 3, 6
"Self-made man," 5
Sexist society, 64
Sex and race study, 105–120
    access to mentors, 109
    characteristics of mentor or sponsor, 110
    developmental relations at a large corporation, 108–118
    instrumental help, 113–115
    protégé characteristics, 110
    protégés by race and sex, 111, 115
    socioemotional (psychosocial) help, 113–115
    and structural approach, 106–108, 116–117
    types of support, 109–110, 113–115
Sexual harassment, 219
Sexual relations with mentors, 4–5, 73–74
Skewed groups, 126–127
Social class, 100, 108, 189–210, *see also* Classism; Developmental relationships
    and academic mentoring, 189–210
    in the academy, 204–207
    advice for working-class and lower-class students, 208
    and cultural capital, 199–201
    definitions of, 191–195
    myth of the American dream, 194–195
    and "passing," 198–201, 203, 208
    tips for mentors, 207
    transitions of, 201–204
    working-class vs. middle class, 192–201
Social identity theory, 202
Social learning theory, 123
Sponsor, 15, 27, *see also* Developmental relationships; Mentors
    characteristics of, 110
    definitions of, 122
Sponsorship, 180–187

Standardized tests, 26
Stereotypes of men and women, 64, 71–72
Stratification of mentoring, 222
Structuralism, 106–108, 116–118, *see also* Sex and race study; Gender and role modeling study
    in role modeling, 126–128, 135
Suffrage movement, 93–94

T

Taboo subjects, 38
TAs, *see* Graduate teaching assistants
Telemachus (in Greek mythology), 4, 63
Terrell, Mary Church, 93
"The Mentor Connection: The Secret Link in the Successful Woman's Life," *New York Magazine*, 5
Theory testing by practice, 173–188
    affirmative action pilot program, 180–187
    mentoring circles, 174–180
Tokens, 36–37, 116, 126–127
Transition (between classes), 201–204
Transparency (in qualitative research), 100–101
Triple jeopardy, 100
Truth, Sojourner, 93

U

U.S. Commission on Civil Rights, 50
"The Uses of Anger: Women Responding to Racism " (Lorde), 92–93

W

White boys' network, 10
White guilt, 38–39

White middle-class men and the importance of mentoring, 3–4
Women, *see also* Black women
    in the labor force, 64

    in management, 98–99
Women's Movement, 5, 93–94
Working Woman (annual survey), 95–96
Workplace 2000, 243